CONGRESS,
THE PRESIDENT,
AND
POLICYMAKING

AMERICAN POLITICAL INSTITUTIONS AND PUBLIC POLICY

Stephen J. Wayne
Series Editor

VICTORY
How a Progressive Democratic Party Can Win and Govern
Arthur Sanders

THE POLITICS OF JUSTICE
The Attorney General and the Making of Legal Policy
Cornell W. Clayton

A KINDER, GENTLER RACISM?
The Reagan–Bush Civil Rights Legacy
Steven A. Shull

CONGRESS, THE PRESIDENT, AND POLICYMAKING
A Historical Analysis
Jean Reith Schroedel

RISKY BUSINESS
PAC Decisionmaking and Strategy
Robert Biersack, Paul S. Herrnson, and Clyde Wilcox, Editors

PUBLIC ATTITUDES TOWARD CHURCH–STATE RELATIONS
Clyde Wilcox and Ted G. Jelen

AMERICAN POLITICAL INSTITUTIONS AND PUBLIC POLICY

CONGRESS, THE PRESIDENT, AND POLICYMAKING

A Historical Analysis

JEAN REITH SCHROEDEL

M.E. Sharpe
Armonk, New York
London, England

Library of Congress Cataloging-in-Publication Data

Schroedel, Jean Reith.
Congress, the President, and policymaking:
a historical analysis
/Jean Reith Schroedel.
p. cm. — (American political institutions and
public policy)
ISBN 1-56324-176-5 (H)–ISBN 1-56324-177-3 (P)
1. Separation of powers—United States—History.
2. Legislation—United States—History.
3. United States—Constitutional history.
I. Title.
II. Title: Congress, the President, and policymaking.
III. Series.
JK305.S45 1994
320.4′04′0973—dc20   93-28578
CIP

Printed in the United States of America

The paper used in this publication meets the minimum requirements of
American National Standard for Information Sciences—
Permanence of Paper for Printed Library Materials,
ANSI Z 39.48-1984.

∞

BM (c)   10   9   8   7   6   5   4   3   2   1

For my not entirely unpleasant partner, Paul

CONTENTS

Tables and Figures

Tables

Figures

Foreword

The allegations have been frequent and continuous. Something is wrong with the policymaking process. During the second term of the Reagan administration the concern was spiraling deficits. Presidential budgets were ritually pronounced "dead on arrival" while appropriations bills were amalgamated into huge, veto-proof, continuing resolutions. During the Bush administration, the charge was "gridlock" and "stalemate" as Congress and the president seemed at loggerheads, unable to agree on legislative policy solutions to the nation's economic and social problems.

The Clinton administration broke the gridlock during its first year but at a cost to the president's reputation and the Congress's integrity. Concerns were voiced that the president had given away too much to build a winning coalition, that members of Congress had "rolled" him for the benefit of their constituencies and ultimately, their own reelection. The criticism was that those in Congress were still preoccupied with short-term, parochial interests rather than longer-term, national concerns; that PAC money continued to flood congressional coffers and affected legislative decisionmaking; and that structural reform that undercut the power of committee and subcommittee chairs remained on the back burner.

All of these factors—gridlock, dealmaking, and pernicious, self-interested pressure—have contributed to low public esteem for the country's political institutions and leaders *even when agreement has been reached on major public policy issues*. Over the last two decades there has been a steady decline in the confidence people have in their governing institutions. National surveys conducted by the National

Opinion Research Center reveal such an erosion of the public's trust in Congress and the executive branch:

People's Confidence in Government*

	Congress			Executive Branch		
	Great Deal	Only Some	Hardly Any	Great Deal	Only Some	Hardly Any
1973	24%	59	15	29	50	18
1983	10	64	23	13	54	29
1993	7	50	41	12	53	32

*Question: I am going to name some institutions in this country. As far as the people running these institutions are concerned, would you say you have a great deal of confidence, only some confidence, or hardly any confidence at all in them?

Source: National Opinion Research Center as cited in *The American Enterprise*, November/December 1993, p. 94.

What is wrong? Are public perceptions out of whack or are Congress and the presidency not functioning effectively? Professor Jean Reith Schroedel's study, *Congress, the President, and Policymaking: A Historical Analysis*, provides a much needed longitudinal perspective for answering these questions.

Schroedel begins on the assumption that the prevailing literature on congressional-presidential relationships presents an either/or perspective that overemphasizes institutional conflict, presidential initiatives, and executive dominance or impotence. What is needed, she argues, is a theory that examines the evolution of this relationship within the constitutional framework in which it was set and still functions. She calls this theory "dynamic constitutionalism" and applies it to the evolution of presidential-congressional relationships. Her application reveals a rather different pattern of interaction from what much of the literature would suggest.

Not only does Schroedel provide a new perspective, but she also provides a historical application of it. Her work spans a large part of the entire period of congressional-presidential interaction. This enables readers to discern patterns of institutional relationships as well as see how the development of the modern activist state, the administrative structure of the executive branch, and the internal organizational and operational changes of Congress have affected this relationship over time.

Naturally, Schroedel cannot examine all legislation. Her focus is on banking—the bills, the committees that consider them, the floor debate and action, and presidential involvement. Three case studies take readers deeply into the intricacies of the legislative process from policy initiatives to legislative outcomes, providing a rich portrayal of the forces that impinge on congressional decisionmaking.

These case studies are supplemented by a quantitative analysis of all 160 years of banking legislation. Schroedel examines the legislation at point of introduction, committee deliberation, and floor action. Success rates of the various participants are calculated and serve as a basis for drawing conclusions about initiatives, influence, and outcomes.

This is a very impressive work, not only for what it concludes about the evolving relations between Congress and the presidency but also for what it implies about the study of those relations. Schroedel has provided a framework and a methodology for assessment. In this way, she has made an important contribution to our understanding of government, how it was designed to work, and how that design continues to shape institutional interactions and affect congressional decisionmaking.

Stephen J. Wayne
Georgetown University

Preface and
Acknowledgments

Many people assisted in the writing of this book. Most fundamentally I owe a debt of gratitude to my parents, Robert and Genevieve Schroedel, who made politics an important part of my childhood. Some of my earliest memories are of handing out campaign brochures for a neighbor, Bill Hume, who ran for state representative in the Thirtieth District in Washington state. I can remember my mother telling me that it did not matter that he lost the race—the important thing was that we had participated in the democratic process. Given my upbringing, perhaps it was preordained that I would become a political scientist. After all, how many parents give their eleven-year-old daughter a copy of *The Federalist Papers* for bedtime reading?

My interest in historical approaches to the study of American politics was piqued during my first semester at the Massachusetts Institute of Technology. I had naively thought that Walter Dean Burnham's basic course on American politics would not be too difficult an introduction to graduate school. The very first class meeting disabused me of any illusions that I might possess any knowledge about the subject. I could not even identify the references made, much less make any contribution to the discussion. I did, however, emerge from that class with a strong desire to understand American politics and a commitment to historical approaches. As will become clear in Chapter 6, the theories of executive-congressional relations put forth by Samuel Huntington and Stephen Skowronek were important influences on my thinking about the evolution of American political institutions.

This book is an outgrowth of research begun in 1985. Like most dissertation research it has gone through many a different iterations, and along the way I accumulated many research debts. My dissertation committee, composed of Walter Dean Burnham, Donald Matthews, and Charles Stewart, deserves my heartfelt thanks for all the hours spent reading through various drafts. Along the way many other colleagues helped by reading parts or all of the manuscript. I think their input helped focus my thinking and helped me produce a clearer piece of scholarship. Specifically, I wish to thank Bruce Ackerman, John Coleman, David Mayhew, Daniel Mazmanian, Donald McCrone, Paul Peretz, Sarah Ritchie, Barbara Sinclair, Stephen Skowronek, Rogers Smith, and Sue Thomas. Thanks are due also to Michael Weber and Stephen Wayne for their assistance and patience in seeing this project through to completion.

There are other debts that will never be repaid but which at least deserve to be acknowledged. The folks working in the interlibrary loan departments at the University of Washington, Cornell, Yale, and the Claremont Graduate School are to be commended for their help in finding a myriad of obscure and out-of-print documents. The men and women who shelve books in the subbasement of the Library of Congress were also a great help in locating materials; moreover, I appreciate their efforts in keeping my spirits up and their gift of a birthday cake. I am grateful to the Yale University Social Science Faculty Research Fund for providing grant money.

My research assistants, Jennifer Liu, Rachel Roth, and Bruce Snyder, also deserve my thanks. Rachel Roth spent many hours poring through reports from the Treasury Department and Office of the Comptroller of the Currency in a futile attempt to identify the policy positions of the broader executive branch. Jennifer Liu and Bruce Snyder assisted in the identification of bills reported out of committee and the copyediting. They did an excellent job and deserve a special commendation. I am sure they will go on to make significant academic contributions.

Finally, my most important debt is to Paul Peretz, who somehow manages to be both my harshest critic and greatest source of support. Thank you for everything.

CONGRESS,
THE PRESIDENT,
AND
POLICYMAKING

1

Introduction

*The Constitutional Convention of 1787 is supposed to have created a
government of "separated powers." It did nothing of the sort. Rather,
it created a government of separated institutions sharing powers*
(Neustadt 1960: 33).

It is a truism that the government of the United States differs from
other advanced industrial nations in the degree of separation between its
executive and legislative functions. While most nations have an executive
who is chosen directly from the legislature, the United States was the first
country to elect the executive and legislative branches separately and
remains one of the very few to do so. This is one of the main reasons why
the question of policy leadership is more complex in the United States
than in most other countries. The American system, unlike parliamentary
systems, lacks a formal hierarchical or organic link between the executive
and the legislative branches of government.[1] Furthermore, long periods of
divided party control of government in the United States are common.[2]

The purpose of this research is to study what effect this institutional
division and forced sharing of powers has on policymaking in this
country. Unlike previous constitutional studies, which focused on the
formal powers of each office, this project utilizes the Constitution to
generate testable propositions about how the legislative process has
developed in the United States. The basic argument is that by establishing a government composed of functionally separated branches that
are required to share legislative responsibilities, the Founders determined the broad outlines of subsequent developments. This dynamic
constitutionalism considers not only the formal division of power but

3

also the differential impact that changes over time in the economy and society have on the two institutions.

The United States of the Founding Fathers was a very different entity from what exists today. At that time there were approximately four million people in the country; almost all of them lived within about 200 miles of the Atlantic Ocean and earned their living through farming or related commercial activities (Lee and Passell 1979: 52). Although the public was certainly concerned about the administrative inefficiencies of the Articles of Confederation, its primary concern was the protection of liberty.[3] By institutionally separating the legislative and executive functions of government, the Founders created a bulwark against tyranny, but they also erected impediments to governing. Many critics (Cutler 1988; Sundquist 1980) have contended that in the contemporary period the need for government to respond quickly to crises outweighs the need to guard against tyranny and that the separation of powers has resulted in governmental "deadlock." But, as will be argued in the following chapters, the Founders also created incentives for an interinstitutional division of labor and cooperation.

The ahistorical character of most of the research on the legislative process also inhibits the identification of which aspects are enduring and which are particularistic. One needs a historical approach to distinguish among aspects of the institutional interaction that are relatively stable, those undergoing change, and those caused by the idiosyncrasies of individual actors.[4] In the absence of a historical perspective, a very real tendency exists either to "see contemporary equilibria as both inevitable and enduring" or to overstate the impact of individual institutional actors (Swift and Brady 1991: 61–62). Although understandable, these two tendencies can lead to an overemphasis on institutional stability and a failure to recognize that individual institutional actors are constrained by their environment. Scholars have become aware of the impact of the endogenous factors limiting the options of policymakers but are much less cognizant of the impact of gradually changing exogenous forces. If one studies only a relatively short period of time, subtle changes in either the institutional or the social environment that may presage more general transformative shifts can be easily overlooked. For example, a historical perspective is critical not only to understanding the current governability crisis and "deadlock" but also to understanding earlier phenomena, such as the relationship between the unsuccessful agricultural third parties of the 1880s and 1890s and the overthrow decades later of Speaker Cannon and the decline of Aldrichism.[5]

The Constitution and Shared Legislative Responsibility

Dynamic constitutionalism holds that when the relational categories of the Constitution are imposed on the living web of societal institutions, they cause certain patterns of interaction to be replicated over time. Although unable to predict future social developments, the Founders' decision to create a government of "separated institutions sharing power" established a framework for subsequent developments. The most important effect is to channel natural institutional developments in a way that allows for growth, but biases it in the direction of preserving the essential balance of powers between Congress and the president established in the Constitution.

The Centrality of the Constitution

This placement of the Constitution at the forefront of the research agenda may strike some as a return to arcane "legalistic" studies of the previous century. In one sense this is accurate; nineteenth-century scholars (Ford 1898; Stanwood 1898; Woodward 1825) placed the formally defined powers of the various offices at the center of their research, but as Eulau noted:

> It is not unusual to refer to this work (nineteenth-century constitutional scholarship) as "legalistic," at times in a rather contemptuous manner. What those using the term have in mind is by no means clear, but it presumably refers to the alleged hair-splitting, nit-picking nature of law-related discourse. But behind the hair-splitting and nit-picking loomed the great constitutional issues of parliamentary government as it emerged in the nineteenth century, notably the conflicts over representation and the separation of powers. (Eulau 1985: 2–3)

While much of this nineteenth-century debate about representative government took place within the European context, American scholarship was also influenced by these ideas. For example, Woodrow Wilson's well-known 1885 book, *Congressional Government,* was explicitly modeled after Walter Bagehot's 1872 study of the British parliamentary system. But Wilson's primary concern was a peculiarly American problem—the difficulty inherent in the sharing of legislative powers between the president and the Congress, which he called "a radical defect in our federal system" (Wilson, 1956 edition: 187).

The advent of the behavioral revolution in the 1950s led scholars to downplay the importance of institutional arrangements in shaping policy outcomes and to focus on the relationships between groups. Constitutional analysis was relegated to the subfield of constitutional law and became divorced from the study of actual policymaking. While most scholars of legislative and presidential politics continue to refer to the Constitution, it is treated as an ancillary factor rather than a central determinant of outcomes.

Dynamic Constitutionalism

This research aims to demonstrate why it is essential to our understanding of policymaking that the Constitution be returned to the forefront of analysis—not because of an interest in esoteric debates about the true intent of the Founding Fathers, but to recognize the Constitution as a major determinant of legislative behavior. Dynamic constitutionalism holds that the United States has a bounded system of governance whose parameters were defined by that document. While these boundaries may not be completely impermeable, they did establish clear limits on the types of changes that may be allowed under our system of government. In particular, developments that in other societies have led to greatly enhanced relative power for the executive branch have been checked by the Constitution and translated into greater power for both the executive and legislative branches in the United States. Constitutional provisions also have encouraged, albeit not mandated, other institutional developments.

This separation between executive and legislative functions has often led scholars to focus solely on the conflictual aspects of policymaking in this country, but the Constitution also creates incentives for an interinstitutional division of labor and cooperation. This division of labor is most likely to occur when an issue has higher salience for one branch than for the other. As will be shown, there are systematic differences in the degree of salience that the two branches accord to different types of policies, and these differences derive from specific constitutional provisions. Cooperation occurs when both Congress and the president agree that new legislation needs to be enacted. It follows that cooperation is more likely at times when both branches feel threatened by a crisis or when their perceptions of what is needed are similar.

Policymaking Within a Bounded System

The most obvious way that the Constitution establishes the parameters of policymaking is through its assignment of governing functions to both the legislative and executive branches of government. By defining the basic legislative responsibilities of each branch, these provisions establish the primary incentive system for a division of labor and cooperation.

The Founding Fathers clearly intended for the legislative branch of government to be predominant. Madison in *Federalist Paper* 51 expressed this when he wrote, "But it is not possible to give to each department an equal power of self defense. In republican government, the legislative authority necessarily predominates" (Madison, Hamilton, and Jay, 1987 edition: 320). The Constitution reflected this sentiment by assigning a wide range of formal legislative powers to the Congress. In Article 1, Section 8, Congress is given the power to collect taxes, borrow money, regulate commerce, establish rules governing naturalization, coin currency, establish post offices, secure patents, create courts, raise and support armed forces, declare war, and "make all Laws which shall be necessary and proper for carrying into Execution the foregoing Powers, and all other Powers vested by this Constitution in the Government of the United States, or in any Department or Officer thereof." In addition to these positive legislative powers, Congress is also assigned negative powers, such as the power of confirmation over executive appointments and impeachment, which allow it to check the power of the president.

The Constitution assigns far fewer formal legislative powers to the president. While the office of the president now plays a much larger legislative role than could have been imagined even a century ago, Congress continues to be the primary legislative actor. A major reason is that the Constitution places severe constraints on what the president may do in the legislative arena. The president can make suggestions, but he cannot introduce legislation into the House or the Senate. Instead, he must rely on members of the legislature to introduce and guide a bill to passage. While the veto gives the president some power over ongoing legislation, it is primarily a negative power.[6] This fundamental asymmetry in the assignment of formal powers provides the underpinnings for the interbranch division of labor and cooperation.

Over the past 200 years the constitutional provisions governing executive-legislative relations have undergone only the most minimal change.[7] Only two constitutional amendments have altered the balance of power between Congress and the president. Somewhat surprisingly, both structural changes have strengthened the policymaking power of Congress vis-à-vis the president. The passage of Seventeenth Amendment in 1913 indirectly increased the popular legitimacy of Congress by mandating popular elections for the Senate. The Twenty-second Amendment, which was passed in 1951, directly curtailed the power of the president by the establishment of presidential term limits.

These formal constitutional limitations on presidential legislating serve as a real check on the aggrandizement of his legislative role. One indication of presidential dissatisfaction with these limits is the aggressiveness with which both Democratic and Republican presidents have pursued the line-item veto.[8] There are two real implications of the constitutional limitations on presidents. First, the limits increase the chance of having large areas of legislative responsibility that will be at most of minimal interest to presidents. Second, the constitutional limitations provide even modern presidents serving during an era of divided party control an incentive to achieve some sort of limited rapprochement with the Congress. Every president is forced to come to grips with this essential fact of American political life—he can accomplish nothing legislatively without the cooperation of some members of Congress.

Additional Constitutional Impetus

In the past, policy formation has often been viewed as a zero-sum game in which leadership by one branch of government comes at the expense of the other.[9] Instead it can be visualized as a game in which direct zero-sum gains are bounded by the Constitution, but indirect non-zero-sum moves are possible that can temporarily change the balance between the two sides. This is because not all power in the United States is in the hands of the federal government. Over the past 200 years both Congress and the president have increased their absolute power by taking over responsibility for areas previously controlled by the states, localities, and the general populace. Moves of this nature can result in one branch, usually the executive, temporarily increasing its relative power vis-à-vis the other, but the latter will respond by using the Constitution to re-establish the balance or make a power grab in another area to re-establish its relative position.

Becoming caught up in the immediate sound and fury on Pennsylvania Avenue and failing to recognize the less conflictual aspects of their legislative interaction are far too easy. In addition to the boundary-setting provisions that mandate certain relationships while prohibiting others, other constitutional provisions push the two branches toward rejection of a zero-sum approach to legislating. These provisions provide a stimulus for the two branches to divide their legislative responsibilities and to cooperate more explicitly on some types of policies but do not require it. Hence, they are more susceptible to external countervailing pressures. A division of labor exists when each branch of government plays a distinctly different role in the legislative process and defers to the other within its sphere of interest. This implicit deference can occur on a specific type of legislation or at a particular point in the policymaking process. Scholars have long recognized a tendency for Congress to defer to presidential expertise in foreign affairs and defense matters.[10] In contrast, there has been scant recognition that other constitutional provisions lead to the opposite result—presidential deferral toward Congress. Three of these less stringent provisions provide an incentive for a president to defer to Congress—one of which also provides a reason for interbranch cooperation.

The first such constitutional provision is the difference between presidential and congressional electoral constituencies delineated in Article I, Section 2, and Article II, Section 1. In order to be elected, presidents must create far broader electoral coalitions and accept more trade-offs than are necessary for members of Congress (Edwards 1980: 36). This difference is likely to be reflected in different policy priorities. A president must also take policy positions on the major national issues of the day, while members of Congress need to consider the policy issues of most importance to their much smaller constituencies. This does not mean that legislators are concerned *only* with parochial matters. Scholars such as Maass (1983) and Fenno (1973) have shown that members' interests extend beyond the narrow concerns of their districts. The difference in electoral constituencies does, however, imply that the scope of congressional concerns will encompass matters of both parochial and national interest. This difference gives presidents an incentive to defer to members of Congress on the more routine and parochial legislative matters.

Second, differences in the internal structures of Congress and the office of the president make it more likely that these more parochial matters will be primarily the purview of the legislature. Article II, Section 1, of the Constitution creates a hierarchically organized executive branch of government and vests the entire "Executive Power" in the president. In contrast, Article I of the Constitution creates a decentralized and bicameral legislature without even a theoretical leader. The Constitution provides that no member of Congress shall be significantly more powerful than any other member. These differences in the internal structure serve to reinforce the tendency for the president to concentrate on national issues, while allowing members of Congress more latitude to pursue the policy interests of their smaller constituencies. Just as the chief executive officer of a large firm has no time to be concerned with the minor, day-to-day matters of running the corporation, the president lacks the time to be involved in more mundane legislative matters. This, however, is one area where the development over time of a large executive branch bureaucracy may have changed the effects of this particular constitutional provision.

Finally, the legislative activities of presidents and members of Congress are influenced by the differing time frameworks that govern the lengths of their terms in office.[11] In general, legislators have a longer time horizon than do presidents because there are no statutory limitations on their tenure. No structural reasons state that a member of Congress must accomplish his policy aims in a limited period of time. In contrast, presidents have at most ten years to accomplish their policy objectives. With the exception of President Franklin D. Roosevelt, the terms of office of earlier presidents were governed by tradition, while those of later ones were statutorily limited by the Twenty-second Amendment to the Constitution. In reality the window of opportunity for presidents wanting to make changes is far less than the ten years. After the honeymoon period of the first term is over, they face a cycle of declining influence. Ironically, at the same time as their influence is waning, their understanding of the job of chief executive is increasing. The way out of this dilemma, as Paul Light succinctly put it, is to "move it or lose it" (Light 1982: 218).

This difference in the possible length of time that one may serve in office affects the division of labor in two ways. First, it provides an additional incentive for presidents to focus on only the most important issues. Because a chief executive's tenure in office is limited, he is likely to choose to spend his political capital primarily on the most important policy initiatives. Second, it is more likely that Congress will be disproportionately responsible for the political incubation of new policy ideas and that presidential involvement will occur later in the policy process. As the size of the executive branch has grown, presidents have been able to become involved both in more issues and at an earlier point in the policymaking process. However, differences in the policy preferences between presidents and the bureaucracy may act as a counterbalance to this phenomenon.[12] This purported independence of the bureaucracy has led some to go so far as to describe the administrative state as a "fourth branch" of government.[13]

This development of a large administrative state in the twentieth century is only one of the factors that may have changed the way the two branches interact over time. Other institutional developments, such as the enormous growth in congressional and White House staff, may also have affected the pattern of policymaking. But endogenous institutional innovations should not be viewed as divorced from underlying transformations in the broader society. The growth of the administrative state and the creation of infrastructural supports within each branch of government were a direct result of a historical evolution in the socioeconomic base of the country. The movement away from an agrarian-based society in the latter part of the nineteenth and early part of the twentieth century triggered the growth of administrative state.[14] While not affecting the boundary-setting aspects of the Constitution, these broader social developments are likely to have influenced the overall pattern of executive-congressional interaction. In particular, they may have exerted countervailing pressure against the constitutional impetus toward cooperation.

Propositions

Even though socioeconomic conditions and institutional developments may have altered the relationship to some degree, the basic argument in this research is that these constitutional provisions throughout our country's history have heavily influenced how Congress and the president enact policies. The provisions dealing with the assignment of formal legislative powers, electoral constituencies, internal structures, and time frameworks were used to generate the following series of testable propositions about how the pattern of executive-congressional interaction on legislation has evolved over time.

1. Congress will continue to bear the primary responsibility for the development of most legislative initiatives.
2. The early development and political incubation of most policies will occur within Congress, and there will be only minimal presidential involvement in the early stages.
3. Presidents will devote the bulk of their attention to the most important policy initiatives while members of Congress will be responsible for the development of a far wider range of policies.
4. Presidents will need the support of key congressional actors if they are to see their initiatives enacted.

In subsequent chapters the ability of these four propositions to capture the patterns of interaction in setting policy will be explored in great detail.

Conventional Approaches to Policymaking

Even though extensive bodies of literature have grown up to deal with the many aspects of policymaking within each institution, there have been only minimal attempts at making a connection between the presidential and congressional scholarship.[15] Presidential scholars have devoted an enormous amount of energy to studying policymaking under particular administrations or to making comparisons between administrations.[16] Congressional scholars have devoted an equally large amount of attention to studying the impact of committees, subcommittees, political parties, and elections on policymaking within Congress. Although this research has greatly increased our understanding of particular aspects of policymaking, its piecemeal character makes generalization difficult.[17] Not only are the various subspecialties within the presidential and congressional literatures often studied in isolation from one another, but traditionally few have tried to create an integrated theory of how Congress and the president jointly influence the legislative process.[18]

The failure to consider the ways that the Constitution has shaped the roles played by Congress and the president in policymaking has led also to an overemphasis on the conflictual and zero-sum aspects of the relationship.[19] Most postwar scholars (Corwin 1957; Huntington 1973; Lippmann 1955; Rossiter 1960) believe that in the nineteenth century the president was largely uninvolved in policymaking and that Congress was the initiator of policies. In the twentieth century, however, the president was thought to have increasingly dominated the legislative process, while Congress's role became mainly that of a passive reactor to presidential initiatives. Walter Lippmann went so far as to describe the executive branch as "the active power of the state, the asking and proposing power" and the legislature as "the consenting power, the petitioning, the approving and criticizing, the accepting and the refusing power" (Lippmann 1955: 31).

Much of this early postwar research was criticized because it was based on anecdotal accounts and case studies (Amlund 1969; Edwards 1990; Heclo 1977; Sperlich 1975). This criticism is no longer particularly relevant because in the last fifteen years significant advances have been made in applying quantitative methodologies to the study of the interaction between the president and Congress in creating legislation.[20] Despite the many differences between this quantitative work and the earlier qualitative work, their underlying assumptions are the same: policy leadership is a zero-sum game, which modern presidents have dominated. There are two reasons for this shared assumption.

The first reason is derived from the structure of research. As Kuhn noted, the accepted theories within a given school of research "define the legitimate problems and methods of a research field for succeeding generations of practitioners" (Kuhn 1970: 10). Political science is no different from other disciplines in that most research falls within the boundaries of clearly defined subfields. As was noted earlier, no clearly established body of literature is devoted to studying the interaction between the president and Congress in establishing policy.

The second reason is that presidential activity on legislation generates media attention, while the quiet and frequently inconspicuous work of representatives and senators often goes unnoticed. Even though a president's program is a relatively small part of Congress's legislative workload, it generates far more attention than do other pieces of legislation. Hence, the current assumption of executive dominance is understandable.

But in another sense this assumption of a zero-sum game is a bit surprising. Some of the most significant legislation of the postwar period, such as the Taft-Hartley Act of 1947, the War Powers Act of 1973, and South African sanctions in 1986, were initiated by Congress without the support of the president. There also have been numerous case studies, for example, the 1968 Sundquist study of policymaking in the Eisenhower, Kennedy, and Johnson years and Birnbaum and Murray's 1988 study of tax reform, which have ascribed to Congress a legislative role equally important to that of the president. These studies describe a much more involved process of give-and-take in policymaking than is traditionally posited. They found that many laws, even those most strongly associated with a particular president, can be traced back to congressional initiatives that had not passed in previous sessions.[21] While not denigrating the important legislative role of presidents, these scholars argue that Congress is much more important than is generally acknowledged.

Furthermore, as early as 1946 Chamberlain found in his study of the legislative histories of ninety major laws that Congress played at least as important a role as the president (Chamberlain 1946). Moe and Teel (1971) in their update of Chamberlain's analysis found very similar results. For many years these two works stood out as unique in their commitment to studying the joint influence of both the president and Congress and to integrating scholarship from both areas of research.

However, none of these earlier quantitative studies changed the conventional view of policymaking as a conflictual process dominated by presidents in the modern era. Peterson's recent critique of the "presidency-centered" perspective and his development of the alternative "tandem-institutions" perspective represent the first serious attempt at redressing this institutional myopia that has prevented the development of a truly joint view of policymaking (Peterson 1990). Although the importance of this work in helping to change the character of scholarly discourse cannot be overstated, Peterson's work suffers from some serious limitations.

First, even though Peterson argues that his perspective is one of "tandem institutions," his decision to limit his study to a subset of presidential initiatives means that he has actually started from a "presidency-centered" perspective. An approach treating Congress and the president as co-equal institutions would necessarily include a broader range of bills.

Second, Peterson's "presidency-centered" perspective is evident in his downplaying of the significance of the fact that many presidential initiatives originate within Congress (Peterson 1990: 47–48). Although his point that becoming a part of a president's program increases an initiative's prominence has merit, the adoption of a truly "tandem-institutions" perspective would also involve consideration of the role Congress plays in the development of the initiative before it is embraced by a president. In particular, one needs to consider Kingdon's perspective that bill introductions by members often serve to keep ideas alive during lean times. It is part of what Kingdon describes as the "softening up process" (Kingdon 1984: 137 and 190–91).

Finally, by studying only the 1953–84 period Peterson is unable to assess the effect of long-term social, political, and economic transformations of the roles played by the president and Congress regarding legislation. Peterson acknowledges this but does not attempt to remedy it when he discusses Skowronek's "political time" theory (Peterson 1990: 101–2).[22]

The theory of dynamic constitutionalism is frankly designed to present an alternative to the prevailing view of presidential dominance of an often conflictual legislative process. The use of the Constitution as a predictor of institutional interaction ensures that there is no implicit bias toward one branch at the expense of the other. The distinction between the boundary-setting constitutional provisions and those that encourage but do not require certain patterns of behavior is unique to this project. The strength of this approach is that it allows one to test whether there is a division of labor and a higher degree of cooperation than was previously recognized. This project differs from earlier scholarship in that it is explicitly co-institutional and diachronic.

Organization

The subsequent chapters will be organized around a series of thematic questions raised by the theory of dynamic constitutionalism. An attempt will be made to identify overall patterns of interbranch interactions and then show how changing social conditions affect those patterns.

Chapter 2 will focus on the linkages between research goals and the choice of methodologies. In particular, the methodological aims and trade-offs inherent in the treatment of Congress and the president as co-institutions and in historical research will be explored in some depth. Part of the chapter will be devoted to a discussion of the reasons for focusing on a single policy area and the justifications for the one chosen. Finally, the reasons for utilizing both qualitative and quantitative methodologies in one research project will be explained.

Chapter 3 will be devoted to a detailed exposition of three case studies. The legislative histories of the policy initiatives will be traced from the point of their initial introduction onto the legislative agenda and will conclude with their final passage into law decades later. These studies will be used to illustrate the various patterns of legislative interaction that occur in the passage of actual specific policy proposals. One of the most notable factors in the case studies is the effect of temporal shifts in the broader social environment in changing the definition of what is politically possible and how that, in turn, alters the interactions between the president and members of Congress.

In Chapter 4 quantitative methodologies will be used to study the role of congressional committees in moving policy initiatives from the systemic to the formal agenda. The emphasis will be on how committees exercise their autonomous "gatekeeping" function. The primary data set used in the analysis consists of 6,578 bills introduced into the House and Senate over the past approximately 160 years. Particular attention will be paid to the activities of presidents and committee chairs and to changing patterns of interaction over time.

In Chapter 5 the primary emphasis will be on the passage of legislation. An attempt will be made to identify which actors have the greatest influence on floor decisionmaking. In addition, the conditions that help or hinder the passage of legislation, such as unified party control and changes in the economy will be explored. Here too both the general pattern of interaction and differences over time will be presented.

In Chapter 6 alternative theories about presidential leadership will be analyzed and tested. The first half of the chapter will focus on zero-sum theories of executive dominance, most notably Huntington's view that the presidency is far better able than Congress to provide leadership in the modern world. In the second half cyclical theories, such as Skowronek's "political time" thesis, which explicitly incorporates a historical dimension, will be tested. Finally, these theories will be contrasted with dynamic constitutionalism.

The concluding chapter offers a general assessment of executive-congressional relations. It returns to the theoretical concerns raised in the first chapter and shows how well they have been answered. The long-term implications of the constitutional separation and sharing of responsibility will be revisited and assessed in light of the preceding chapters. Overall patterns and historical trends will be offered.

Notes

1. In a parliamentary system of government, where the executive and legislative functions are fused, a majority in the parliament virtually guarantees that legislation endorsed by the prime minister or the cabinet will be passed. As LeLoup and Shull noted, even though the Christian Democrats under German chancellor Helmut Schmidt had only a four-vote majority in the 1970s, they were able to win every key legislative vote (LeLoup and Shull 1993: 5).

2. Between 1946 and 1992 we have experienced twenty-eight years of divided party control of government. While there have been many periods of divided control in the past, this era has been unique in the amount of concern about governmental "stalemate" and "gridlock." During the long period of divided government in the last quarter of the nineteenth century, there were no comparable outpourings of concern about a governability crisis. See Mayhew's (1991) summary of the literature on divided government.

3. James Madison, in *Federalist Paper* 51, spoke for both the Federalists and the Anti-Federalists when he wrote, "Ambition must be made to counteract ambition. The interest of the man must be connected with the constitutional rights of the place. It may be a reflection on human nature that such devices should be necessary to control the abuse of government. But what is government itself but the greatest of all reflections on human nature? If men were angels, no government would be necessary. If angels were to govern men, neither external nor internal controls on government would be necessary" (Madison, Hamilton, and Jay, 1987 edition: 319–20).

4. It is particularly difficult to distinguish between general patterns of presidential behavior and the idiosyncrasies of individual presidents because of the "N of one" problem. The "N of one" problem refers to the constraints on quantitative analysis caused by having only one president at any given time. The small number of presidents makes it difficult to generalize about the nature of the office. See Edwards (1990: 37); King (1975: 174); and Spitzer (1983b: 2–3) for a more extended discussion of the impediments to quantitative research.

5. Even though these earlier agrarian movements and the dramatic institutional changes in Congress were separated by decades, scholars such as Brady and Althoff (1974); Brady, Brody, and Epstein (1989); and Schroedel and Snyder (1992), using an historical framework to analyze Congress, have found a link between the mass-based Populist protest and subsequent Progressive era reforms within Congress.

6. Hamilton, writing in *Federalist Paper* 123, laid out two reasons why the chief executive needed to have at least a partial veto over legislative acts. The first

was that the president needed its power because of "the propensity of the legislative department to intrude upon the rights and to absorb the powers, of the other departments" (Madison, Hamilton, and Jay, 1987 edition: 418). But Hamilton viewed the veto also as "a salutary check upon the legislative body, calculated to guard the community against the effects of faction, precipitancy, or of any impulse unfriendly to the public good, which may happen to influence a majority of that body" (Madison, Hamilton, Jay, 1987 edition: 418).

7. The recognition of only minimal constitutional change in the provisions governing executive-congressional relations should not be taken as implying constitutional stasis. At least as far back as McCloskey's (1960) history of the Supreme Court, there has been an understanding that interpretations of the Constitution can dramatically alter the law. See also Ackerman (1991) for a more recent theory of historical changes in constitutional law.

8. The line-item veto would give presidents the power to veto part of a bill while allowing the rest to become law. Forty-three state constitutions give their governors some version of the line-item veto power. Most advocates of a presidential line-item veto believe that it would restrain congressional enactment of pork barrel legislation. Interest in the line-item veto has increased dramatically over the past decade as federal deficits skyrocketed. See Berch (1992) for an up-to-date review of the literature on the line-item veto.

9. Lawrence Chamberlain warned against this tendency when he wrote, "The legislative process is not like a see-saw where as one end goes down the other must automatically go up. It is, rather, like a gasoline engine which operates most efficiently when all of its cylinders are functioning. When the president becomes unusually active, there is a tendency to assume that the congressional cylinder has ceased to function. Such is not necessarily the case" (Chamberlain 1946: 14).

10. This congressional deferral has its roots in the Constitution's designation of the president as "commander-in-chief" and his pre-eminent position in treaty-making as set out in Article I, Section 2. More generally, presidents have used the plenary powers and a narrow interpretation of enumerated powers to buttress their position in foreign and defense policy. Since there is no specific constitutional clause assigning overall responsibility for the conduct of foreign policy, it was a source of some early conflict between the president and Congress. See Fisher (1985: 252–325) for a thorough discussion of the historical developments. Eventual presidential supremacy in this area was achieved by presidents combining the plenary powers doctrine and the doctrine of exclusion as applied to the powers enumerated in the Constitution. The plenary powers theory holds that the United States government can exercise the same foreign affairs powers as any other sovereign nation even though most of these powers are not mentioned in the Constitution. When this theory is combined with a belief that Congress can act only in the areas specifically outlined in Article I of the Constitution, an opportunity was created for presidents to claim those powers for themselves as part of their general grant of the "Executive Power" (Pious 1979: 333–34).

11. The current movement toward limiting the terms of members of Congress may change the incentive structure for legislators by shortening their time framework, but these measures will almost certainly face constitutional challenges. Although there are no exactly comparable cases that can be used as a precedent, one case will certainly be drawn on in any ruling dealing with limitations on

congressional service. In 1969 the Supreme Court in *Powell* v. *McCormack,* 395
U.S. 486, held that a state's right to elect and send to Congress whomever it
wishes can be overturned only if the person elected fails to meet the qualifications
laid out in Article I, Section 5, of the Constitution.

12. Although many scholars have studied the conflicts between presidents and
their subordinates, Heclo's (1977) path-breaking study is a particularly good starting point for those interested in this issue. Gormley (1989) examines the consequences of bureaucratic reforms of the 1970s and 1980s.

13. The description of the bureaucracy as a "fourth branch" of government
appears to have originated with the Brownlow Committee, which in its 1937
report referred to independent regulatory commissions as "a headless 'fourth
branch' of government, a haphazard deposit of irresponsible agencies and uncoordinated powers" (Brownlow 1937: 40). Although the Brownlow Report applied
the term only to independent agencies, the "fourth branch" label has subsequently
been applied to the entire federal bureaucracy.

14. According to Stephen Skowronek, the American government cannot be
classified as a state in the European sense for the first hundred years of its
existence. American state building was a direct response to the emergence of
industrially based capitalism between 1877 and 1920. Increased demands on the
government to act as an economic guarantor of well-being led to the creation of a
full-fledged administrative state (Skowronek 1982: 5–14).

15. While there have been some attempts at understanding the causes of divided government, there have only been a few analyses of the overall policymaking relationship between Congress and the president. Aside from traditional
constitutional law analyses and studies of presidential influence, only minimal
interest has been evident in developing a theoretical understanding of how the two
branches jointly interact in setting policy. Mezey's (1989, 1991) development of
the representational model of Congress's role in policymaking is an interesting
update of Huntington's (1973) arguments about why the presidency is better
suited than Congress is to meet the policy demands of the late twentieth century.
LeLoup and Shull (1993) use case studies to illustrate the following possible four
patterns of policy interactions: deadlock/extraordinary resolution, presidential
dominance, congressional dominance, and consensus/cooperation.

16. Peter Sperlich, in a famous quotation, described presidential scholarship in
the following manner: "It is a quite common observation that the quality and
quantity of literature on the American presidency, apart from strictly biographic
materials, is exceedingly poor" (Sperlich 1975: 412). While most would argue
that there has been significant improvement in the past two decades, the relative
paucity of quantitative measures of presidential performance has hindered the
development of comparisons across administrations. Some of the more recent
works making these type of comparisons include Edwards and Wayne (1990);
Kernell (1986); Lowi (1985); and Spitzer (1983a) .

17. See Loewenberg, Patterson, and Jewell (1985) for an in-depth discussion
of the methodologically sophisticated, albeit fragmented, character of current legislative research.

18. Bond and Fleisher (1990) devote much of their second chapter to an
excellent critique of the "presidency-centered" and "Congress-centered" approaches to the study of policymaking. Although critical of both approaches for

their institutional myopia, Bond and Fleisher's own research clearly falls within the "presidency-centered" school, since their primary concern is to discover the sources of presidential success.

19. One example of this tendency to view the two branches in competition is former House Republican Leader John Rhodes's description of Congress as "little more than a glorified echo chamber for the Executive Branch of government—usually content to approve or disapprove, rarely willing to initiate" (Johannes 1974: 356).

20. Political power researchers (Bond and Fleisher 1980, 1990; Edwards 1976, 1980, and 1989; Edwards and Wayne 1990; Harmon and Brauen 1979; Zeidenstein 1980, 1983) working within the Neustadtian tradition have studied the relationship among a president's standing in public opinion polls, electoral success, and his depiction in the media and congressional support for his legislative program. Other political scientists associated with the rational choice variant of the "new institutionalist" tradition have studied general patterns of presidential coalition building (Sullivan 1988) and the influence of a threatened veto on congressional appropriations decisions (Kiewiet and McCubbins 1988).

21. Johannes described as "stealing" the tendency of presidents to claim Congressional initiatives as their own (Johannes 1974: 359).

22. Stephen Skowronek's "political time" theory is an attempt to apply the historical variant of "new institutionalism" to the interaction between the president and Congress on legislation (Skowronek 1986, 1984). It is discussed in more detail in Chapter 6.

2

Linking Goals
and Methodologies

Methodological Objectives

Every research project involves making subjective decisions about
the trade-offs necessary to achieve particular research goals. Each
researcher weighs whether the advantages of a particular approach or
methodology outweigh its disadvantages. Scholars will inevitably
disagree about the subjective choices made by an individual researcher.[1] Since there are neither completely value-free methodologies nor perfect empirical indicators, the best approach is to make the
reader aware of the linkages between research goals and the choice
of methodologies and the reasons why specific methodological trade-
offs were made.

This study of how Congress and the president historically have
attempted to overcome the governing paradox of being constitutionally separate but functionally related institutions entailed significant research trade-offs. The project was designed to highlight
some previously understudied aspects of the executive-congressional interaction in the legislative arena: the effect of the constitutional separation and forced sharing of legislative responsibility
on the degree of interbranch cooperation from both a co-institutional and a diachronic perspective. The maximization of these research goals led to concomitant decisions about the trade-offs
necessitated by those choices.

Co-institutional Perspective

The first aim was to devise an empirical measure emanating from neither a "presidency-centered" nor a "Congress-centered" perspective. The development of an empirical measure that is not implicitly biased toward one of the institutions requires a much broader approach than has previously been used by scholars. For example, an approach limiting itself only to studying initiatives that have presidential support has already biased its results in a manner that overstates the importance of the president.[2] Treating Congress and the presidency as co-equal institutions would entail the inclusion of initiatives lacking presidential involvement as well as those explicitly opposed by presidents.

The use of a more inclusive co-institutional empirical measure would have several concrete research advantages over the measures used in earlier research. It would allow an assessment of whether there are systematic differences between the types of legislation supported by presidents and those without presidential involvement. Given the constitutional incentives described in the previous chapter, the assumption is that presidents are much more likely to be involved in only the most important pieces of legislation, but little empirical evidence supports the strength and durability of this tendency. Standard measures, such as Congressional Quarterly's Presidential Box Score, are limited because they consider only items that have been on the legislative agendas of postwar presidents.[3]

It would also be desirable to have an empirical measure that compares the treatment of initiatives at different key decisionmaking junctures in the legislative process. The measure needs to be able to distinguish both the overall progression of an initiative toward passage and the speed of that movement. Are more presidentially supported measures reported out of committee than those without presidential support? Do these measures move through the different stages toward passage faster than other measures? What happens when initiatives are supported by committee chairs? Is the movement faster and are the passage rates higher on initiatives where there is explicit cooperation between the president and congressional leaders?

Finally, the measure needs to allow an assessment to be made of the impact of presidential opposition on legislative outcomes. The sheer number of opportunities to stop or slow a bill's progress suggests that the addition of presidential opposition up to and including the veto would make it difficult for congressional supporters to succeed in enacting legislation. Although such a premise is intuitively appealing, the overall effectiveness of presidential opposition has not been quantitatively measured.[4] Recent research indicates that only approximately 7% of presidential vetoes are overridden by Congress, but no one has assessed the impact of presidential opposition on stopping or slowing bills before they are passed.[5] Given the difficulty that Congress has in overriding the veto, the mere threat of presidential opposition may be enough to kill a bill's chances of moving through the stages toward passage.

In research, just as in real life, there are no free lunches. Some research advantages are associated with a more fully developed co-institutional perspective, but disadvantages are as well. In this case the major research trade-off involves the loss of detailed information about legislation. If one studies only major policy initiatives, especially those with presidential support, obtaining information about the behind-the-scenes maneuvering that occurs is easy. It is much more difficult and in many cases impossible to gain that type of information about routine and minor bills that lack presidential involvement. For example, legions of scholars are currently studying the congressional wheeling and dealing over the North American Free Trade Agreement. In contrast, few people know anything about the recent role of Congress in determining the qualifications of men involved in the Big Brothers organization in Washington, D.C.[6]

Diachronic Perspective

The second research aim was to develop an empirical measure incorporating a diachronic perspective able to detect the more subtle and slow-moving shifts in the underlying pattern of interinstitutional interaction. Without a long-term historical approach, those aspects of the interbranch relationship that have remained relatively constant and those that have pushed most strongly against the parameters established by the Constitution cannot be identified. Has the division of labor between the branches remained constant throughout the period studied? Has the level of explicit cooperation changed over time? Has the effectiveness of presidential opposition increased over time, and if so, by how much? Are there key historical junctures where changes have occurred or are most of the changes too subtle and inchoate to be associated with a particular era?

Previous research has not addressed these research questions. The ahistorical focus of that research has led to a failure to recognize the potential significance of slower and more subtle changes in the broader social environment on legislative decisionmaking. Their scholarship's limited temporal scope has produced a static formulation of executive-congressional relations. This is the first project designed to measure the more prolonged patterns of institutional adaptation brought about by the movement from a predominantly agricultural to an industrial and possibly postindustrial society.

Again the trade-off necessary to achieve this historical perspective involves the sacrifice of some other forms of information. Although uncovering hidden politicking around more obscure contemporary pieces of legislation may be difficult, obtaining records about the maneuvering associated with any but the most important nineteenth-century policy initiatives is impossible. For example, a researcher wanting to discover why the House Post Office and Roads Committee in the Forty-third Congress failed to report out a bill establishing a class three post office in Lafourche, Louisiana, would not be able to examine committee records because they were not kept, nor would she be able to ask any of the participants what happened because they are all dead. Many times it would be difficult even to ascertain whether the committee held hearings on the bill. Within the executive branch of government no reliable records exist of which bills were supported by the members of the administration during the nineteenth century.

Only a few reliable sources of information remain about a wide range of policy initiatives from the nineteenth century. Probably the most important sources of information about nineteenth-century bills are the Library of Congress's microfiche and paper copies of the text of legislation introduced into the House and the Senate. During the early years there are gaps in the numbering sequence of bills, indicating that some have been lost. With the exception of a handful of bills from the first half of the nineteenth century, the Library of Congress records also list the primary sponsor. That problem was eliminated with the start of the *Congressional Record* in 1873. Determining whether measures were reported out of committee in the early years requires examination of the *Congressional Globe* and *House Journal* to see if the bills came up on the floor of the entire chamber during that session, but even then one cannot be sure that the item discussed is the same one. Neither the *Congressional Globe* nor the *House Journal* use the official number and/or title of the bill when reporting floor action.

The only reliable and comparable source of information about the legislative positions of different presidents is the published records of their papers, messages, and speeches. While there are extensive records of the private positions of some presidents, for others there is virtually no information.[7] Because of the comparability problem, only the public positions are used in this research project. This means that presidential influence will be to some extent undermeasured; the problem is unavoidable because of the necessity of using a roughly comparable measure across the different presidencies. However, this is partly mitigated by the systematic undermeasurement of the influence of congressional actors. The measure of congressional influence, sponsorship of legislation, also fails to capture other important ways that members of Congress can affect legislative outcomes. This is particularly true of chairs, who can influence outcomes through their power to set the agendas of their committees, choose expert witnesses, and control committee staff.

The positions taken by other members of the executive branch of government on nineteenth-century bill are impossible to identify. No reliable records remain even of the positions of cabinet members on bills affecting their jurisdictional areas. Because of this problem, the role of the executive branch as a whole will be understated. Having this kind of information would certainly be desirable, but the penchant of individuals serving in the executive branch, even in the cabinet, to work at cross-purposes with the president is well documented.[8] Since relying solely on quantitative analysis of the bills would not capture the role of the broader executive branch, this study will also draw heavily on case studies and illustrative examples to fill in this gap. The case studies, which detail the legislative histories of three policy proposals, provide a sense of some of these interactions.

Defining Research Limits

Because over 400,000 bills have been introduced into Congress since its inception, limitations on the scope of legislation studied need to be justified. A researcher cannot possibly study more than a small portion of the total. This project's research design limits that scope in two significant ways. First, the time period, limited to the Eighteenth through Ninety-ninth Congresses (1823–1986), was chosen because it coincides with the beginning of both institutionalization within Congress and industrialization throughout the country. Despite some controversy about exactly when industrialization began (Porter 1973: 28), scholars unanimously agree it began no earlier than the 1820s. North (1961: 189) identifies 1820–50 as the "critical period" of the country's economic development, when the economy took off and industrialization began.[9] Although the genesis of institutionalization is also difficult to determine, the Eighteenth Congress is a plausible starting point for the research. Within the House of Representatives the speakership and committee system were well developed by the mid-1820s, and even the Senate, slower to institutionalize, had begun the process (Peters 1990: 37; Smith and Deering 1990: 27–32).

Second, difficulties in assuring the randomization of any cross-section of bills mitigated in favor of limiting research to all the legislation introduced in a single policy area. The strategy of analyzing a single policy area ensures that data set will include bills of varying significance. The alternative approach of studying a subset of bills from different policy areas cannot assure this mix of important, routine, and minor legislation. For example, Chamberlain (1946) studied the legislative histories of ninety major laws passed over a fifty-year period. Moe and Teel (1971), in their update of Chamberlain's research, employed a similar research design. It is, however, difficult to generalize from these findings; the subsets are atypical because each of the laws was extremely important and was enacted. The pattern of legislative leadership may vary systematically with differences in policy importance, and one is likely to find differences between those initiatives that passed and those that did not. More recent studies by Peterson (1990) and Bond and Fleisher (1990), which examine subsets of presidential initiatives and important roll-call votes during the postwar period, are also atypical of the entire legislative universe.

Choice of a Policy Area

Since only legislation from a single policy area is studied, the area must be chosen carefully. Ever since Wildavsky published his seminal article, "The Two Presidencies," scholars have argued that Congress and the president have different patterns of interaction on foreign policy than they do on domestic policy.[10] The initial decision of whether to pick a foreign or domestic policy area was relatively simple. The enormous additional difficulties in obtaining information about foreign policy initiatives was a consideration, but more important, since the vast majority of bills are designed to enact domestic policies, it made sense to consider only those. One could not draw generalizations based on a study of foreign policy bills. Moreover, foreign policy has traditionally been an area of presidential dominance, so any results would be biased in that direction.

In making the decision about which domestic policy area to choose, three factors were paramount. First, the legislation in the policy area had to vary in the degree of importance. It had to include bills of the highest importance, as well as those of minor significance, so that generalizations about possible differences in interaction caused the level of significance can be drawn. Second, the policy had to be on the legislative agenda throughout the period studied. Otherwise, it would be impossible to assess which aspects of executive-congressional interaction had remained the same and which had changed over time. Finally, in keeping with the desire to have a truly co-institutional perspective, the policy could not be one in which either the Congress or the president have traditionally been viewed as dominant. The policy area chosen, banking regulation, is the only one that meets all three of these criteria.

Since commercial bank assets equal approximately 40% of the aggregate resources of the financial sector, the public's stake in the banking sector is enormous (Rose and Fraser 1985: 141). The amount and quality of housing available, the rate of inflation, regional growth, urban renewal, and the funding of schools are just a few of the public's concerns affected by bankers' decisions. For these reasons, some banking bills will always fall into the highest category of importance. However, there are a large number of bills of moderate and even minor importance. For example, most would agree that legislation establishing prison terms for bank robbers is of moderate importance and that a bill allowing a small bank located in a Massachusetts town to change its name is of only minimal significance. The criteria used in classifying legislative importance are discussed at great length in the Appendix.

Not only is the well-being of the banking system essential to the country's economic health, but banking is also a policy area that has figured prominently on the public agenda throughout the entire history of the United States. Unlike most domestic policies, banking policy contains a clear, unambiguous grant of federal authority going back to the Constitution, making it a policy area particularly well suited to this type of historical analysis. Most of the other policy areas that are currently considered important components of the domestic agenda, such as health care, welfare, and economic stabilization, were not within the purview of the national government during the nineteenth century. Many of the issues that were important then, such as Indian policy, land development, postal service, and war pensions, are relatively minor concerns today. Banking policy is virtually the only policy area that was prominent throughout the entire period.

Finally, it is important to examine a policy area in which neither the president nor Congress is traditionally viewed as being dominant. If the policy was one where either branch had an inherent advantage, generalizations would be even more difficult. Lowi (1964) classified regulatory policies, such as banking, as an area not traditionally dominated by either branch.[11]

No other domestic policy area meets these three criteria as effectively as does banking regulation. The few other domestic policies that have been on the national policy agenda for the entire period either fail to meet the test of including bills that differ in terms of the level of significance or are biased toward one branch of government. For these reasons, banking policy is a particularly suitable test case. Readers who lack a background in this particular policy area will find the following synopsis a useful introduction to American banking practices. Those who are already familiar with the area should feel free to skip this section.

A Brief History of Banking Policy

During the last 160 years the forms of bank regulation have spanned the entire range of possibilities—from absolute, tight control exercised by a central bank to completely unregulated laissez-faire banking in which anything was possible. At different times, federal law has mandated the establishment and in some cases the dismantling of a host of government regulatory agencies. To cope with the varying requirements of regulatory law, the banks in turn have developed distinctive institutional arrangements during different historical periods. In a like manner, a wide range of banking practices has been alternately permitted and prohibited.

At the most general level, the major changes in regulatory law, institutional arrangements, and practices were an outgrowth of the underlying social and economic transformations within the broader society. However, the specific forms that these changes took were often shaped by the underlying conflicts among different financial sector interests. This section traces the most important changes in the laws governing banking operations through five historical periods: 1823–60, 1861–1912, 1913–32, 1933–60, and 1961 onward. These periods were chosen because they coincided with major shifts in the country's political economy.

Early Banking Practices

In the 1820s banks fell into two general classes: commercial center banks, which paid their capital in specie and whose assets were short-term loans to merchants, and state-chartered country banks located in the agricultural regions, where specie was scarce and whose primary capital was the credit of the state. The country banks located in the South and West favored easy credit to facilitate regional economic growth, which was primarily based on agriculture.[12] In contrast, the commercial center banks of the Northeast were primarily concerned with providing capital to commerce and industry and maintaining the value of currency. However, it is overly simplistic to think of the regions as having separate economies; already in the mid-1820s the transportation revolution was laying the groundwork for a national economy.[13]

Most of the early banking bills were designed to provide competitive advantages to individual small banks. Few of these bills were actually enacted into law. Federal regulation of bank activities was provided by the Second Bank of the United States (hereafter referred to as the BUS), which acted as general creditor to the other banks. By pressing for the payment of notes, the BUS exercised restraint on the entire system, so that the capital scarce country banks were often unable to make loans to farmers. The country banks' increasing hostility to the BUS is evidenced by the following Supreme Court cases: *McCulloch* v. *Maryland* (1819), which sought to have the BUS declared unconstitutional, and *Bank of the United States* v. *Planters Bank* (1824), in which the BUS went to court to force a debtor bank to pay. The larger banks in New York and Philadelphia also resented the BUS because it was a potent economic competitor.[14] The money center banks were particularly jealous of the BUS's role as a depository for government funds.

The 1828 election brought into office a coalition opposed to the BUS. Traditional historians such as Schlesinger (1945) have seen the Jacksonian revolution as the triumph of popular control over economic privilege, while revisionist historian Hammond (1957) saw it as a conflict between entrepreneurial elements in the West and conservative old money in the East. Post-Hammond scholars have split between those giving primacy to economic explanations (Temin 1969) and those more concerned with political explanations (McFaul 1972; Sharp 1970). The most plausible explanation is that the Jackson coalition was just that—a coalition of economically and politically diverse groups united largely by their opposition to the Monster Bank.

The importance of presidential leadership in breaking the Bank of the United States is absolutely clear. Andrew Jackson first attacked the BUS in 1828, seven years before it was due to be rechartered, and made the power of the bank a central issue in his 1832 re-election campaign.[15] When supporters of the BUS made a tactical error and tried to pass a bill rechartering the bank three years early, Jackson vetoed the legislation and Congress was unable to override the veto. When Jackson was re-elected in the fall, he believed that the electorate had given him a mandate to destroy the BUS and transferred government funds to state-chartered banks.[16]

From the time the Bank of the United States's charter expired in 1836 until the passage of the National Bank Act in 1863, there was no federal regulation of banks. At the national level, different interests within the dominant Jackson coalition battled over establishment of the Independent Treasury Plan to remove all government funds from the banking system. In 1840 the Democrats succeeded in passing legislation designed to create an Independent Treasury, but after the Whigs regained control of Congress the Independent Treasury Act was repealed. The congressional divisions over banking issues prevented the enactment of any other significant legislation during this period.

State lawmakers continued to struggle over questions of bank regulation. Some states responded to widespread bank closures during the Panic of 1837 by enacting laws prohibiting banks from operating within their state boundaries. The most common response of state legislatures was to pass a "free banking law," which eliminated most of the barriers that had prevented entrepreneurs from entering into the banking business. Typically the laws provided that: (1) any person or group could form a bank without a special act of the state legislature; (2) note issues had to be supported by some form of security; (3) a bank had to maintain a specie reserve equal to a specific percentage of deposits; and (4) state bank examiners would periodically examine each bank. The ability of the state laws to protect bank customers varied from state to state.[17] The "free banking laws" served as the model for the next major federal regulatory law, the National Bank Act of 1863.

In the 1850s the commercial center banks developed a new institutional arrangement, the clearinghouse, to restrain the country banks from issuing excessive amounts of notes that were not backed by deposits. Clearinghouses required country banks to keep deposits in city banks to cover their checks. Balances were settled daily. After the Panic of 1857, the clearinghouse movement spread rapidly because few well-capitalized money center banks would honor checks from rural banks that were not part of the system (Klebner 1974: 26–27).

The Comptroller of the Currency

The election of Abraham Lincoln in 1860 and the Civil War were watershed events in the history of the nation. In social, political, and economic terms, the Civil War is often used to mark the end of one era and the beginning of another. In one sense, the Civil War only accelerated changes already under way, most notably the transportation revolution that facilitated the shift from an agrarian society to an industrial one.[18] But in another sense, the war itself had a tremendous effect. The more than half a million soldiers killed in the Civil War is quadruple the rate of World War II. Goldin and Lewis (1975: 304–9) estimated the direct costs of the war at over $6 billion in 1860 dollars.

Lincoln experienced great difficulty in raising the more than $2.25 billion necessary to fight the Civil War and in controlling currency fluctuations without a central bank. In his first Annual Treasury Report, Secretary Salmon Chase proposed the establishment of a system of nationally chartered banks regulated by the new Office of the Comptroller of the Currency to overcome these problems. A variety of appeals were used to pull together a highly unlikely coalition to enact such a system in the National Bank Act of 1863. Western Republicans were won over by appeals to nationalist sentiment that equated states' rights with respect to slavery and secession to state control over money and banking (Hammond 1970: 321 and 326). At the same time, large Eastern banks were led to believe that the National Bank Act was the first step toward currency stabilization and cartelization, which would allow them to eliminate the country banks (Eccles 1982: 49).

Much to the chagrin of the banking community, post–Civil War comptrollers of the currency interpreted the Act's statement that a bank's "usual business shall be transacted at an office or banking house located in the place specified in its organization certificate" to be a prohibition against branching by national banks (Eccles 1982: 49). As a result banks were reluctant to switch from state to national charters, leading Congress to pass an act to force banks into the national system through the imposition of a tax on all state bank notes. If Congress had not acted in this manner, there would have been no national banks, and by extension, no national regulation of the banking system.

Until superseded by the Federal Reserve Act of 1913, the National Bank Act was the most important banking law in the country. It established three important precedents in banking regulation: national supervision, minimum capital requirements, and the maintenance of specified reserve requirements.

While the new national system did eliminate the hodge-podge of state bank notes and reduce the number of bank failures, it also encouraged the pyramiding of reserves in New York City. In order to take advantage of the call money market, country banks in the summer and winter deposited part of their reserves in the New York City banks. This resulted in a double counting, as both the New York City banks and the country banks counted those funds as part of their required reserves. A credit squeeze occurred in the spring and fall when the country banks withdrew their funds to make farm loans. These actions brought on the liquidity crises of 1873, 1893, and 1907.

Progressive Era Reforms

In the first two liquidity crises the calls for banking reform subsided once the crisis passed, but 1907 was different because of the heavy involvement of foreign banks. After depleting domestic funds, speculators turned to European banks for additional capital. When these funds were cut off in 1907, the credit squeeze was far worse than ever before (Eccles 1982: 51–52). In the ensuing panic, which spread from the weaker interior banks to the more powerful Eastern banks, nineteen national and eighty-three state banks failed because of insufficient funds (Kennedy 1973: 8).

After the 1907 crisis, Congress established the National Monetary Commission to make recommendations for comprehensive banking reform. Despite a consensus that changes in the regulatory structure were necessary, Congress was deadlocked on the issue from 1907 until 1913. The entire banking community united behind a proposal put forward by Senator Nelson Aldrich (R, Rhode Island) for a central banking system run entirely by bankers. The country bankers supported the Aldrich plan because it proposed fifteen independent regional associations that they felt would protect them from being swallowed up by the larger Eastern banks. After the Pujo Committee investigations into the abuses of money trusts, radical Democrats, Populists, farmers, and the general public were chary of any plan putting control of the system in the hands of bankers (Krooss 1983, Vol. 3: 165–66). Partisan conflicts kept even the more conservative Democrats from uniting behind the Aldrich Plan.

The stalemate was broken in 1912, when the Democrats gained control of both legislative chambers and the White House. Immediately after the election, Carter Glass (D, Virginia), the new chair of the House Banking and Currency Committee, began work on a bill to establish a national reserve system. Although Woodrow Wilson had given no indication during the campaign of his position on banking reform, he became a strong backer of the bill. As a Democrat, Wilson was able to garner support for Glass's bill that incorporated many of the features of the defunct Aldrich Plan (Kolko 1963: 224–28). That bill became the Federal Reserve Act of 1913, which established an advisory Federal Reserve Board and twelve autonomous regional banks. Each regional bank was headed by a board of nine directors (six selected by the member banks and three appointed by the national Federal Reserve Board). Each regional bank sought to influence credit in its region by changing the discount rate (i.e., raising or lowering the interest member banks paid for loans from the reserve banks) or by buying or selling on the open market (Kennedy 1973: 11).

Structural weaknesses that were built into the Federal Reserve System prevented it from exercising strong control over the policies pursued by the nation's banks. First, the lack of central control over the twelve regional reserve banks meant that they often worked against each other (Kennedy 1973: 11–12). Second, banks could completely avoid federal regulation through continuing charters with the less stringent state systems (Kennedy 1973: 7). Third, although the Federal Reserve System could pump money into the system, it lacked the authority to control banks' use of funds (Kennedy 1973: 210–11). Because of these loopholes, the Federal Reserve System was unable to prevent banks from making risky investments in securities and real estate during the 1920s (Kennedy 1973: 13).

The Impact of the Great Depression

By the time Roosevelt came into office in 1933, the country was in the midst of an economic collapse. More than a quarter of the work force was unemployed, the country's manufacturing output had dropped 50%, and the financial system had virtually collapsed. Between 1930 and 1933, 773 national banks and 3,604 state banks failed (Eccles 1982: 82). The new administration moved quickly to assert control over the banking system. Its first proposal was the 1933 Emergency Banking Act, which gave the president authority to close and open banks. This was the only administration proposal that can be attributed almost solely to the executive branch. The administration's other banking proposals reflect at least as much of a congressional imprint as executive influence (Chamberlain 1946: 450–52) and were sponsored by the chairs of the House and Senate banking committees.

The Glass-Steagall Act of 1933, a comprehensive bank reform measure, was the result of this collaboration between the White House and the banking committees. The Act strengthened the nation's banks by severing the links between commercial and investment banking, increasing the power of the Federal Reserve System to control credit, permitting branch banking where allowed by state law, and establishing the Federal Deposit Insurance Corporation (FDIC) to provide federal government guarantees of deposits.

The Bank Act of 1935 was another product of extensive executive-congressional interaction. It was designed to prevent a recurrence of the regional reserve banks' mistakes of the 1920s by centralizing power within the Federal Reserve System. The Act gave the president the power to appoint members of the Federal Reserve Board and to confirm the elected heads of each of the regional reserve banks. The Act also gave the board the authority to alter the reserve requirements of each of the regional reserve banks and placed the seven governors of the board on the twelve-person Open Market Committee.

Contemporary Banking

There were few problems with this system until the 1960s, when the entire financial sector began to experience a major structural transformation. The dominant position of American commercial banking came under sustained attack from both foreign banks and other sectors of the domestic financial community. Foreign banks, which were not subject to restrictions on branching, reserve requirements, and antitrust laws, made impressive inroads in the market (*Fortune* 28 August 1978: 95). Existing law limited the interest rates that banks could offer on savings accounts to far below market rates, which left them vulnerable to competition from savings and loans and mutuals. At the same time, credit unions, mutuals, and savings and loans launched an assault on banking's traditional monopoly on checking accounts.

Most of these specialized "savings intermediaries" were born in the late nineteenth century because the commercial banks ignored the needs of ordinary citizens and small businesses for savings accounts. Because banks were strictly interested in demand deposits and short-term loans, the thrifts were able to take over the small savings niche. The thrifts paid interest on the deposits and put most of the funds into the home mortgage market (Salamon et al. 1975: 6). By the 1960s, when the small savings niche had become sufficiently lucrative to attract the interest of the bankers, the thrifts were firmly entrenched. With the aid of their allies in the construction industry, the thrifts were able to convince Congress to place ceilings on the interest rates that banks could offer on savings accounts, giving the thrift industry an advantage in the mortgage market.

Much of this encroachment on the traditional bank market was facilitated by computer-age technology. The segmentation of the financial industry was rendered obsolete when fund transfer could be accomplished merely by pushing a button. Thrifts, which had been prohibited from offering checking accounts, could offer share draft accounts that served the same function as checking accounts but did not explicitly violate the law. Technological development had outpaced the development of the regulatory structures.

When the regulatory agencies failed to resolve these sectoral conflicts, the affected institutions looked to the courts for relief. The courts were reluctant to get involved and gave Congress until 1 January 1980, to enact comprehensive banking regulation that would resolve these conflicts (Patterson 1979: 322). Congress responded by passing the Depository Institutions Deregulatory and Monetary Control Act of 1980, which sanctioned the use of automatic transfer services, checking account substitutes, and remote service units. It also established a Depository Institutions Deregulatory Committee to phase out interest rate ceilings over the next ten years (*Congressional Quarterly Weekly Report* 12 April 1980: 965).

Even though the Reagan administration was committed to deregulating the financial sector, Congress was able to block most of its attempts to change banking law. For example, the Garn–St. Germain Depository Institutions Act of 1982 is fairly limited. The administration's major deregulation proposal, a plan to repeal the Glass-Steagall Act's separation of commercial and investment banking, was blocked in 1983 and 1984 by House Banking Committee Chair St. Germain (*Congressional Quarterly Weekly Report* 2 February 1985: 188). This meant that much of the deregulatory momentum shifted from the legislative to the administrative arena.

Methodological Approach

Since both qualitative and quantitative approaches to the study of executive-congressional interaction in policymaking have distinctive strengths, each is utilized in this study. One obvious advantage of the main qualitative approach, case studies, is the ability to provide a detailed and in-depth understanding of a process. If one wants to understand the give-and-take of actual policymaking, case studies are the appropriate methodology.

Williamson, Karp, and Dalphin identify two additional functions of qualitative research (1977: 17–24). The first function, exploration, is widely accepted as a necessary part of any type of ongoing research. Scholars use insights gained through an intensive study of one case to generate hypotheses about the broader world. The second function of qualitative research, making conceptual or analytic generalizations, is less well received. Critics of the case study method charge that reliance solely on case studies increases the danger that the cases studied may not be typical. Williamson, Karp, and Dalphin try to refute that charge by arguing that contextual differences should not be allowed to obscure universal social forms of interaction:

> Good social science also seeks to uncover generic forms of phenomena that may vary in empirical content—underlying forms of social life. We can assert that human behavior presents itself in constant behavioral forms that differ only in content. If we accept the notion that specific analytical generalizations can be made, and that these generalizations cut across contexts varying in empirical content, we begin to see the importance of the case study. One task of sociological analysis is to reveal universal social forms that display themselves in a variety of empirical contexts. (Williamson, Karp, and Dalphin 1977: 22)

The main qualitative analysis in this project is an in-depth analysis of three case studies that illustrate some of the most important aspects of interaction between the president and Congress in setting policy. The legislative histories of these policies will be traced from the time they were first introduced as bills until their passage. A particularly useful characteristic of the case studies is that they allow a contextualization of the role played by institutional actors, such as members of the broader executive branch, that could not be adequately analyzed solely through quantitative measures. These case studies provide insights into the impact of constituency groups, external events, and the bargaining necessary to build a winning coalition. In one sense these case studies are exploratory, in that they identify questions that will be addressed more fully in the data analysis. But in another sense the case studies allow one to make generalizations about underlying forms of behavior.

By using quantitative methods one can avoid the controversy over the typicality of case studies. The main advantage of quantitative methods is their identification of broad patterns. Hence, this approach is particularly useful for testing generalizable hypotheses. The core of this project will involve an examination of the roles played by presidents and members of Congress in banking legislation over the past approximately 160 years. The primary data set is the 6,578 banking bills introduced into the House and Senate during that time period.[19] These data can be understood only through the use of various statistical techniques, which illuminate the broad patterns of executive-congressional behavior and permit some conclusions to be drawn about the factors affecting that behavior.

Notes

1. For example, one of the biggest current disagreements among researchers is between scholars utilizing sociologically based models of congressional behavior and advocates of spatial models derived from economically based models of rationality. Recently, scholars from both schools have begun to justify their particular approaches. For example, Strom (1990: xi–xiii) does an excellent job of explaining exactly what a spatial modeling approach can and cannot be used to explain. While certainly arguing that his approach is superior to the alternative, Strom is to be commended for clearly explaining his choices.

2. Even the recent research, which attempts to develop a "tandem-institutions" perspective, utilizes a research design that overstates the importance of the president. As was pointed out in Chapter 1, Peterson (1990), who is responsible for popularizing the term "tandem institutions," biased his results by only studying presidential initiatives. LeLoup and Shull (1993) also utilize the "tandem-institutions" perspective, but their research design was also implicitly biased toward the president. Their decision to limit their study to an in-depth analysis of the legislative histories of sixteen important laws understates the role of Congress, which bears a disproportionate responsibility for routine and minor legislation.

3. The Congressional Quarterly Box Score also suffers from other methodological problems. According to Bond and Fleisher, the box scores have five additional methodological limitations: (1) the reliability of the measures, (2) difficulties in handling compromises, (3) aggregation problems caused by limiting their time framework to only yearly measures, (4) problems with distinguishing between congressional failure as opposed to inaction, and (5) other important instances of executive-congressional interaction, such as decisions on presidential appointments, are omitted (Bond and Fleisher 1990: 55–59).

4. There have been a variety of studies (Copeland 1983; Hoff 1991; Lee 1975; Rohde and Simon 1985; Taylor 1971; Watson 1988) assessing the impact of presidential vetoes on the ultimate passage of legislation into law, but there have been no studies exploring the effect of the other forms of presidential opposition.

5. Presidents Washington through Reagan vetoed a total of 2,469 bills; 1,050 of these were pocket vetoes that Congress could not override. Congress actually succeeded in overriding only 103 of the 1,419 non-pocket vetoes (*Congressional Quarterly Weekly Report* 7 January 1989, table on p. 7).

6. Senator William Armstrong (D, Colorado) on March 1, 1990, introduced an amendment to S1430, the National and Community Services Act, to prohibit gays and lesbians from volunteering to work with organizations such as Big Brothers in Washington, D.C. When this amendment was defeated, he introduced a similar amendment to the District of Columbia Appropriations bill for fiscal year 1991.

7. There is a wide variation in the amount of information available about the different men who have served in the Oval Office. Some presidents, such as Franklin Roosevelt and Lyndon Johnson, have been widely studied. This stands in marked contrast to the amount of information available about some of the less well known nineteenth-century presidents, such as Millard Fillmore and Chester Arthur. But only minimal information is available about the private and behind-the-scenes maneuvering of some twentieth-century presidents. For example, Cal-

vin Coolidge was an extremely private man with few confidants. Not only are there no insider accounts of the Coolidge presidency, there are no collections of private papers from the Coolidge presidency. President Coolidge burned almost all his private papers.

8. Recent conflicts, such as those between President George Bush and his Housing secretary, Jack Kemp, are quite restrained when compared with those of the nineteenth century. For example, President Abraham Lincoln reputedly appointed his former Treasury secretary, Salmon Chase, to the chief justice's position in the Supreme Court in an attempt to end Chase's continual intriguing against the president. Chase and Lincoln had repeatedly clashed over wartime policies and civil service appointments (Charnwood 1917: 328–29, 406–8, and 429–30.)

9. The "takeoff" thesis was first put forth by the economist Walter Rostow in the 1950s. His most complete exposition of the thesis can be found in his 1960 book. Later scholars have criticized Rostow for either picking too late of a date for "takeoff" or argued that there was a gradual increase in economic output instead of a rapid increase (David 1967; North 1961; Porter 1973).

10. Wildavsky (1966) argued that presidents are more successful in winning congressional support for foreign and defense policies than for their domestic agendas. Most subsequent scholars found a similar pattern of greater support for defense and foreign policy initiatives, although the differences declined in the 1970s (LeLoup and Shull 1979; Peppers 1975). More recently, Bond and Fleisher (1990) have found evidence disputing the original "two presidencies" thesis. They discovered that Republican presidents get higher levels of support from Democratic members of Congress on conflictual foreign policy votes than on domestic policy votes, but that Democratic presidents get approximately the same level of cross-party support on both types of votes.

11. An inverse relationship may exist between the degree of institutional bias and the level of conflict. For example, Peterson found that there was greater interbranch conflict over regulatory policies than any other (Peterson 1990: 179). Hence, if one finds cooperation on regulatory policies, such as banking, the level of cooperation is likely to be even higher on less conflictual types of policies; this study, if anything, understates the prevalence of interbranch cooperation.

12. The need for capital in the West took primarily two different forms. First, even though the purchase price for public land was as low as $1.25 an acre, it still cost the average family the equivalent of three years' wages and years of back-breaking work to establish a working farm able to support a family at subsistence level. See Danhof (1969) and Primack (1962) for a detailed discussion of the high costs associated with setting up Western farms. The second reason for the capital shortage was endemic to agricultural production. In the spring and the autumn, farmers borrowed heavily from local banks in order to plant and to harvest their crops, thereby causing a cyclical credit squeeze. During bad years, when either the weather was bad or the price for agricultural crops low, farmers had difficulty paying off their accumulated debts.

13. Between 1849 and 1884, the United States went from having only 6,000 miles of railroad lines to having a total of 202,000 miles of railroad lines, or 43% of the total railroad tracks in the entire world. By 1894 the country's industrial output equaled the combined total of Britain, France, and Germany (Chandler 1965: 21–40).

14. The BUS was a major competitor to the money center banks. In 1830 the BUS made approximately 20% of all bank loans in the country, was responsible for issuing about 20% of all notes in circulation, and held about one-third of the total bank deposits and specie in the country (Van Deusen 1959: 63).

15. The exact origins of Jackson's hatred of the Bank of the United States are unclear, but certainly his opposition hardened after hearing from associates that the BUS had worked against him in several states in the 1828 election (Van Deusen 1959: 64).

16. On 26 September 1833, Treasury Secretary Roger Taney announced that beginning on 1 October federal government deposits would be placed in private banks rather than the BUS. This announcement had a tremendous impact on the functioning of the BUS. Public deposits in the bank dropped from $7,600,000 in August 1833 to $3,100,000 in February 1834 (Hammond 1957: 419 and 434).

17. While some states had very good records of protecting depositors and noteholders, other states, particularly those that did not carefully regulate the type of security required to be kept on deposit, had poor records. Louisiana, which carefully regulated bank security deposits, had a very good record, but Michigan, which allowed banks to use land mortgages as security, became a haven for "wildcat" banks that were little more than con operations. See Rockoff (1974, 1975) for further information on the impact of "free banking" laws.

18. The transportation revolution made it economically feasible to ship products to markets located hundreds or even thousands of miles away. For example, after the Erie Canal was completed in 1825, the price of hauling a barrel of pork from Cincinnati dropped from $10.00 to $3.50 (Lee and Passell 1979: 132–33). Rail transportation, which developed over the next thirty years, had the additional advantage of being able to move commodities cheaply over long distances that were not accessible by water transport.

19. For most of the statistical analyses, the 1,440 duplicate bills were eliminated from the data set. Many similar bills are commonly introduced during a Congress, particularly in the last twenty-five years. If each of these bills is counted separately, the effectiveness of support from presidents can be underestimated. See the Appendix for a more detailed discussion of the methodological implications of eliminating the duplicate bills.

3

A Tale of Three Policies

Overview

As was pointed out in the preceding chapter, case studies are useful because they raise questions that might be missed in a solely quantitative study and facilitate in the construction of generalizable hypotheses. In addition, case studies convey a richness of detail and provide a feel for the actual give-and-take that occurs in setting policy. This greater texture is particularly important in a study such as this, where much of what has occurred is not amenable to aggregate data analysis. The size of the undertaking and absence of reliable records made the quantification of some important aspects of the policymaking process impractical. For example, the private negotiations of individual actors are not conducive to quantitative analysis. But these sorts of questions are an important part of the creation of a fully co-institutional view of policymaking over time.

Dynamic Constitutionalism and Case Studies

The theory of dynamic constitutionalism holds that certain characteristic patterns of legislative interaction can be traced to the Constitution, and that these patterns are replicated in the enactment of different laws. Although this theory will be tested at the macro level in the quantitative chapters, some lessons can best be gleaned from micro-level studies. The three cases analyzed in this chapter are atypical in that the need for detailed information required the study of more important policy initiatives, yet they do allow some testing of the four propositions outlined in Chapter 1.

Dynamic constitutionalism holds that Congress will be primarily responsible for the development of most legislative initiatives. Although the importance of the policies studied in this chapter will at least partially decrease this tendency, one should pay close attention to whether Congress played a greater role than the president in the development of the legislation. More specifically, was Congress disproportionately responsible for the early development and political incubation of the policies? For example, did private or public actions by members of Congress serve to keep the initiatives alive at some critical early point? Were there differences between the behind-the-scenes roles played by committee chairs and other legislators? Did presidential backing occur at a later point in the development of these policies? And finally, did presidents need the support of key congressional actors if they wanted to get initiatives enacted?

In addition to these questions directly derived from the theory, other questions could not be addressed in the quantitative analyses but can be explored in these case studies. Most notably, the case studies allow an assessment to be made of the role played by the broader executive branch, which cannot be quantitatively measured. Attention can also be paid to the activities of extragovernmental groups in changing legislative outcomes. Because case studies illustrate the types of maneuvers employed by these outside groups to kill or sustain a measure, they have an advantage over quantitative methods. They are particularly useful in demonstrating how the actual content of the proposed policies changed over time to satisfy the demands of different actors. They also vividly illustrate how changes in the broader social environment, especially economic crisis, can profoundly alter conceptions of what is and is not politically feasible.

Choice of Case Studies

In one sense the choice of only three policies out of the thousands of possibilities available over the past century and a half was difficult. No policy or handful of policies can be seen as entirely typical. Each is in some way unique. Three factors were paramount in the choice of policies. First, it was important to examine initiatives whose entry onto the political agenda coincided with some of the more significant transformative shifts within the broader society. A second, possibly related, consideration was the choice of a historical period that encompassed crucial turning points in interbranch relations. And finally, it was important that the policies be diverse in terms of their degree of prominence and in the coalitions mobilized to support or oppose passage.

The turn of the century, probably better than any other period in our country's history, satisfies the first of these conditions. The period encompassing roughly the last twenty-five years of the nineteenth century and the first two decades of the twentieth century has been described as one in which America was embarked on a "search for order" (Wiebe 1967). It includes the Gilded Age, the Populist movement, and the Progressive Era. However characterized, the time was one of profound change, marking the transition from an agrarian to an industrial society, polity, and economy. Positions on the most contentious political issues of the era—banking and currency, tariffs, transportation, monopoly power—reflected disagreements on the scope, as well as the propriety, of that transition.

The latter part of the nineteenth and early part of twentieth century was also a period of profound change within both the legislative and executive branches of government. The homogeneity of the congressional parties and the stranglehold of the Republican leadership over policies dissolved during this period. The overthrow of Czar Cannon in the House and the less dramatic decline of Aldrichism in the Senate signified the end of the era of "Boss Rule," which had been characterized by "responsible parties" that were highly cohesive and homogeneous and in which leadership was centralized (Brady and Althoff 1974) and strictly hierarchical (Swenson 1982). By the end of the Progressive Era, Congress had become a far different institution—one with far lower levels of party voting, weaker overall leadership, and a system of dispersed institutional power.

At approximately the same time, the executive branch of government was undergoing its own transformation, albeit in the opposite direction. The triumph of large, hierarchically organized corporations in the private sector led to demands for similar structures in the public sector. Many scholars believe that the trends toward centralization within the executive branch and the decentralization in the legislative branch culminated in a radical transformation in the balance of power between the institutions, such that congressional dominance of the legislative process was replaced by presidential hegemony.[1] However, the argument in this work is that these moves by the executive branch generated in turn a series of countermoves by Congress, which resulted in policy leadership being exercised by committee chairs.

Despite the time period limitation, there were still thousands of possible initiatives from which to choose case studies. The overarching prominence of the Federal Reserve System made its inclusion a necessity. The creation of a central banking system was certainly the most important banking policy innovation in the twentieth century. In the course of researching the Federal Reserve System, it became clear that a full understanding of the politics surrounding the creation of the central bank was impossible without also understanding the development of the postal savings system and of guarantee insurance for deposits. The long legislative histories of these two less well known initiatives were intimately connected with that of the Federal Reserve System. The fate of one of the three policies repeatedly hinged on that of the others. However, the three policies were designed to accomplish different aims and engendered radically different responses from elite and popular groups.

The origins of all three of the cases can be traced back to the economic disruption of the last quarter of the nineteenth century. Some of the same individuals and groups played important roles in enacting each of the policies into law, but the particular positions taken varied enormously from case to case and across time. Each of these policies was unique in terms of its response to the surrounding conditions and the final impetus to passage. Each generated different coalitions, both inside and outside government, working on its behalf. Each was the subject of a unique bargaining process on the road to passage. Each illuminates changes in the underlying relationship between the two branches of government, as presidents became more active and power within Congress was dispersed to the committees.

The Postal Savings System

The first of the three initiatives introduced into Congress was a proposal to create a system of postal savings banks. Postal savings banks were government-run savings banks or depositories at local post office branches. First established in Britain in 1861, postal savings banks were subsequently instituted in most of Western Europe by 1890 and in thirty countries worldwide by the turn of the century. While the specific features of postal savings varied among countries, most systems typically paid interest on deposits and set minimum and maximum account limits. The deposited funds were used by the particular countries for various governmental purposes.[2] Because post offices were much more numerous than banks in most of peripheral America, postal savings was seen as a way to establish rudimentary banking throughout the country. Postal savings banks also allayed public fears about the power of the Eastern money center banks.

Early Development

HR797, introduced by Republican representative Horace Maynard from the agricultural state of Tennessee on 18 December 1873, proposed a national system of savings banks run by the Post Office. The bill would have allowed individuals to deposit up to $1,000 in accounts paying a maximum of 4% annual interest. The postmaster general would deposit the funds in a special Treasury account, which could be used for a variety of investment purposes (HR797, 18 December 1873).

While certainly influenced by the postmaster general's 1871 recommendation that the United States consider establishing postal savings banks such as existed in Britain and Canada, Maynard's bill was primarily a response to the bank failures and agricultural distress brought about by the Panic of 1873. In 1870 there were only three bank suspensions in the entire country. There were ten during the next year, but in 1873 that figure increased to forty-one (Bureau of the Census 1975: 1038), primarily in the hard-hit agricultural regions of the country.[3] By placing savings under the control of the federal government, Maynard's proposal would have protected small savers from losing their deposits in times of economic crisis.

Although Representative Maynard was the chair of the House Banking and Currency Committee, he was not able to get HR797 favorably reported out of his committee. Instead, the bill was sent with an adverse recommendation to the Committee of the Whole. As was typical with negative recommendations, the leadership refused to bring the measure up on the floor of the House of Representatives during the Forty-third Congress (March 1873–March 1875).

The Forty-third Congress was the last time that a bill to create a postal savings system was introduced into the Banking and Currency Committee. The committee was seen as intractable in its opposition to postal savings plans, which would undercut the position of private banking. Maynard's status as a Republican leader during an era of unprecedented Republican hegemony made his failure even more notable. At this time not only did the Republican Party control the presidency, but it also held a greater than two-to-one majority in each of the houses of Congress.

During the Forty-fourth Congress (March 1875–March 1877), Representative Samuel Cox, a New York Democrat, introduced another postal savings bill. Even though the House had a strong Democratic majority and Cox was then the chair of the House Banking and Currency Committee, he sent HR1840 over to the Committee on the Post Office and Post-Roads, where he thought it had a better chance of being reported out favorably.

In one sense, Cox's maneuvering failed because the bill died in committee. In another sense, he did succeed because by the time the Forty-fifth Congress (March 1877–March 1879) convened, postal savings had become an important political issue. The number of bank failures since 1871 increased dramatically. Two hundred and thirty-nine banks failed during the two years in which the Forty-fifth Congress was in session (Bureau of the Census 1975: 1038). Between 1876 and 1878, the prices of wheat, wool, and cotton fell another 5.16%, 14.02%, and 13.08%, respectively (Bureau of the Census 1975: 208). During those years, in just two agricultural states, Ohio and Illinois, the losses through state-chartered banks were greater than all the losses to creditors of national banks since they were first chartered (Wanamaker 1891: 8).

Legislators facing the wrath of destitute constituents found postal savings a good initiative with which to be associated. During the Forty-fifth Congress there were ten bills to create a postal savings system introduced into the House, and for the first time one was introduced into the Senate. Eight of the bills were sponsored by Republicans and the remainder by Democrats. All were sent to the respective committees on the Post Office and Post-Roads, and one House bill was reported favorably out of committee but not voted on by Congress.

When agricultural prices stabilized and the number of bank suspensions decreased during the Forty-sixth Congress (March 1879–March 1881), congressional interest waned. No postal savings bills were introduced in that Congress. However, President Rutherford B. Hayes became the first president to advocate the creation of a postal savings system in his Fourth Annual Message on 6 December 1880 (U.S. President, 1897, Vol. 10: 4574). Three other chief executives followed Hayes's example, and eight postmasters general also endorsed the creation of a postal savings system. The relative reluctance of chief executives to support postal savings legislation is consistent with constitutional incentives favoring congressional policy incubation.[4] It also illustrates possible differences in policy priorities between a president and other members of the executive branch with more parochial constituencies. The inability of these presidents and their postmasters general to succeed in moving postal savings legislation through congressional committees also highlights their limited influence during the early stages of congressional decisionmaking.

When agricultural prices dropped and bank suspensions started increasing again during the Forty-seventh and Forty-eighth Congresses, congressional interest in the proposal grew modestly. Two bills were introduced in the Forty-seventh Congress (March 1881–March 1883) and three in the subsequent Congress. Despite the backing of President Arthur, the bills went nowhere (U.S. President, 1897, Vol. 10: 4639).

The Debate Heats Up

The Forty-eighth Congress (December 1883–March 1885) was the first in which evidence can be found of public support for a system of postal savings banks in the *Congressional Record* (U.S. Congress, *Congressional Record,* 48th Congress, 1884: 261, 262, 350, 399, 649, 875, 1284, 2235). During its first session petitions from charities and labor groups implored Congress to establish a postal savings system. Nineteen similar groups sent petitions on behalf of the system in the first session of the Forty-ninth Congress (U.S. Congress, *Congressional Record,* 49th Congress), probably in response to the sharp 1883–84 jump in bank failures from thirty-three to sixty-three (Bureau of the Census 1975: 1038).

The continuing interest of farm organizations and labor groups is understandable; their members would presumably use such a system. F.D. Wimberly, representing the National Farmers Union, explained why his members supported the creation of a government-run postal savings system: "Many men are fearful of banks; many men have got to believing that banks steal; many men are ignorant and prejudiced, and they range from the simple thick-headed negro and the utterly ignorant white man up to men of that class who have got to be pretty prosperous" (F.D. Wimberly's testimony before the Committee on the Post Office and Post Roads, 17 March 1910: 171).

Middle-class groups such as the State Charities Aid Association supported postal savings banks as a means of teaching middle-class values to the poor. As Kemmerer wrote, "Whatever else a postal savings bank may be, it is without exception an institution working principally through the post offices, and its primary object is the encouragement of thrift among the poorer classes by providing safe and convenient places for the deposit of savings at a comparatively low interest rate" (Kemmerer 1911: 465). Postmaster General John Wanamaker argued that a postal savings system would give poorer citizens a stake in the society and provide protection against "disorder and anarchy" (Wanamaker 1891: 4).

In a quite remarkable article in the *Annals of the American Academy of Political and Social Sciences,* Edward Heyn tried to win middle-class support for postal savings by arguing that the system would prevent crime. He used evidence from Britain to show that fewer old people are murdered when they keep their money in postal savings banks because thieves are less likely to rob individuals who have less cash on hand (Heyn 1891: 489). Heyn usually made less emotional appeals to the middle class. Through the use of European and Canadian examples, he tried to show that postal savings banks would facilitate the circulation of money and provide resources for government borrowing (Heyn 1891: 463–84).

Additional arguments in favor of a postal savings system focused on the lack of banking facilities, especially in the Western states. In 1890 there were 921 savings banks in the entire country. Six hundred and thirty-seven of these banks were purely mutual and the other 284 were the much smaller stock savings banks. Of the 637 mutual savings banks all but eleven were located in the New England and Mid-Atlantic states. The remaining eleven mutual savings banks were distributed as follows: Ohio 4, Indiana 5, Wisconsin 1, and West Virginia 1. The much weaker stock savings banks were concentrated in the Western states. Two hundred and nineteen of these banks were located in the Western states and territories (Wanamaker 1891: 9). Agitation on behalf of postal savings proposals continued to grow as the country approached the turn of the century. In the six-month period from September 1890 through February 1891, Postmaster General Wanamaker found that press reports were running almost four to one in favor of creating a postal savings system (Wanamaker 1891: 46–72). The *Manufacturer's Record* headline proclaiming "The South Needs Savings Banks" was typical (*Manufacturer's Record* 14 February 1891). Northeastern newspapers usually couched their support of postal savings in terms of deposit safety:

> A Government bank could never fail in a Republic to the extent of being beyond power to pay its depositors. This is but one of the arguments that may be adduced in favor of such an institution, but it is all-sufficient, albeit the incidental benefits of post-office banking would be many and widespread. (*Troy Standard* 26 November 1890)

Western newspapers, such as the *Duluth Times* in a 4 December 1890 article, stressed the benefits to isolated communities, many of which lacked banking facilities during that time.[5]

The state legislature in Minnesota passed a resolution on 9 February 1897 asking Congress to establish a postal savings system (U.S. Congress, *Congressional Record,* 54th Congress, 1897: 1789). Shortly thereafter Congress received a similar petition from the legislatures in Montana (*Congressional Record*, 55th Congress, 1897: 6).

In terms of partisan politics, by the end of the nineteenth century much of the agitation on behalf of a postal savings system came from third parties. Representatives and senators from the Farmer's Alliance, Independent, Fusionist, and Populist parties introduced legislation to establish the system. The Union Labor Party became the first political party formally to favor postal savings through the adoption of a plank in its 1888 party platform (Johnson and Porter 1973: 83). The People's Party approved similar planks in their 1892, 1896, 1904, and 1908 platforms (Johnson and Porter 1973: 91, 105, 135, and 155). Both critics (Bicha 1976; Hofstadter 1985) and supporters (Hicks 1931) of agrarian movements such as Populism view the implementation of the postal savings bank system as one of their major legacies, although its initial introduction predated and its final enactment postdated the agrarian zenith. The Populists were instrumental in placing the idea of postal savings on the national political agenda and keeping it there throughout the 1890s.

In terms of party support, 1908 was a watershed year; both the Democratic and Republican parties passed resolutions at their conventions favoring postal savings (Johnson and Porter 1973: 147 and 159).

The Democrats, however, viewed postal savings as less desirable than achieving deposit guarantees. "We favor a postal savings bank if the guarantee bank cannot be secured, and that it be constituted so as to keep the deposited money in the communities where it is established" (Johnson and Porter 1973: 147). The Prohibition and Independence parties also came out in favor of the system (Johnson and Porter 1973: 153, 154, and 156).

Organized opposition outside Congress came primarily from the American Bankers Association (ABA). Its earliest clear statement of opposition, J.H. Thiry's 1898 article in the *American Banker*, argued that postal savings banks were not only unnecessary but also an unwarranted government intrusion into the private sector (*American Banker* 26 January 1898). This article was later submitted to the Subcommittee of the Post Office and Post Roads as representing the position of the American Bankers Association.

Although agitation on behalf of postal savings increased after the Panic of 1907, the American Bankers Association at its annual convention took a position strongly opposed to postal savings. Arthur Reynolds, chair of the ABA's Federal Legislative Committee, condemned both postal savings and deposit insurance when he said:

> No bill has been presented which would really prove beneficial to the country. On the contrary all have been burdened with measures sure to prove detrimental, not only to the banks, but the individual depositors as well, by impairing the ability of the banks to adequately provide and care for the very desirable feature of active bank accounts, curtailing the use of individual credit, and giving to the dishonest a cloak by making such finds immune from all process of law, and particularly inviting the several withdrawals of large sums from commercial channels by making such deposits not subject to taxation, and such banks are proving a serious menace to the financial credit of the countries in which they are in use. (American Bankers Association 1908a: 282)

As support for the plan increased over the next year, the ABA decided that more activist measures were needed to stop it. Under the leadership of Lucius Teeter, president of the Chicago Savings Bank and Trust Company and chair of the Committee on Postal Savings Banks of the Savings Bank Section, the ABA organized a national propaganda campaign to defeat postal savings.

On 24 November 1908, the ABA's Committee on Postal Savings Banks sent a packet of materials to all banks in the country. It contained a copy of the bill introduced by Senator Thomas Carter (D, Montana), the report of the 1908 convention opposing such a plan, several addresses opposed to the proposal, and a synopsis of all the arguments against postal savings. The bankers were urged to use this material in preparing newspaper articles on the subject. The circular closed with these instructions: "Each banker receiving these press suggestions is requested to present them to the publisher of the local newspaper, with the request that editorials and write ups be prepared setting forth the arguments showing the real tendency and effects of postal savings bank legislation." In recognition of the need to appear spontaneous and unsolicited, the small type following the instructions read: "Please remove this slip when handing to newspaper" (American Bankers Association 1908b).

The circular summarized eleven different arguments against postal savings banks. They ranged from the unwarranted intrusion of the federal government into the private sector to specific harms likely to occur within the banking industry if such a proposal were adopted. Some of the material was specifically directed against the Carter bill (U.S. Congress, *Congressional Record* 15 December 1908: 258–59).[6]

The strongest opposition within Congress came from the Republican leadership of both the House and Senate. Speaker Cannon (R, Illinois) and Senate Majority Leader Aldrich (R, Rhode Island) over the years had used their leadership positions to prevent postal savings plans from coming up for a vote. This allowed members to avoid taking a public position in opposition to this politically popular initiative.

The Enactment of Legislation

By the opening of the Sixty-first Congress (March 1909–March 1911), it was much more difficult for these two leaders to continue stonewalling on postal savings. The position of congressional proponents of postal savings legislation had been strengthened by two important developments. First, Cannon's and Aldrich's opposition was undercut by the Republican Party's endorsement of the plan at the 1908 convention. Second, President William Howard Taft decided to make the passage of postal savings one of his primary legislative goals (Anderson 1968:

125–26). Unlike previous presidents, who had publicly endorsed the proposal but privately ignored it, Taft added private arm twisting to his laudatory public pronouncements. Given the rise of the Insurgent movement within the Republican Party, Cannon's and Aldrich's positions had grown tenuous. Taft was able to reach an agreement with Cannon and Aldrich; in return for his agreement not to support the Insurgents, they would aid him in pushing his legislative program (Anderson 1968: 100).

During the Sixty-first Congress five bills to create a postal savings system were introduced into the House and two bills were introduced into the Senate. The best received was S5876, introduced by Senator Thomas Carter. This was the bill against which the ABA had begun mobilizing its nationwide propaganda campaign.

When Subcommittee Number Two of the House Committee on the Post Office and Post Roads held hearings on postal savings banks, Lucius Teeter, representing the American Bankers Association, said:

> We hold that the postal savings banks could add an unnecessary burden on the Federal Government, that there is not the need or demand for it that many people think, and that its establishment would derange the present developing banking system of the country and inconvenience the multitudes as compared to a few who might be served. (Teeter in testimony before Subcommittee Number Two of the House Committee on the Post Office and Post Roads on 25 February 1909: 113)

Approximately one year later, when passage of a postal savings bill appeared likely, the ABA committed $1 million to an education campaign to halt passage (*Chicago Banker* 5 February 1910), and Teeter took a different approach in his congressional testimony. Instead of opposing the proposal directly, Teeter argued that a change as radical as postal savings needed more study. He suggested that bills be referred to the newly created National Monetary Commission or a similar body (Teeter in testimony before the House Committee on the Post Office and Post Roads on 16 March 1910: 4).[7] Despite his efforts and those of the ABA generally, both the House and Senate moved closer to passage.

Aldrich's New Year's Day agreement to join with Taft and support passage initially appeared to increase the likelihood that the Senate would pass some type of bill. The question seemed to have been what type of postal savings plan the Senate would pass.[8] However, by March suspicious Insurgents threatened to kill postal savings. They saw Aldrich's conversion as an attempt to take money away from their communities and concentrate the funds in the hands of Eastern national banks. Their fear was buttressed because S5876 called for the investment of collected funds in 2% bonds held by the national banks (Hechler 1964: 159).

When Nelson Aldrich fell ill and was unable to shepherd the legislation through the Senate, there was a real possibility that postal savings might be dead in the session. The Republican Party was split between the regulars and the Midwestern Insurgents, and the Democrats were not likely to resurrect a policy for which President Taft could claim credit. When an Insurgent-Democratic coalition tried to filibuster until the end of the Sixty-first Congress, Taft threatened to keep Congress in session until December in an institutional war of attrition (Anderson 1968: 132). The ailing Aldrich was recuperating in Florida when President Taft telegraphed him to say the bill would die unless he returned to push it through (Stephenson 1930: 367).

After returning, Aldrich got an amended version of the bill approved by the Senate in a fifty-to-twenty-two vote. The Republicans, including staunch opponents of earlier postal savings legislation, voted unanimously in favor of the bill. This unanimity was a bit surprising, since Insurgent Republicans had added a series of radical amendments before its passage, the most important of which was the Borah amendment prohibiting the investment of postal savings funds in bonds paying less than 2.25% per annum.[9] It would have precluded investment of funds in 2% national bank bonds.

To understand the apparent conversion of postal savings opponents into proponents, the dispute must be placed within a historical and institutional context. Although institutional changes in Congress and philosophical divisions were beginning to erode the homogeneity of congressional parties, the decline of partisanship was evolutionary rather than immediate. The Senate of 1910 was at the end of an era in which "each [party was] concentrated at a distinct point on the continua of socioeconomic status and policy space" (Brady, Brody, and Epstein 1989: 206). The Republican Party had unequivocally supported postal savings in its convention only two years earlier, and a Republican president had made the enactment of the policy an important part of his agenda. While this particular Senate bill did not

have his unequivocal blessing, President Taft was committed to sign-
ing a postal savings bill before the end of the legislative session
(Hechler 1964: 159).

Senate Insurgents expected their Insurgent colleagues to follow suit
in the House and pass a version of postal savings that resembled the
radical Senate bill. President Taft, however, was able to prevail upon
House Insurgents to join ranks with regular Republicans to withdraw
the radical Senate amendments (Hechler 1964: 161). The president
vehemently opposed the Borah amendment (U.S. Congress, *Congressional Record* 22 June 1910: 8735).

The House Post Office Committee wrote a virtually new postal
savings bill while retaining the Senate bill number. The most critical
changes were the deletion of the Borah amendment and the addition of
a provision establishing that 5% of deposited funds be held as a reserve, 30% be invested in government bonds, and 65% be invested in
local banks, subject to withdrawal "for investment in bonds or other
securities of the United States, but only by direction of the president,
and only when, in his judgment, the general welfare and the interests
of the United States so require" (S5876, as amended 7 June 1910,
section 9). Democrats on the House Post Office Committee lamented
the change as "the first step toward a central bank."[10] They produced a
Minority substitute of S5876 that required that 95% of postal savings
funds be deposited by the government in banks located where the
deposits were made.

With assistance from the president, on 7 June Speaker Cannon got
the House to agree to rules that allowed for votes on the Majority
postal savings bill (the unamended House version of S5876) and the
Minority substitute, prohibited floor amendments, and limited debate
to eight hours. Voting on the restrictive rules followed party lines, with
157 (93.5%) Republicans and only 2 (1.6%) Democrats voting for
them. The votes on the Minority and Majority bills also followed party
lines, with virtually all the Democrats voting for the Minority bill and
Republicans favoring the Majority bill.

In the end, the more conservative version of postal savings passed the
House on a 195–102 vote. Even though Democrats had traditionally supported postal savings, very few voted in favor of the bill. In the Senate,
only one Democrat voted for Thomas Carter's bill (U.S. Congress, *Congressional Record* 5 March 1910: 2761). Twenty-two Democrats voted
for the House version (U.S. Congress, *Congressional Record* 9 June

1910: 7768). On 22 June, the Senate voted forty-four to twenty-five to concur with the more conservative House version of the bill. Only one Democrat voted with the majority (U.S. Congress, *Congressional Record* 22 June 1910: 8741).

Because the House and Senate versions were so different, many observers believed a compromise was impossible before the end of the legislative session. To break the impasse President Taft canceled plans to leave Washington and summoned congressional leaders to a series of meetings at the White House. First, Taft told the leaders that he would veto any postal savings bill that included the 2.25% bond requirement in the final Senate bill. Then, when it appeared a filibuster would emerge and no legislation would be passed, the president bluntly threatened to veto two bills—a river and harbors bill, which contained funding for hundreds of projects across the country, and a public buildings bill, which affected every state in the country, unless the Senate passed postal savings legislation substantially similar to the House version (U.S. Congress, *Congressional Record* 22 June 1910: 8735).

At the end of three days of debate, the Senate on 22 June voted forty-four to twenty-five to pass the more conservative House version of postal savings legislation. Over 90% of Republican senators, but only two Democrats, voted in favor of the bill. The bill that President Taft signed into law three days later was a considerably more conservative piece of legislation than had been proposed by Representative Maynard thirty-seven years earlier. Instead of paying 4% interest on accounts of up to $1,000 as Maynard had proposed, the new postal savings banks would pay only 2% interest on accounts of up to $500 (*Postal Savings Act* 1910).

Although private American savings banks paid higher interest on deposits than in any other country in the world, the bankers succeeded in getting Congress to set at 2% the interest rate that the new postal savings banks could pay, which was lower than the rates paid by any foreign postal savings systems (Kemmerer 1911: 485), and approximately half the rate that private banks paid on savings accounts at that time.[11] The low interest rate coupled with the $500 maximum allowed in any account, clearly assuaged the banking community's fears about competition. The national banks would also benefit because the funds could be used to purchase their 2% bonds.

The concessions obtained by the banking community do not mean that the law failed to provide real benefits to the populace. For many citizens the postal savings system was the only alternative to keeping their savings under the proverbial mattress. At the time the law was passed, on average only one bank handled savings accounts for every 270 square miles. Post offices were located every fifty square miles (Kemmerer 1911: 467). The South had an average of one bank for every 418 square miles and one post office every 35 square miles, or one bank for every 13,600 people and one post office for every 1,120 people (Kemmerer 1911: 471–73). For these people the law made a significant difference in their lives; they had a safe place to deposit their limited savings.

When postal savings was first introduced, congressional proponents had to work around hostile majorities on the Banking and Currency Committee to keep the initiative alive. Without political incubation, postal savings would have died before support could be built both within Congress and around the country. Later, unrelenting popular agitation kept postal savings on the political agenda. Much of this support, especially during the 1890s, came from third parties. Without their continual pressure postal savings easily might have disappeared from the political agenda. The forces arrayed against its passage were formidable. In the private sphere the powerful and well-organized banking sector, which had opposed the initiative at every step, had managed to kill more than one hundred bills before finally failing to stop the weakened S5876. Within Congress the leadership had for many years kept postal savings from being voted upon by the members. Eventually a concerted effort on the part of congressional backers and President Taft first won over congressional leaders and then made postal savings banks a reality. In describing Taft's success, Hechler wrote, "Such triumphs as this were few and far between for the president, but none was more clearly his" (Hechler 1964: 162).

Depositors' Guarantee Fund

Proposals to create a depositors' guarantee fund were another response to the rash of bank failures in the periphery. The guarantee fund proposals were loosely modeled after the New York Safety Fund, created in 1826. Under the New York Safety Fund, each state-chartered bank paid a portion of its capital into a fund administered by the state comptroller for the protection of depositors. Although investor confidence engendered by the Safety Fund enabled New York bankers to be the first to resume specie payments after the Panic of 1873, it was not enough to prevent the elimination of the fund as a result of the pressure induced by the Panic (Eccles 1982: 46). Proponents of deposit insurance plans argued that the problem with the New York Safety Fund was its relatively small size. Instead of individual states establishing safety funds for state-chartered institutions, the national government would establish a national fund to guarantee deposits in both state and nationally chartered banks.

Early Development

Three proposals introduced in the first session of the Forty-ninth Congress (March 1885–March 1887) essentially tried to create a national safety fund. The first of these bills was HR3740, introduced by Representative William Price (R, Wisconsin) on 11 January 1886. This was quickly followed by HR5683, which was introduced by Representative John Hutton (D, Missouri) on 15 February 1886. The last of the three bills, HR6240, was introduced on 1 March 1886 by Representative Charles Brumm (R, Pennsylvania), who was also affiliated with the Greenbacker Party during part of his legislative career.

The three bills were similar. Each proposed to raise twenty million dollars to create a Treasury Department fund to protect depositors from national bank failures. The only real difference among the bills dealt with the manner by which moneys for the fund were to be generated. Price's bill called for the funds to be raised by placing a semiannual fee on national bank circulating notes (HR3740 11 January 1886). The other two bills sought to replace all existing taxes on national banks with a semiannual duty of "one-half mill on the dollar upon their average monthly deposits" (HR5683, 15 February 1886 and HR6240, 1 March 1886).

Even though Hutton and Brumm were members of the House Banking and Currency Committee, they could not get the bills reported out of committee. In this they were not alone; over the next thirty-two years, more than fifty bills were introduced into Congress to create a depositors' guarantee fund, and every one died in committee. Not until the Democratic Sixty-fifth Congress (1917–19) was a bill finally reported out of committee.

Even though deposit insurance initially had adherents from both sides of the aisle, over the years it increasingly became associated with

Populists and the left wing of the Democratic Party. The heart of the Populist movement, located in the South and West-Central region, was battered by a series of crop failures after 1887 that culminated in the national depression of 1893. Between 1892 and 1898 seventy-five state banks and thirty-two national banks in Kansas suspended operations (Blocker 1929: 9).

In 1897 Populist politicians began to advocate state deposit insurance schemes, beginning with Kansas state representative F.P. Gillispie's introduction of the first state plan. One year later the state bank commissioner, John W. Breidenthal, also advocated such a plan in his annual report, and Kansas governor John Leedy called the legislature into special session to consider a deposit guarantee plan. The plan passed the state senate but lost by four votes in the house. Similar legislation was introduced into the state houses of Oklahoma and Nebraska. Interest in state deposit plans waned when the agricultural economy picked up (Blocker 1929: 9).

The Debate Heats Up

When the economy worsened again in 1907, interest in national deposit insurance plans re-emerged. Between 1907 and 1908 there were 246 bank failures (Bureau of the Census 1975: 1038). In response the 1908 Democratic Party platform strongly endorsed a deposit guarantee fund (Johnson and Porter 1973: 147). The great Fusionist William Jennings Bryan made deposit insurance one of the central tenets of his 1908 presidential campaign (Trescott 1963: 161). Bryan, who had always encountered difficulties in expanding his base into the industrial East, saw advocacy of deposit insurance as a way to appeal not only to his core agricultural constituency but also to industrial workers (Koenig 1971: 453).

The period also witnessed renewed interest in state deposit insurance plans. When, despite all the agitation at the national level, no legislation was reported out of committee, the proponents of deposit insurance once again shifted their attention to the state level. On 17 December 1907, Oklahoma passed the first state plan guaranteeing the deposits of state-chartered banks (Blocker 1929: 10). During the 1908 election campaign in Kansas, both the Democratic and Republican parties came out in favor of state deposit insurance plans; when the new state legislature met in 1909 a plan was passed into law (Blocker

1929: 10). Texas passed similar legislation that year, and by 1917 six contiguous Midwestern states, plus Texas and Washington, had established state-run deposit insurance plans (Economic Policy Commission 1933).

As the 1912 election approached, the Democratic Party, unsuccessful in every presidential election since Grover Cleveland's 1892 success, was hungry for a victory. Because the Republican Party's Taft and Roosevelt factions were feuding, the Democrats entered their convention hopeful of victory. They had lost three times under the banner of the Great Commoner and so strongly sought to avoid his taint of radicalism that the 1912 platform under which Woodrow Wilson ran ignored all Populist programs, including deposit insurance. J. Laurence Laughlin of the National Citizens League, a business group dominated by banking interests, called the platform's banking plank "meaningless" and claimed victory over the absence of a plank endorsing deposit insurance (Laughlin 1933: 97–98).

Because Wilson gave little indication of his position on banking issues during the campaign, his role in reforming the banking system remained unclear, as did the direction of Democrats in Congress. Not since the Fifty-third Congress (March 1893–March 1895) had there been a Democratic majority in both the House and Senate. Reformist elements in the Democratic Party were anxious to finally have an opportunity to shape banking policy.

The split between the more conservative Wilson Democrats and those closer to the Populist tradition (to be discussed more fully in the next section, on the Federal Reserve System) affected the legislative fate of plans for a deposit guarantee fund, which was itself intimately tied to that of the Federal Reserve System. A bill (HR7837) introduced by Carter Glass (D, Virginia) to establish the Federal Reserve System passed the House of Representatives with very few changes. In the Senate, however, more radical Democrats under the leadership of Senator Robert Owen (D, Oklahoma) amended the bill to include a provision on deposit insurance.

Opponents of deposit insurance rallied both inside and outside Congress. The American Bankers Association strongly opposed deposit insurance since its 1908 convention (American Bankers Association 1908a); before that time most of the leading bankers had opposed the plan, but the ABA had not taken a formal position (American Bankers Association 1905).

The American Bankers Association's opposition was premised on both constitutional and policy grounds. Festus Wade, in his address to the Thirty-fourth Annual Convention, argued that the assessments necessary to create the fund were a violation of the Fifth Amendment's protection of private property because they would take property unjustly from the stockholders of solvent institutions to pay the creditors of insolvent ones (American Bankers Association 1908a: 276). In addition, he argued that federal protection of deposits would encourage the creation of unsound institutions. Depositors' funds were guaranteed, so they had no incentive to seek sound institutions; instead they would be attracted to those paying the highest rates, even if those rates were the result of speculative practices (American Bankers Association 1908a: 278).

The National Citizens League under the leadership of J. Lawrence Laughlin also strongly opposed the inclusion of deposit insurance in the Federal Reserve Act. In its publications on banking reform, the League's arguments are similar to those put forth by the ABA against deposit insurance (Laughlin 1912: 344–45). Laughlin also tried to persuade congressional leaders that inclusion of such a provision in the Federal Reserve bill would kill its chances of passing. Carter Glass, the sponsor of HR7837, had been supporter of William Jennings Bryan at the 1896 Democratic Convention.[12] Even though Glass had never espoused Bryan's Populism, Laughlin still feared that he was amenable to a guarantee of deposits. Laughlin attempted to persuade Glass that a deposit guarantee would kill the bill and eventually succeeded in procuring Glass's opposition to its inclusion (Laughlin 1933: 131).

Bryan's silence on deposit insurance aided conservative Democrats in their struggle against a deposit guarantee provision. As Wilson's secretary of state at the time, Bryan did nothing to aid the cause of deposit insurance. Although part of his acquiescence may be attributable to his position in the Wilson administration, it also derives from his efforts on behalf of another unrelated part of the bill.

Without minutes of the proceedings, it is difficult to know exactly what transpired in the conference committee charged with resolving the differences between the House and Senate versions of the Federal Reserve Act. However, the leadership in both chambers did stack the membership of the conference committee with reliable party line Democrats. For example, Senator Gilbert Hitchcock (D, Nebraska), who was the second-ranking Democrat on the Banking and Currency Committee, was left off the committee because the Democratic leadership felt he could not be trusted (Glass 1927: 214). Moreover, the House and Senate Democrats met separately and reached an agreement before letting the Republicans into the meeting (Glass 1927: 214–15).

The bill produced by the conference committee did not contain a deposit insurance provision. In his autobiography Carter Glass did not divulge how this came about, but many years later one version appeared in Thomas Love's 1934 testimony before the House Banking and Currency Committee. The former Texas insurance commissioner said that when the conference committee eliminated deposit insurance from the Federal Reserve Bank Act, members agreed that it would be postponed only until the regular session of Congress that fall (1913), when a more comprehensive bill would be introduced. Comptroller of the Currency John Skelton Williams had agreed to collaborate with Senator Owen from Oklahoma in preparing the bill, but this agreement was "forgotten" with the outbreak of World War I (Love in testimony before the House of Representatives Committee on Banking and Currency on 1 May 1934: 102).

While it is difficult to assess the veracity of Love's testimony without corroboration, Senator Owen did introduce a comprehensive bill on 10 December 1915. Despite his power as chair of the Senate Banking and Currency Committee, Owen's bill was not reported out of committee. As the war wound down in 1918, Senator John Shafroth (D, Colorado), who was also on the Banking Committee, introduced a similar bill, S4426, on 23 April 1918. With Owen's assistance the bill was reported out of committee, but went no further.

Perhaps as a result of distractions of the war, the momentum necessary to pass national deposit guarantee disappeared during World War I. The war years coincided with the height of state-level movements for deposit insurance. The strongest backers of state guarantees of bank deposits were Midwesterners, and when state-based plans were adopted they probably felt that the need to struggle for national plans was less urgent.

Interest waned to such an extent that by the Sixty-eighth Congress (1923–25) no bills to create deposit insurance were introduced. This cannot be attributed to any decline in the number of bank failures, because bank suspensions in 1920 jumped to 168, almost triple the number of suspensions in 1919 (U.S. Bureau of the Census 1975: 1038). The number of suspensions continued to rise throughout the 1920s

(U.S. Bureau of the Census 1975: 1038). Although bank failures were concentrated in the agricultural region, in the first half of the decade there was little agitation for national deposit insurance, possibly because Midwesterners believed that their savings were protected by the state deposit guarantees. The situation had changed dramatically by the end of the 1920s. Agricultural prices, which had begun to decline in 1920, continued to fall throughout the period.[13] The failure of large numbers of undercapitalized state banks put an enormous strain on the state deposit guarantee funds. In states where participation of state-chartered banks in the deposit guarantee funds was voluntary, most state banks withdrew to avoid the assessments to pay off insolvent banks; in states with mandatory participation, the state banks tried to switch to national charters. In either case the result was the same: insufficient funds to pay off the depositors of the failed banks. By 1929 none of the state plans was operating (Blocker 1929; Economic Policy Commission 1933).

The situation worsened dramatically with the onset of the Great Depression. In the unprecedented economic collapse caused by the stock market crash of 1929, national income fell from $87.4 billion in 1929 to $41.7 billion in 1932. By 1932 almost one out of every four workers, or at least thirteen million people, was out of work at the time of the 1932 elections. Wage payments dropped from $50.0 billion in 1929 to $30.0 billion in 1932 (Schlesinger 1957: 248). Even more so than in ordinary times, people needed to have confidence in the banking system and know that their savings were secure. But during the Depression, banks throughout the country—not only in the Midwest—failed in unprecedented numbers. In 1930, 1,352 banks suspended operations and another 2,294 closed their doors in the next year (U.S. Bureau of the Census 1975: 1038). The health of the country's banking was one of the paramount issues in the 1932 election.

The Enactment of Legislation

These bank failures, coupled with bankruptcy of the state insurance plans, brought deposit guarantees back onto the national political agenda. A clear indication of changes in the perception of the politically possible can be found in the 1932 Democratic and Republican party platforms. The two main parties joined the Prohibition Party in a call for the creation of a guarantee fund (Johnson and Porter 1973: 338, 350, and 332). More radical parties, such as the Farmer-Labor Party and the Socialist Party, called for expanding the postal savings system to encompass all forms of banking (Johnson and Porter 1973: 333 and 352).

During the Seventy-second Congress (1931–33) twelve bills to create a deposit insurance fund were introduced into Congress, and the American Bankers Association launched a major campaign to forestall their success. The Economic Policy Commission of the ABA circulated pamphlets with statistical analyses of the failures of the state-based plans and predicted disastrous results if a national system were implemented (Economic Policy Commission 1933). In testimony before the House of Representatives, Thomas B. Paton, the ABA's general counsel, argued that deposit guarantees were "impractical, unsound, misleading, revolutionary in character, and subversive to sound economics," basing his conclusions on the failure of the state deposit guarantee plans (*Congressional Record* 25 May 1932: 11225–27).

However, the credibility of the ABA had never been lower than in 1932. Revelations from the Pecora Committee that examined stock exchange practices undercut the credibility of the entire financial community.[14] The committee used broad subpoena powers to grill leading bankers about shady stock exchange practices and the blurred or nonexistent distinction between commercial and investment banking. For example, Charles E. Mitchell of National City Bank admitted to income tax evasion in 1929 by selling stock worth $2.8 million to a relative at a "loss" and then buying it back later. Mitchell also testified that his bank secretly set up an undisclosed "loan fund" of $2.4 million for use by bank officers. The officers did not have to pledge collateral or pay interest on the loans, the proceeds of which were invested in the stock market. Only 5% of the money was repaid (Pecora Committee Hearings, 21 February 1933: 1812–14. See U.S. Congress Senate Committee on Banking and Currency. 1932–34.).

Despite the obvious economic distress in the country and the low credibility of the banking community, the deposit insurance bills went nowhere. Although the ABA was partly responsible, much of this inactivity could be attributed directly to partisan bickering between the White House and Congress. The 1930 election gave the Democrats a six-vote majority in the House, and the Senate maintained a one-vote Republican majority. Each side was completely stymied without cooperation from the other.

Until the end of his administration Herbert Hoover refused to compromise on the Democratic deposit insurance plan. On 17 February 1933 a Democratic group representing the House Banking and Currency Committee asked then lame-duck President Hoover to agree to a plan to guarantee all bank deposits. Despite his endorsement of some form of deposit insurance on three different occasions, Hoover refused to support the $3-billion plan unless President-elect Franklin Roosevelt gave assurances that he would maintain the gold standard, preserve sound currency, and balance the budget (Sullivan 1936: 91).[15] Hoover hoped to use the negotiations as a way to force the incoming administration to make a commitment "to the abandonment of ninety percent of the so-called new deal" (Schlesinger 1957: 477; Schlesinger 1958: 4). Roosevelt was unwilling to provide Hoover with these assurances, and the banking system continued to deteriorate in the months preceding the inauguration.

Even after Roosevelt took office on 4 March 1933 obstacles remained in the way of passing deposit insurance. Roosevelt had strong Democratic majorities in both houses of Congress, but not all the leadership was committed to it. Carter Glass, whom Laughlin had feared was a backer of the plan twenty years earlier, turned out to have reservations. In an argument with Roosevelt, Glass said:

> Is there any reason why the American people should be taxed to guarantee the debts of banks, any more than they should be taxed to guarantee the debts of other institutions, including the merchants, the industries, and the mills of the country? (Smith and Beasley 1939: 357)

Eventually the combined efforts of the other congressional leaders and Roosevelt succeeded in convincing Glass to support deposit insurance. The chair of the Senate Banking and Currency Committee, Senator Duncan Fletcher (D, Florida) introduced a bill to establish deposit insurance, but most of the support coalesced around a House bill, HR5661, introduced by House Banking and Currency Chair Henry Steagall (D, Alabama) on 17 May 1933. One indication of the strength of support for the bill was a petition signed by 100 House members, who pledged to vote against any motion to adjourn the session until bank guarantee legislation was passed (U.S. Congress, *Congressional Record* 12 June 1933: 5826).

Outside the capital, the American Bankers Association's media campaign was overwhelmed by the public sentiment in favor of the legislation. Mainstream newspapers, such as the *Philadelphia Record,* took strong editorial positions in support of bank deposit guarantees (*Philadelphia Record* 27 May 1933). Other less respectable groups came out in favor of the proposal. The demagogue Father Charles Coughlin exhorted his twenty million radio listeners to support deposit insurance.[16]

> We are demanding legislation that will have some milk of human kindness in it; that will have some drop of God's justice in it to care for a people of a land that is teeming with wealth, filled with corn, crowded with factories, all of which, as far as we are concerned, may as well be in the depths of the Atlantic Ocean, because we must get down on our bended knees to worship at this god of gold. Surely we are asking for nothing that is un-Christian or unconstitutional when we petition for work, when we raise our voices for an opportunity to pay our debts, or when we ask for a guarantee for the savings of a lifetime which perforce we must deposit in a bank. (Coughlin 15 January 1933 radio broadcast)

Passed on 16 June 1933 as part of Roosevelt's famous "First One Hundred Days," the Banking Act of 1933 dealt with much more than deposit insurance. The Federal Deposit Insurance Corporation was created as an amendment to the Federal Reserve Act of 1913. Section 12B(e) required that all banks that are part of the Federal Reserve System must become stockholders in the Federal Deposit Insurance Corporation. Hence, forty-seven years after the legislation was first introduced into Congress, and twenty years after being eliminated in conference committee, deposit insurance became part of the Federal Reserve Act. In the intervening years a total of eighty-four bills designed to create such a plan had been introduced into Congress.

In one sense the creation of the FDIC illustrates the limits of the power of economic elites in times of crisis. Unlike the postal savings system, this legislation, essentially the same as initially proposed in 1886, made no concessions to the banking industry. In another sense the struggle to pass deposit insurance illustrates the increased power or at least tacit acceptance of big business and the banking community in the twentieth century. Unlike earlier periods of economic depression, the 1930s was notable for its relatively mild castigation of moneyed interests. It has been argued that Americans had become socialized into acceptance of the corporate monolith and were no longer motivated by personal animus against the "robber barons" of the nineteenth century. Trust-busting and class-based radicalism had been supplanted by bureaucratic and incremental solutions to market failures. In that context, only after almost half a century of continual agitation, a Democratic landslide, and, most important, the worst economic decline in the nation's history did the legislation pass.[17]

Once again, congressional backers associated with third-party groups helped keep the initiative alive until economic crisis brought it to the forefront of the political arena. Yet even in the midst of the Great Depression partisan wrangling slowed its passage. In contrast to their actions on postal savings, the chairs of the House and Senate banking committees played crucial roles in crafting the final law. It took massive public pressure and unified legislative and executive branch support finally to push the measure through the legislative labyrinth.

The Federal Reserve Act

From the time of Andrew Jackson's veto in 1832 of the Bank of the United States until the passage of the Federal Reserve Act in 1913, the United States had no central bank. Although many proposals called for creating a new central bank in the years preceding the Civil War, none of them could be considered precursors to the Federal Reserve plan. All these proposals were based directly on the defunct Second Bank of the United States.

Early Development

The first bill to create a central bank along lines similar to the Federal Reserve System was not introduced until the Forty-ninth Congress (March 1885–March 1887), when Representative Lewis Payson (R, Illinois) introduced HR7666 on 12 April 1886. The bill was referred to the House Banking and Currency Committee a few days later. HR7666 proposed a Board of Management of the Revenue and Currency, whose members would be elected or appointed from ten regional districts. This board would be charged with the regulation of the money supply (HR7666, 12 April 1886).

In many respects, HR7666 was an unimportant piece of legislation. The bill was never reported out of committee, and there is no indication that it had any influence on subsequent central bank proposals.

Its sponsor was neither an influential member of Congress nor a member of the Banking and Currency Committee. The importance of HR7666 lies in its place in the evolution of thinking about banking policy. HR7666 may have had a more direct impact on the thinking of people who later became important in the development of the Federal Reserve System. Nelson Aldrich (R, Rhode Island) was already a member of the Senate and on the Finance Committee at this time and may have heard of the bill, although there is no evidence that this happened.

No similar bills were introduced until after the turn of the century, when the 1907 money market panic brought banking reform back onto the political agenda. Unlike most of the earlier downturns, which were confined primarily to the agricultural regions, the Panic of 1907 struck the Eastern money centers. A year earlier, when interest rates had reached their highest point in forty years and reserves came close to the legal minimum, the money market loosened in the winter, and many people thought the crisis had been avoided. However, in 1907 reserves declined again as bank loans increased. Stock market speculation further increased uncertainty such that when the Knickerbocker Trust Company suspended operations in late October, it triggered a run on the other trusts and banks. The liquidity crisis became so severe that the call money rate reached 125 percent (Krooss 1983, Vol. 3: 165). In the aftermath of the crisis, which Krooss termed the most severe money market crisis in American history (Krooss 1983, Vol. 3: 164), legislators and bankers seriously began to consider structural reform of the banking system.

The Debate Heats Up

In 1908 and again in 1910 Representative Charles Fowler (R, New Jersey) introduced legislation that influenced subsequent thinking about banking reform. Fowler was an important Republican leader and chaired the House Banking and Currency Committee during the Fifty-seventh through the Sixtieth Congresses (March 1901–March 1909). The first of these bills, HR12677, would have created banknote redemption centers under the Office of the Comptroller of the Currency. Member banks were to vote for a seven-member board at each of these redemption centers. Bank examiners would be selected by these boards and all bank failures would be borne by the member banks of a district. A bank guarantee fund, financed by a 5% tax on each national bank's average sum of deposits, would protect against losses to depositors from bank failures (HR12677, 1 January 1908).

Fowler's insistence on a deposit guarantee alienated virtually the entire banking community and the old guard Republican leadership. A. Barton Hepburn, the president of Chase National Bank and a leading member of the National Sound Money League, told Senator Nelson Aldrich that the bill was "the worst piece of proposed legislation ever submitted to Congress" (Livingston 1986: 181). Speaker Cannon opposed HR12677 and backed an entirely different piece of legislation without deposit guarantees that twice passed the Republican caucus (Hechler 1964: 42). An angry Fowler refused to report the party bill, which later became the Aldrich-Vreeland Act, out of the Banking and Currency Committee and began to align with Insurgent Republicans against the Speaker of the House. To punish this rebellion, Cannon removed Fowler from his chairmanship of the Banking and Currency Committee (Hechler 1964: 42).

Fowler subsequently introduced HR23707, which called for the creation of a complete banking system, into the Sixty-first Congress (March 1909–March 1911). Retaining the banknote redemption centers from HR12677, the bill included new features such as regional districts, a bankers' council, a board of control, and a Federal Reserve Bank (HR23707, 29 March 1910). Not surprisingly, given Fowler's removal from leadership on the Banking and Currency Committee, the bill was not reported out of committee.

Ignoring both of the Fowler bills, Congress passed a stop-gap measure, the Aldrich-Vreeland Act of 30 May 1908. Designed to provide short-term relief for bankers if another crisis occurred, it provided for the issuance of emergency currency if liquidity crises occurred during the next couple of years. The Act was little more than a thumb-in-the-dike measure. Its authority expired in 1914. Some legislators hoped to use the intervening years to formulate a comprehensive plan for reorganizing the banking system, while others hoped that the passage of time would kill the reform movement. Both groups hoped that the National Monetary Commission, which was created by the Aldrich-Vreeland Act, would serve their purposes. The commission's mandate was to "inquire into and report to Congress at the earliest possible date practicable, what changes are necessary or desirable in the monetary system of the United States or in the laws, relating to banking and currency" (Aldrich-Vreeland Act, Section 18, 30 May 1908).

Paradoxically, Senator Nelson Aldrich, who was appointed chair of the National Monetary Commission, had initially opposed its creation, agreeing only to include it as part of the bill to help win Insurgent support. Senator Albert Beveridge (R, Indiana) convinced him that the opposition would accept the rest of the bill if a commission were established to "make a careful, honest and scientific study of the whole subject of our monetary system" (Stephenson 1930: 328–29).

Given Aldrich's background as a defender of the status quo and his reluctant acquiescence in its creation, the National Monetary Commission was not expected to fulfill Beveridge's lofty expectations.[18] But Aldrich surprised his detractors when he proposed that the commission interview European bankers about possible alternative banking structures. Aldrich's biographer calls him "very shrewd in making up the commission" (Stephenson 1930: 334). It comprised three distinct groups, distinguished by their relative cosmetic and pragmatic importance. The first included the most "prestigious" individuals, who could not go to Europe and therefore would not be involved in the real work of the commission. The second was made up of those who wanted to go to Europe but did not particularly want to be involved in the substantive efforts of the commission. The final group, consisting of early-day "policy wonks," wanted to study the issue thoroughly and effect policy change.

During his trip to Europe, Aldrich's three advisers tutored the members on banking. These three advisers, while not technically members of the National Monetary Commission, wielded enormous influence. H.P. Davidson, an expert on practical banking, had been recommended to Aldrich by his long-time friend J.P. Morgan. A. Piatt Andrew, an assistant professor at Harvard, ran banking tutorials on the ship. George Reynolds, president of the American Bankers Association, was the final adviser to the commission. These three men and Aldrich formed the heart of the National Monetary Commission (Stephenson 1930: 335).

Before the European trip Aldrich had not believed in major banking reform. He had favored only legislation to allow banks to issue currency backed by bonds during times of economic crisis (West 1974: 69–70). While in Germany, however, Aldrich became convinced that currency should be based on commercial assets and returned home favoring a central bank with asset-based currency (Stephenson 1930: 339–40; Warburg 1930, Vol. 1: 56–57).

The November 1910 meeting of the Academy of Political Science illustrates the close ties among the National Monetary Commission, the academic community, and the business elite. At the meeting the academy, along with the New York Chamber of Commerce and the Merchants Association of New York, sponsored a national monetary conference at which the members of the National Monetary Commission were the guests of honor. Twenty-two governors and twenty-four chambers of commerce sent official delegates. Leading bankers, such as Frank Vanderlip, J.P. Morgan, A.B. Hepburn, and George Reynolds, were active participants, and J. Laurence Laughlin, who six months later helped found the National Citizens League, presented one of the major conference papers (Livingston 1986: 203–4).

Not until the end of 1910 did the National Monetary Commission attempt to draft a bill. Reynolds was not involved in the actual writing, but the other two advisers were part of a group that assisted Aldrich in drafting the bill. They were joined by Paul Warburg, an investment banker in the firm of Kuhn, Loeb, and Company, and Frank Vanderlip, a vice president of the National City Bank of New York (West 1974: 71–72). The bill that these men produced drew on many proposals, particularly Warburg's United Reserve Plan, which had been discussed in financial circles since the Panic of 1907 (West 1974: 72). Although the authors' primary ties were to Eastern money center banks, their bill incorporated concessions designed to win support from smaller banks located in the periphery. Such a compromise was necessary because of the long-standing distrust of Southern and Western bankers toward any plan that might increase the power of money center banks. Their fear was not unfounded, because bankers in the thirteen Eastern states then held two-thirds of the country's cash (Kettl 1986: 18).

In one concession to the country bankers, the bill drew on the regional structure from the Payson bill, both of the Fowler bills, the Aldrich-Vreeland Act, and the United Reserve Plan. Another concession was the decentralization of control originally proposed by Victor Morawetz, a member of the American Economic Association and the Academy of Political Science (West 1974: 60 and 62).

Given the close collaboration between the banking community and the National Monetary Commission, the banking community's support was not surprising. In the previous year, in a survey of 5,613 state and national banks, 60% favored the creation of a central bank. The remainder were not so much opposed to central banking as dubious of its autonomy from Wall Street control (Warburg 1930, Vol. 1: 57–58). As discussed above, the Aldrich Plan contained specific concessions designed to allay these fears. At the 1911 convention, the American Bankers Association specifically supported the Aldrich Plan in a resolution (American Bankers Association 1911).

Other sectors of the business community also rallied behind the Aldrich Plan. The National Board of Trade at its 1911 Monetary Conference passed a resolution introduced by the Chamber of Commerce of New York State, the Merchants Association of New York, and the New York Produce Exchange endorsing the plan (Warburg 1930, Vol. 1: 62–63). Aside from the American Bankers Association, the single most important business group involved in lobbying on behalf of monetary reform was the National Citizens League for the Promotion of a Sound Banking System. Many ABA members were also active in the National Citizens League, modeled after the Indianapolis Monetary Commission of 1897.[19]

The National Citizens League, formed in May 1911 as an explicitly nonpartisan group dedicated to banking reform, supported many features of the Aldrich bill but never endorsed it by name. The specific endorsement of a Republican measure would have undercut the league's nonpartisan character (Laughlin 1933: 61). The league saw its task in broader terms than mere mobilization on behalf of a particular bill. It tried to change public sentiment through "a comprehensive campaign of education for some kind of a national reserve association" in forty-five states (Laughlin 1933: 57, 63). While certainly aiding the Aldrich bill, this education was designed to affect public opinion and have an effect on both Democratic and Republican reform efforts. Although the league tried to present itself as a business group separate from the banking community, it had very close ties with the American Bankers Association. At its 1912 convention the ABA unanimously passed a resolution endorsing the education campaign of the National Citizens League (American Bankers Association 1912).

The Aldrich bill generated intense opposition for several reasons. The bill was introduced at the same time that the Pujo Committee revelations about the Money Trust were dominating the news coverage.[20] The opposition to the Aldrich bill also went well beyond what would normally have been expected because of the strong dislike of Senator Aldrich. In Congress Aldrich was the leader of the Republican old guard and had acquired many enemies among Republican Insurgents, as well as among Democrats (Wilensky 1965: 2–3). More important, from the beginning of his stay in Congress Aldrich had strongly defended Eastern economic elites against attacks from the agricultural South and West. Early in his political career Aldrich made a name for himself as a champion of Eastern manufacturers by opposing the Interstate Commerce Commission Act (Stephenson 1930: 62). He earned additional enmity from the agricultural sections of the country for his consistent opposition to tariffs on raw materials. Eastern manufacturers wanted to obtain cheap foreign raw materials, while the West wanted to protect its products from foreign competition (Stephenson 1930: 348). Aldrich led tariff battles in 1883, 1888, 1890, 1894, 1897, and 1909.

This last tariff battle was still fresh when the National Monetary Commission report containing the bill was presented to Congress (Laughlin 1933: 36). H.P. Willis, in an article in the *Journal of Commerce,* argued that any bill introduced by Aldrich would be defeated solely because of the hostility that people felt toward Aldrich (*Journal of Commerce* 14 April 1911). Friends of Aldrich tried to persuade him to allow the bill to be submitted with another sponsor, but he refused (Warburg 1930, Vol. 1: 76).

Even Aldrich eventually concluded that his bill was not going anywhere, so he allowed it to die. How much of the bill's death was attributable to personal or partisan animosity directed toward Aldrich and how much to the Pujo Committee's revelations in 1912 is unclear. Eccles cast most of the blame on public sentiment generated by the Pujo Committee hearings (Eccles 1982: 53).

The Enactment of Legislation

Banking reform had to wait until after the 1912 elections. Senator Aldrich was retiring, ensuring new leadership in Congress even if the Republicans remained in control. While Taft was running for office again, there was a reasonable chance that he would lose as a result of the divisions within the Republican Party. In the months before the election, Taft avoided the highly divisive bank reform issue. Neither the Republican nor the Democratic party platforms of 1912 called for a complete overhaul of the banking system such as the Aldrich bill would have done. The Republican banking plank was composed of generalities such as "It (the Republican Party) is committed to the progressive development of our banking and currency system" (Johnson and Porter 1973: 185). The Democrats, as well as the Progressives, were explicitly opposed to the Aldrich bill (Johnson and Porter: 171, 179). Even though Bryan did not run in 1912, he still occupied a preeminent position within the party and had helped write the party's plank on banking. Bryan's antipathy toward the Aldrich Plan was well known. He called such a central bank "a gigantic money trust. It is hard enough to control the financiers when there is some little competition between them—it will be a hopeless task when the finances of government are turned over to them" (Koenig 1971: 464).

As was pointed out earlier, Woodrow Wilson gave no indication of his position on restructuring the banking industry during the campaign. This uncertainty did not, however, deter Carter Glass, who expected to become the new chair of the House Banking and Currency Committee, from acting during the time between the election and the inauguration. While Representative Arsene Pujo (D, Louisiana) had chaired the more glamorous subcommittee investigating the money trusts, Glass had headed up a subcommittee on banking reform. Glass's chief subcommittee expert was H.P. Willis, who was also affiliated with the National Citizens League, and on 26 December 1912, Glass and Willis met with President-elect Wilson to discuss their ideas for a divisional reserve bank. Even though Willis and Glass credited Wilson with changes in the bill they were drafting, how many of these originated with the president is unclear. For example, they said Wilson initiated the idea of a Federal Reserve Board to oversee the system, but the concept had already been promulgated by Laughlin of the National Citizens League (West 1974: 93). Although Wilson's familiarity with the writings of the National Citizens League was dubious, he had taught political economy at Princeton and some of his colleagues there were deeply involved in banking reform (West 1974: 90–91).

Except for his discussions of the bill with President Wilson and Treasury Secretary William McAdoo, Glass kept the text secret until after the members of the Banking and Currency Committee were appointed on 3 June 1913. After the committees were constituted, Glass began a series of discussions with key actors including Senator Owen, the new Senate Banking and Currency Committee chair, who was preparing his own central bank plan (Glass 1927: 95–96).

Although Glass's final bill (HR7837) was not introduced into the House until 29 August 1913, early drafts of the bill (HR6454) provoked controversy throughout the late spring and summer. William Jennings Bryan, the undisputed leader of the Populist wing of the party and recently appointed secretary of state, told President Wilson in early May that he would have to oppose the Glass bill (Link 1954: 47). Initially, Glass showed the bill only to the Democratic members of his committee, and even the reaction of such an ostensibly favorable audience was described as "almost a riot" (Iden 1914: 19).

Representatives Otis Wingo (D, Arkansas) and James Ragsdale (D, South Carolina) were early committee opponents of the legislation. They favored a much more radical Populist plan: an "agricultural" currency, which would allow a farmer to store his agricultural products in a warehouse and obtain loans secured by the warehouse receipts (Iden 1914: 18–19).[21] To help overcome the divisions between radical and mainstream Democrats, President Wilson invited the Democratic members of the committee to a June 20 White House meeting on the bill (Glass 1927: 129–30; Iden 1914: 19).

As word about the bill spread beyond the committee, Democrats, particularly those from the farm belt, mounted a campaign against it. Opposition within the Democratic caucus was led by Representative Robert Henry (D, Texas), who as chair of the House Rules Committee had a great deal of formal and informal power within the House. He also favored the more radical plan with "agricultural" currency (Smith and Beasley 1939: 121). Representative Henry claimed to have Bryan's support in his attacks on the Glass bill (Smith and Beasley 1939: 121).

President Wilson had, however, already taken steps to convert his secretary of state. The most important of these steps involved a change in little more than the terminology. Wilson convinced Glass to call the notes issued by the federal reserve banks government notes instead of banknotes. Throughout much of his political career Bryan had advocated government issues, and Wilson felt that he could be convinced to support the Federal Reserve bill if it called for the creation of government notes. When Glass protested to Wilson that this was just a semantic change and there would be no government obligation, Wilson replied, "Exactly so, Glass. Every word you say is true; the government liability is a mere thought. And so, if we can hold to the substance of the thing and give the other fellow the shadow, why not do it, if thereby we may save the bill?" (Glass 1927: 125). Wilson's strategy succeeded, and Bryan decided to support the Glass bill.

The opposition led by Representative Henry collapsed after Bryan sent a letter to Glass, stating that he supported President Wilson's efforts on currency reform and wanted the bill to pass (Glass 1927: 138–39). With most of the radicals seemingly placated, the Democratic caucus then voted 168–9 in favor of the Glass bill (Glass 1927: 141). Victory within the caucus provided the impetus for the bill to be favorably reported out of committee without amendments and to pass in the House, where the Democrats held a 291–127 vote majority.

The banking community also raised some objections to the Glass bill, primarily over the composition of the Federal Reserve Board. The bankers favored a banker-run board while Senator Owen's own proposal included a board appointed entirely by the president. Glass at first tried to strike a compromise, but when President Wilson strongly argued against any form of banker control Glass changed his position (Glass 1927: 112–16).

Even though the bankers raised objections to some of the provisions of the Glass bill, they were much happier with it than with the other alternatives. They were completely opposed to the "agricultural" currency plan of Wingo, Ragsdale, and Henry. The Owen bill (S3099) was also peppered with many more objectionable provisions from their perspective, particularly its provision creating a deposit insurance system. The American Bankers Association neither endorsed nor condemned the Federal Reserve bill. After the bill's passage in the House, the ABA's Currency Commission invited the presidents of forty-seven state bank associations and the representatives of 191 clearinghouses to a September meeting on the proposed legislation. Its middle-of-the-road position was probably typical of the feelings of the banking community in general.

> Whereas although the pending measure has many excellent features and recognizes certain principles fundamental in any scientific banking system, yet it is believed that the application of those principles may in certain respects be made in ways that will more surely avoid a credit disturbance and more efficiently attain the desired benefits for the whole. (American Bankers Association 1913)

This statement, presented to the Senate Banking and Currency Committee hearing on HR7837, closely resembled the testimony of J.H. Tregoe of the National Association of Credit Men (Tregoe in testi-

mony before the Senate Committee on Banking and Currency on 24
September 1913, Vol. 2: 1039). Although the banking community
viewed the Glass bill as less than ideal, its criticisms were not directed
at killing the measure. There are indications that the Glass bill enjoyed
significant support in other parts of the business community. For example, the U.S. Chamber of Commerce, the New York Economic
Club, and the Merchant's Association of New York supported the
proposal (Livingston 1986: 222).

After passing the House, the Glass bill was referred to the Senate,
where the Democrats again split on the measure. In October the
Senate Banking and Currency Committee held closed hearings on the
bill, at which Democratic senators O'Gorman, Reed, and Hitchcock
refused to go along with the administration in supporting the legislation (Iden 1914: 24). President Wilson tried everything to bring
the recalcitrant senators into line. After numerous private meetings at the White House failed to sway them, he persuaded his allies
in the Senate to call a Democratic conference on the bill. This appeal
to peer and partisan pressure pulled O'Gorman and Reed back into
the fold, but not Hitchcock (Iden 1914: 24). Since there were seven
Democrats and five Republicans on the Senate Banking and Currency Committee, the vote was six to six on recommending the bill.
As a result, the five Republicans and Hitchcock prepared a negative
report and the six remaining Democrats prepared another report with
a positive recommendation. On 22 November both reports were filed
in the Senate (Iden 1914: 24–25).

The Senate Democratic leadership, working in coordination with the
White House, called the Democratic caucus into daily sessions from
10:00 A.M. until 11:00 P.M. They vowed to continue holding these
sessions until the bill was passed. The members did not want to be
forced into continuing to meet during the Christmas season and endorsed the bill (Iden 1914: 25). Given the Democratic fifty-one to
forty-four majority, the caucus endorsement meant the bill would probably pass the Senate.

On 19 December 1913 the Senate voted fifty-four to thirty-four to
pass an amended version of the Glass bill. The most important of the
amendments was the previously discussed deposit insurance provision,
which was dropped by the conference committee. The conference
committee report was adopted by both houses on 23 December, and
President Wilson signed the Federal Reserve Act into law on the same

day. Even though twenty-seven years had passed since the Payson bill had been introduced, restructuring of the banking system had seriously been considered only since the money market crisis of 1907. The Fowler bills and the Aldrich Plan focused legislative attention over the next three Congresses on the specifics of such a restructuring. The sharp divisions within and between the parties prevented these bills from being favorably reported out of committee. Throughout this period, leading figures from within the banking community worked intimately with congressional leaders in crafting legislation that would be acceptable to the various elements within their communities. But without the Democratic victories in the 1912 election, nothing would have been accomplished.

Much has been written and debated about the extent to which the Federal Reserve Act is a pro-banker piece of legislation. One clue is the extent to which the Act resembles the Aldrich Plan, which was clearly supported by the banking community. In his autobiography, Carter Glass emphasized the ways in which the Act differs from the ABA endorsed Aldrich Plan (Glass 1927: 241). Others, such as Kolko, have asserted that there are relatively few differences between the two pieces of legislation (Kolko 1963: 224–28). Paul Warburg in *The Federal Reserve System* compared the two documents by juxtaposing the texts against one another section by section (Warburg 1930, Vol. 1: 369–406). After looking over the texts, Warburg reached the conclusion that "they are surprisingly akin" (Warburg 1930, Vol. 1: 408).

Another way to assess whether the Act is fundamentally favorable to the banking community is to look at the reactions of different groups to the newly passed law. Carter Glass received letters of congratulation from the National Citizens League, the National Association of Credit Men, the Chamber of Commerce, and the Board of Trade. Although he did not receive formal congratulations from the American Bankers Association, he did get letters from prominent bankers including Warburg, who had been an adviser to Aldrich (Glass 1927: 235). Perhaps George Reynolds, the ABA president, best summed up the feelings of his organization when he said, "I have never refused half a loaf merely because I couldn't get it all" (Smith and Beasley 1939: 98).

The struggle to pass the Federal Reserve Act also demonstrated how partisan differences can scuttle legislation, even when it has the strong support of the congressional leadership. Unlike postal savings and deposit insurance, the key figures in keeping support alive in this case were part of the leadership structure. The Federal Reserve Act also illustrates the importance of leadership by committee chairs. In particular, the aggressive leadership of the House chair and the president were crucial in building the necessary support to ensure passage.

Conclusion

Although each of the three policies analyzed in this chapter represented a response to economic crises, they were treated differently within Congress. Despite acute distress in the agricultural sections of the country, the two popularly based initiatives—postal savings and deposit guarantees—faced major obstacles at each stage of the legislative process. In contrast, the more elite-based proposal to create the Federal Reserve System moved rapidly through the system toward eventual passage.

Congressional adherents of a postal savings system moved their bills from the Banking and Currency Committee to the Committee of the Post Office and Postal Roads because the former committee would not report them out. The leaders within both houses simply refused to allow the few measures that did get out of the Post Office Committees to come up for a vote. Postal savings vividly illustrates the important role that ordinary members of Congress can play in keeping initiatives alive until support from more powerful actors is obtained. Beginning in 1873, more than one hundred bills to create postal savings banks were introduced before passage of a relatively weak version in 1910, and even that version with major concessions to the banking community would not have been considered without a concerted effort by President Taft.

Part of the motivation to pass postal savings was a desire to satisfy public demands for a deposit guarantee fund. There were twenty-one deposit guarantee bills introduced in the Congress before passage of postal savings. The banking industry and its allies within Congress vehemently opposed deposit insurance. Unlike the postal savings plan, the ultimately successful bill creating deposit insurance conceded nothing to the banking community. It still took more than twenty years and a prolonged economic crisis in the agricultural section of the country to convince the chair of the Senate Banking Committee to allow a bill creating a deposit guarantee fund to be reported out of committee. Even that institutional support was insufficient to secure success. Only the Great Depression, a change from Republican to Democratic leadership in both houses and the presidency, and the virtual collapse of the banking system in early 1933 finally convinced Democrats that they had a sufficient mandate from the people to legislate against the wishes of the banking lobby. At that point the committee chairs formed a coalition with the newly elected president to enact the law.

In contrast, the banking industry was intimately involved in all stages of the Federal Reserve System's creation. Leading bankers assisted in the writing of the Aldrich Plan, the direct precursor to the Federal Reserve Act, and one of the authors of the Glass bill was also associated with the National Citizens League. Although the banking community did not achieve all its goals with the Federal Reserve Act, the bankers were satisfied with the final product. The Federal Reserve Act and the other two policies were products of economic crisis. The Payson bill of 1886 was generated by the crisis of 1883, and the more important Fowler, Aldrich, and Glass bills were brought about by the Panic of 1907, an event that brought serious consideration of structural changes onto the political agenda. Panic within the banking community itself probably contributed as much as anything else to passage of the Federal Reserve Act only six years later. While without bankers' support and active advocacy no major change could have been achieved, their actions constituted a necessary but not sufficient condition for change. The Democratic majorities in both houses and the cooperation between Banking Committee Chair Glass and President Wilson were also keys to the legislative success of the Act. The Republicans, without such institutional control, had not been able to generate sufficient support even to report the Aldrich bill out of committee.

Many of the differences in how the proposals were treated can be traced to popular-elite cleavages, yet those proposals had some important commonalities. The political incubation of each of the policies occurred within Congress, and the cooperation of congressional leaders was crucial. In one case, the party leaders of the House and Senate succumbed the pressure from other legislators and the president and provided crucial support. In the other two cases, the leadership originated within the committee structure. Furthermore, presidential intervention provided a significant boost in the late stages. The role of broader executive branch was mixed. In the case of postal savings, the support of postmasters general helped keep the idea alive during lean times. The other two policies received little, if any, help from members of the executive branch. In fact, presidents had to maneuver to prevent members of their cabinet from opposing their initiatives. Party change was necessary to push through the creation of the Federal Reserve System and the FDIC. Although a watered-down version of postal savings was passed without party change, it was at least in part an attempt to head off the perceived greater evil of deposit insurance.

Notes

1. According to Sundquist, the first move toward the president's assuming the role of fiscal manager was the result of the passage of the 1921 Budget and Accounting Act. "Before 1921 a president did not have to propose a fiscal policy for the government, and many did not; after 1921, every chief executive had to have a fiscal policy, every year. That act made the president a leader, a policy and program initiator, and a manager, whether he wished to be or not. The modern presidency, judged in terms of institutional responsibilities, began on 10 June 1921, the day that President Harding signed the Budget and Accounting Act" (Sundquist 1981: 39).

2. See Report No. 1455, House of Representatives, 61st Congress, 2nd Session, 7 June 1910, for brief descriptions of postal saving systems in other countries.

3. Between 1872 and 1876 wheat prices dropped 25.84%, wool prices dropped 44.52% and cotton prices dropped 36.59% (U.S. Bureau of the Census 1975: 208).

4. The seven years between the introduction of postal savings legislation and the first presidential position is more than twice as long as is typical on legislation that presidents end up supporting. That could be because postal savings was a popular rather than an elite-based measure.

5. Schroedel and Snyder (1992) show that the degree of support for postal savings was highest in the West and Midwest and lowest in the Northeast. They also found that the types of postal savings plans introduced by members of Congress varied systematically between the different regions of the country.

6. The American Bankers Association plan to create the appearance of widespread, grass-roots opposition to postal savings backfired when Senator Thomas Carter was given a copy of the circular. Senator Carter had the circular and the instructions entered into the *Congressional Record* (U.S. Congress, *Congressional Record* 15 December 1908: 258–59).

7. The National Monetary Commission, created by the 1908 Aldrich-Vreeland Act, was given a mandate to study the country's monetary system and make suggestions for its improvement. Initially, most observers believed that the Commission would be a means of sidetracking reform efforts. But the chair of the Commission, Senator Nelson Aldrich (R, Rhode Island), surprised his critics by presenting them with a plan for completely revamping the country's banking and monetary systems.

8. Postal savings bills can be analyzed on five key dimensions. Four of these dimensions can be classified as reflecting the social/economic class character of the bill, while the remaining one measures the legislation's stance toward the

participation of women in the system. The class axis of postal savings bills can be measured by examining the minimum deposit required to open an account, the maximum allowed in one of these accounts, the amount of annual interest paid, and whether at least some postal savings funds were required to be returned to the community of origin for investment. Most, but not all, bills included language dealing with each of the five areas. See Schroedel and Snyder (1992) for a thorough discussion of how the class and gender components of the postal savings bills varied across time.

9. The Borah amendment passed, 49–11, with many Republican regulars joining the Insurgents to push it through (Hechler 1964: 161).

10. They took the then unusual step of attaching "Minority Views" to the Committee Report. In addition to criticism of the Committee (Majority) bill, it included a Minority substitute bill. See H. Rep. 1445 (Part 2), 61st Cong., 2nd sess., 7 June 1910, "Views of the Minority."

11. Few records remain of the amount of interest paid on savings deposits of individuals, but in 1910 the Bowery Savings Bank, located in New York City, paid 4% interest on savings accounts. The liquidity shortage in the West and the South made it likely that those regions paid higher interest rates than did money center banks, but there are no records of rates paid in those regions of the country. See Sidney Homer (1977) for a discussion of difficulties in obtaining this type of data and the rates paid by the Bowery Savings Bank.

12. Even though Carter Glass was considered a moderate-to-conservative Democrat, he had been an enthusiastic supporter of Bryan at the 1896 convention (Smith and Beasley 1939: 44).

13. During the decade wheat prices declined 51.93%, wool declined 51.93%, and cotton declined 43.66% (U.S. Bureau of the Census 1975: 208).

14. The Pecora Committee was created on 4 March 1932 persuant to Senate Resolution 84, 72nd Congress. In the Seventy-second Congress the committee was chaired by Senator Peter Norbeck (R, South Dakota). When the Democrats took control of the Senate in the Seventy-third Congress, Senator Duncan Fletcher (D, Florida) served as chair. However, the committee is generally known by the name of its counsel, Ferdinand Pecora (Coren et al. 1989: 48). Transcripts are listed under the formal name, Hearings before the Committee on Banking and Currency; United States Senate, 72nd Congress, 1st and 2nd Sessions, pursuant to Senate Resolutions 84 and 239; 73rd Congress, 1st and 2nd Sessions, pursuant to Senate Resolutions 56 and 97; on Stock Exchange Practices, 1932–34.

15. Hoover spoke in favor of deposit insurance plans in a 15 June 1931 address to the Indiana Republican Editorial Association, in his 8 December 1931 Annual Message, and in his 4 January 1932 Special Message to Congress on the Economic Recovery (Hoover 1934, Vol. 1: 572; Vol. 2: 41, 305).

16. Charles Coughlin (1891–1979), known as the "radio priest," was in many ways a sectarian Huey Long. Capitalizing on widespread anxiety after the Crash of 1929, Coughlin quickly developed a large and loyal following of listeners to his "Radio League of the Little Flower." Among other ideas, he espoused income redistribution and guarantees, abolition of the Federal Reserve System, government control of banking and nationalization of key industries; however, he was antisocialist, anticommunist, and a virulent anti-Semite. He led a political movement, the Union Party, which received less than 2% of the vote in its only

presidential run. After its dismal showing in the 1936 presidential race, the Union Party and Father Coughlin disappeared from public life. (See Brinkley 1982; Marcus 1973; Tull 1965.)

17. This point of view is best expressed in Galambos's (1975) research on the degree of American cultural acceptance accorded big business.

18. After the death of her conservative banker husband, A. Barton Hepburn, Emily Hepburn wrote in the preface to the last edition of his famous book on currency that her husband thought the commission was created to "sidetrack" reform (Hepburn 1924: vii–viii).

19. The Indianapolis Monetary Commission of 1897 was a conservative business group dedicated to ensuring that after Bryan's defeat in the 1896 presidential election the silver issue would never reemerge. Many individuals with ties to the banking community and the ABA played key roles in the Indianapolis Monetary Commission (Laughlin 1933: vii and 3).

20. In 1912 a subcommittee of the House Banking and Currency Committee conducted hearings into major financial institutions' use of elaborate systems of interlocking directorates to control the country's money and credit. Arsene Pujo (D, Louisiana) chaired these investigations. The final report documenting widespread abuses was released on 28 February 1913 (Krooss 1983, Vol. 3: 181–233; Schamel et al. 1989: 68). The timing of these hearings was such that unfavorable publicity about the banking industry dominated the news during the entire period when Senator Aldrich was trying to win support for his banker-run central bank.

21. The roots of their proposal to develop an "agricultural" currency can be traced back to the subtreasury proposal first put forth by Charles Macune of the Farmer's Alliance in 1889. Macune's plan called for the federal government to create a system of agricultural warehouses in every county. Farmers could store their crops in the warehouses while waiting for prices to rise. The warehouses would be empowered to issue "certificates of deposit" for up to 80% of the crop's current price to each farmer. These "certificates of deposit" could then be sold by the farmer to generate cash (Goodwyn 1978: 91–93 and 109–11).

4

Legislation Within Committees

Policy Incubation

Writing about policy incubation, Nelson Polsby in 1969 criticized his colleagues' simplistic view of policymaking:

> It is a cliché of academic political science that, in legislative matters, it is the President who initiates policy, and Congress which responds, amplifying and modifying and rearranging elements that are essentially originated in the executive branch. Not much work has been done, however, on following this river of bills-becoming-and-not-becoming laws back to its sources. Where do innovations in policy come from *before* the President "initiates" them? (Polsby 1969: 65)

Polsby asserted that many of these policy ideas have "been around" for quite a while before the president discovers and makes them his own.

Although several excellent case studies had looked at the development of specific policies,[1] Kingdon's (1984) study stands out as the first empirically based attempt to build a generalizable theory of agenda setting.[2] Kingdon wanted to understand why some items rose out of the "policy primeval soup" while others languished and died there. One of his most important findings was that major policy changes occur when a window of opportunity is created by the confluence of the three process streams: problem recognition, the generation of policy proposals, and a shift in the political climate (Kingdon 1984: 174–75). Kingdon believes Polsby's advice to trace a "river of bills-becoming-and-not-becoming laws back to its sources" to be futile because there is no logical stopping point and the system is so fragmented that no one group consistently acts as a leader (Kingdon 1984: 77–81).

Congressional Origins

While Kingdon's argument has merit, two institutional features point toward an analysis of at least the congressional origins of policies. First and most fundamentally, all legislation must go through Congress. Because the Constitution designates it as the legislative branch of government, Congress is by design a unique participant in the policymaking process. Presidents, members of the executive branch, interest groups, and all other potential participants have a choice about whether to contribute to the development of a particular policy. However, members of Congress have no choice; they must consider all legislation that comes before them.

Because all legislation goes through Congress, the first introduction of legislation is a logical starting point for analysis. This does not mean that all policy ideas originate at this point, only that it is a theoretically justifiable point to begin the analysis. It also provides a clear paper trail not found in other analytic frameworks.[3] Furthermore, as Kingdon notes, Congress is the only entity to play a consistent role in both agenda setting and the choice of alternatives (Kingdon 1984: 38).

The committee system's central role in the coupling of Kingdon's three process streams is a second justification for analyzing policy from the perspective of Congress. While correctly citing Cohen, March, and Olson's (1972) observation that there is a great deal of fluidity among participants in a "garbage can" system, Kingdon fails to consider fully the implications of the committee referral system.[4] Although the way in which members choose to play an active role on any particular piece of legislation is a bit random, chairs of standing committees have always been important legislative actors (Polsby, Gallaher, and Rundquist 1969: 789). They are not the only important participants and have not always been equally influential, yet committee chairs have always played a major role in the development of policies under their committees' jurisdiction.[5] Even when a policy idea originates with another member, the support of the committee chair is often essential for putting together a winning coalition.[6]

Policymaking Within Committees

Because legislation is almost never considered on the floor of the Senate or House of Representatives without having first been approved by a committee, an understanding of the policymaking process requires knowledge of the committee system. In 1884, Woodrow Wilson summarized the feelings of many observers when he wrote, "Congressional government is Committee government" (Wilson 1956: 24). Committees provide the nexus that links congressional specialists, the administration, interest groups, and the general public.[7] Although all standing committees do consider and debate legislation, not all committees are equally likely to initiate policies. Committees with activist members and a high degree of receptivity to outside influences have generally exercised a greater degree of policy innovation.[8]

Committee "Gatekeeping"

Almost all standing committees have three primary policymaking powers: the use of hearings and investigations to gather information, the drafting of bills, and the ability to report or not report legislation out to the larger chamber.[9] These committee powers may be used either to defend the status quo against individuals and groups seeking policy change or to overcome opposition or inertia in order to enact new policies.[10] Since the late 1820s the most potent legislative power of committees has been their ability to determine whether legislation can be considered on the floor. By acting as "gatekeepers" for the chamber as a whole, committees can choose either to obstruct or to aid in the passage of legislation. The refusal of a committee to favorably report out legislation makes enactment of a bill extremely difficult.[11]

The extent to which the committees have autonomously exercised their "gatekeeping" power has varied across time and between chambers.[12] For example, the "gatekeeping" power over reporting legislation onto the floor of the House was not a meaningful political tool for committees until the referral of bills to standing or select committees became the norm in the late 1820s.[13] Before the Civil War, standing committees in the Senate played a relatively minor role. The members of committees generated very few bills; instead, their legislative workload consisted almost entirely of bills already passed in the House. The Senate committees were, however, quite willing to perform the "gatekeeping" function with respect to House-generated bills. Historically, limitations on the autonomous exercise of committee power in the House have come from strong party leaders and from the diffuse power of individual members in the Senate. But it is worth remembering that even in the era of "Czar Cannon,"[14] there were attempts to exercise autonomous committee power over legislation.

Committees and the Constitution

This chapter aims to determine to what extent dynamic constitutionalism described in Chapter 1 affects policymaking within congressional committees. The development of the congressional committee system may itself be considered a product of the institutional separation of the executive and legislative functions in this country. Congressional committees in the United States perform different functions than do committees in parliamentary systems, where committees are given little authority to exercise independent judgment or initiate policy change. Their purpose is, rather, simply to act on the legislative agenda presented to them by the head of the majority party.[15] However, because of the constitutional separation between the executive and legislative functions in the United States, congressional committees are extremely powerful and independent policy actors. Although the Constitution does not establish congressional committees, their genesis and expansion are the natural result of the functional specialization and factionalism engendered by the Founding Fathers.

Because of the constitutional limitations on the formal legislative powers available to presidents, Congress continues to be the "first branch" of government. The ways that Congress chooses to carry out its legislative duties may vary over time, but the basic constitutional responsibility does not. For more than a century and a half, standing committees have been the structural mechanism used by Congress to develop viable policy initiatives and weed out those without merit.[16]

This chapter analyzes how the support of presidents and key congressional actors affects the way that committees exercise their "gatekeeping" power. The extent of presidential influence on committee decisionmaking will be quantitatively measured and contrasted with the influence of key congressional actors. Particular attention will be placed on the differences between the treatment of minor, routine, and important proposals within committees. As was indicated earlier, constitutionally mandated differences in constituency characteristics, in internal structures of the two branches, and in the terms of office give presidents an incentive to focus their attention on the most important policy initiatives. These differences also provide presidents with an incentive to become involved in policy development only at the last stages. The differential impact of presidential support or opposition will be assessed, as will that of different congressional actors. Comparisons will also be made between House and Senate committees' treatment of bills. An additional concern will be to discover to what extent the patterns of interaction on different types of bills are stable and to what extent they have changed over time.

General Differences in Interaction

The first step is the delineation of the general differences between the extent and timing of the legislative activities of presidents and members of Congress, especially committee chairs. The obvious starting point of comparison is the level of involvement of the actors in the determination of the fate of legislation introduced into Congress. As was previously noted, Congress plays at least some role in all legislation and the evidence indicates that presidents are much less prominent legislative actors. Of the 4,927 non-duplicate banking bills studied, presidents supported only 172, or 3.5%, of the total and opposed an additional 80, or 1.6%, of the bills.[17] If sheer numbers were the sole criterion in determining legislative leadership, presidents would be relatively minor actors.

The failure of presidents to take a position on most legislation contributes to the creation of "policy gaps"—areas where Congress, by default, has wide latitude for policy initiation (Price 1972: 332). To a large extent, committee chairs control much of the legislative agenda of their committees and determine to what extent those "policy gaps" will be filled. Chairs can use their discretionary powers to facilitate, delay, or halt the progress of legislation through their committees. Unfortunately, the lack of historical records hinders measuring and comparing different chairs' use of their discretionary powers to set the

Figure 4.1. **Support for Banking Bills: Congressional Sponsors and Presidential Position**

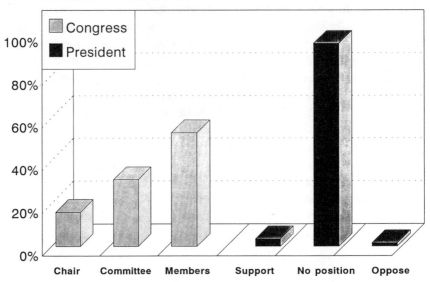

Percent of All Bank Bills

legislative priorities of their committees.[18] Overall, chairs sponsored 784, or 15.9%, of all banking bills, while other members of the banking committees introduced an additional 1,528, or 31.1%, of the bills. The remaining bills were sponsored by legislators who did not serve on the banking committees. See Figure 4.1 for a comparison of presidential and congressional support for legislation.

Of course, not all policies are equally important. Although presidents staked out positions on a relatively small number of bills, their support may have been essential to the passage of the substantively more important bills. In such a case, presidents would have to be deemed major actors irrespective of the number of bills they supported. A composite measure of policy importance, which is described in the Appendix, was used to classify all the bills based on their policy significance. One-quarter were classified as minor, slightly over half were categorized as of routine importance, and the remainder, just under a quarter, fell into the highest category of importance.

This measure was used to determine whether, as postulated in Chapter 1, presidents tend to support the most important legislation. While less than a quarter of the bills were categorized as important, almost half (45.3%) the bills supported by presidents fell into that category, and only fourteen (8.1%) were deemed unimportant. Presidents therefore supported important bills at approximately twice the rate and minor bills at only one-third the rate that might be expected if their support were entirely random.

The congressional pattern of support for bills was more randomly distributed. Even committee chairs sponsored close to the expected number of bills: 211 (26.9%) minor bills, 421 (53.7%) routine bills, and 152 (19.4%) important bills. This is consistent with earlier research (Maass 1983) indicating that members of Congress were concerned with both parochial and major initiatives.

While the relative importance of the different policy actors cannot be definitively determined, the support patterns are suggestive. As expected, given the constitutional incentives, presidents do not consider most legislative initiatives worth their consideration. By default then, most bills involve only the members of Congress.

Eliminating Legislative Chaff

These results may be distorted by legislative chaff, or bills introduced solely to placate insistent constituents. As one senator stated, "You never expect those bills to go anywhere. They are just a printed piece of paper to send out to the constituents to mollify them. You introduce a bill and that is the end of it" (Ripley 1969: 173). If a large number of the bills introduced into Congress every year are legislative chaff rather than actually serious initiatives, then they must be eliminated from consideration in order to assess accurately the role of Congress in policymaking.

The mass public, constituency groups, and congressional committees jointly work to exclude politically unacceptable legislation from serious consideration. Kingdon uses the language of set theory to show how the range of policy options is progressively narrowed.

> Out of the total range of all conceivable policy outcomes (i.e. the full set), the mass public makes some of these options politically improbable, and allows only a subset to be seriously considered. From that mass public subset, constituency elites constrain congressmen further to an elite subset of policy alternatives. From that elite subset, congressmen themselves choose the alternatives which they will allow to be

seriously considered, leaving a comparatively narrow whole House sub-set of alternatives from which the committees are free to choose. (Kingdon 1989: 290)

Kingdon does not rule out the possibility of unacceptable initiatives passing, but describes the chances of this occurring as "unlikely" or "improbable."

According to Oleszek, most bill introductions are simply attempts to calm constituents or claim credit rather than efforts to enact policies (Oleszek 1989: 83). The presence of a great deal of legislative chaff or non-serious bills in the data set can cause significant underestimations of the influence of some members of Congress and the president, by showing them as supporting a great many bills that in reality they did not care about. This can be avoided by distinguishing between the legislative chaff and bills that are "commonly perceived by members of the political community as meriting public attention and as involv-ing matters within the legitimate jurisdiction of existing governmental authority" (Cobb and Elder 1983: 85).

Legislation that has gained this degree of legitimacy is considered part of the systemic agenda. These bills may be divided into two categories: legislation that receives immediate and serious attention after being intro-duced, and that which has some support but needs additional time for attracting a coalition. For purposes of this research, a policy was considered part of the systemic agenda if it was reported out by committee in its first Congress or if more than one bill pursuing the same policy goal was introduced into the House or the Senate during a particular Congress. An initiative must normally have some degree of support for multiple members of Congress to sponsor separate bills to enact the same policy. Although simply reintroducing bills does not guarantee the serious consideration, it often serves to keep an idea alive during lean times (Kingdon 1984: 137).

This somewhat crude mechanism to distinguish legislative chaff from bills that need a longer gestation period resulted in the identifica-tion of 312 policy proposals, involving 2,226 bills, or more than a third of all the banking bills that met this multiple introduction criteria. This ability to distinguish between the two types of legislation is crucial in determining support patterns for policies across time. In the past, case studies were the principal means of studying variability over time in support for initiatives, but the thorny issue of generalizability is always raised with this form of research.

Reanalyzing Involvement

Some significant differences arose in the overall support patterns among the 312 policies. The impact of committee chairs and presidents was approximately twice as great as in the larger data set; chairs were responsible for sponsoring 34.9% and presidents supported 8.7% of the policies. Since presidents opposed an additional 1.3%, they took a position of any kind on 10% of policy initiatives, as opposed to 5.1% of the larger sample.

Two-thirds of policies supported by presidents were categorized as important, as opposed to less than half when the entire data set is analyzed. In a similar vein, 38.5% of those sponsored by committee chairs were categorized as important. This is nearly double the proportion of important chair-sponsored bills that were found when the entire data set was analyzed. Neither chairs nor presidents supported many policies of minor importance.

The larger portion of policies supported by major policy actors and the higher proportion falling into the highest category of importance is a significant, albeit unsurprising, result. Quite plausibly some of the members responsible for the submission of multiple bills to enact these policies will also lobby to win support of more influential policy actors, such as chairs and presidents. These individuals will probably also be more susceptible to lobbying on behalf of more important initiatives.

Timing of Involvement

In many cases the timing of support can be a critical factor in whether a policy lives or dies. As noted in Chapter 3, presidents were minimally involved in the early political incubation of postal savings, the Federal Reserve System, and deposit insurance legislation, and presidential involvement was a crucial but late factor in final passage. In order to determine whether this delayed involvement is typical or anomalous, the length of time between the introduction of the first bill concerning a policy and initial presidential support for the policy was calculated for the 312 policies in the small data set.

For presidents, the mean length of time between bill introduction and support is 3.33 years (with a standard deviation of 9.414 years) as compared with .899 years (with a standard deviation of 3.26 years) between bill introduction and chair sponsorship of similar legislation. The slowness of presidential support identified in Chapter 3 was not an aberration but part of a larger pattern, consistent with the premise that Congress, rather than the president, is primarily responsible for policy incubation. Furthermore, within Congress committee chairs play an early role in policy initiation. However, the high standard deviation in the timing of presidential involvement indicates a much higher degree of variability in the timing of presidential involvement than of committee chairs.

Committee chairs need not be the originators of a particular policy idea in order to become significant early sponsors of legislation. Quite often chairs supplant more junior legislators as the sponsors of legislation because they can "often supply what less senior members pursuing new policies lack: a sense of the possible, an ability to transform good ideas into viable bills, and a capacity for support building" (Johannes 1974: 364). Thus, chairs may be given undue credit for initiating a policy idea while the role of their less senior colleagues is systematically understated.

Reporting Legislation Out of Committee

Congressional committees exercise the positive or negative aspects of "gatekeeping" power principally by making decisions on reporting legislation out for consideration by the whole chamber. The committee may choose to report a bill with or without amendments, rewrite the bill, vote to reject it, or take no action whatsoever—which is tantamount to killing the bill. Because only a small percentage of all bills introduced into a committee are favorably reported out, committees have been described as the "graveyard" for most bills (Oleszek 1989: 81). For example, in the Ninety-ninth Congress only 1,512 out of 9,267 bills (16.3%) were favorably reported out of committee.[19] These bills, which have moved from the systemic agenda onto the narrower formal agenda, are "explicitly up for the active and serious consideration of authoritative decision makers" (Cobb and Elder 1983: 86).

The committee chairs have a great deal of power to determine whether a bill will make it onto the formal agenda. A committee chair can expedite or slow a bill's movement through committee in many ways: the exercise of power over the committee's legislative agenda, the schedule of hearings, the referral to subcommittees, the choice of witnesses at committee hearings, the allocation of committee funds, and the use of staff. Oleszek characterized committee chairs as the "chief 'agenda setters' of committees," and Johannes described them as the "most successful [policy] initiators" (Johannes 1974: 364; Oleszek 1989: 94).

Although scholars have long recognized the influence of committee chairs over legislation under their jurisdiction, no one has systematically measured their influence or compared it to the power of other important political actors. No one knows how the power of committee chairs to get legislation favorably reported out of committee compares to that of other committee members or the president.

Presidential Versus Congressional Influence

When the entire data set of non-duplicate banking bills was analyzed, the role of presidents was generally peripheral to committee action. They exercised surprisingly little influence over whether bills were favorably reported out of committee.[20] Only twenty-seven (15.7%) of the bills supported by presidents were reported out of committee, comprising less than 5% of all bills reported out of the banking committees. Presidents supported an average of one bill reported out of committee every 4.5 years. Perhaps even more dramatic is the relatively limited impact of presidents on the progress of bills they opposed. In the larger data set twelve (15%) of the eighty bills that presidents publicly opposed were favorably reported out against the wishes of presidents. In other words, bills that presidents opposed were almost as likely as those they supported to receive favorable treatment within committees.

The support of chairs has much greater impact on decisions within committees than that of presidents. Slightly over one-third (34.1%) of the bills sponsored by committee chairs were reported out of committee. Chairs successfully guided an average of more than two of their own bills out of committee every year. These 267 bills constitute 41.4% of all legislation reported out of the banking committees during the period studied. In contrast, only 10.5% of the bills sponsored by the other members of the banking committees and 8.4% of the bills sponsored by non-members are reported out. See Table 4.1 for a comparison of presidential and congressional success in reporting legislation out of committee.[21]

Table 4.1

Impact of Congress and President in Getting Bills Reported Out of Committee

	Congress			President		
	Non-committee	Committee	Chair	Oppose	No position	Support
Number	218	160	267	12	612	27
Percent of category	8.4	10.5	34.1	15.0	13.1	15.7
Percent of all bills	33.8	24.8	41.4	1.8	94.0	4.2

Note: The measure of congressional support in this table is primary sponsorship of legislation. There are 4,916 non-duplicate bills, which the Library of Congress records that include the name of the primary sponsor. The percent of category row shows the percentages of all bills within that category that are favorably reported out of committee. For example, the 34.1% under the chair heading means that 34.1% of all banking bills sponsored by the banking committee chairs were reported out of committee. The percent of all bills row shows what percentage each of the various categories contribute to the overall total number of bills favorably reported out of committee.

Adjusting for Importance

Two distinct patterns of interaction could affect the frequency with which bills of varying degrees of importance are reported out of committee. On the one hand, a solid inverse relationship exists between the importance of a bill and its chances of favorable consideration by a committee: 23.7% of minor bills, 10.9% of routine bills, and only 7% of important banking bills were favorably reported out. On the other hand, this inverse relationship may not apply to legislation supported by key actors. The degree of effort expended by presidents and committee chairs may increase as the level of importance escalates, thereby counteracting the increased difficulty in getting through committee obstacles. Then legislation with the support of these key actors might not exhibit the characteristic pattern of declining rates as the level of importance increases.

Bills endorsed by presidents do not follow the normal pattern of declining rates as the level of importance increases. Presidents have only minimal success in getting minor bills successfully reported out of committee. Only one out of thirteen minor bills (7.1%) publicly supported by presidents was reported out. Since this is less than half the average rate achieved by presidents, the presidents probably exerted very little effort on behalf of the minor bills that they publicly endorsed. The rate on bills of routine significance is almost three times as high; sixteen out of eighty routine bills (20%) that presidents supported were reported out of committee. This is consistent with the view that presidents exert more effort as the level of a bill's importance increases. However, on the most important category of bills, even increased presidential effort cannot overcome the barriers against the enactment of major legislative change. Presidents were able to get only ten (12.8%) out of seventy-eight of the most important bills reported out of committee. While lower than the rate presidents achieved on routine legislation, it is, however, nearly twice the normal rate on the most important category of bills.

Generally, presidents needed strong support from committee chairs, or at least members of the banking committees, to get these bills reported out of committee. The one minor bill that presidents were able to maneuver past committee "gatekeepers" was also sponsored by the committee chair. Of the sixteen routine bills reported out of committee that presidents favored, nine had chairs as their sponsors, five had other committee members as sponsors, and only one had a non-committee sponsor. Half of the most important bills with presidential backing that were reported out of committee were sponsored by chairs and the other half had ordinary committee members as sponsors. The wise president will, at the very least, find a committee member to sponsor bills that he favors.

Unlike presidents, who achieve their greatest success on routine bills, all members of Congress experienced declining success as the level of bill importance increased. The difference is probably the result of constituency pressures preventing members of Congress from focusing exclusively on the most important bills. Of the bills they sponsored, committee chairs successfully guided 97 out of 211 minor bills (46%), 130 out of 421 routine bills (30.9%), and 40 of the 152 important bills (26.3%) out of their committees. Similar declining success rates were experienced by ordinary committee members and non-committee members on legislation of increasing importance.

However, while chairs were able to get fewer bills reported out of committee as the level of importance increased, the chairs' total share of all the bills reported out of committee increased. Bills sponsored by chairs only constituted approximately one-third (33.6%) of all the minor bills reported out of committee, but that increased to 47.1% of routine bills and 50% on the most important bills. These figures indicate that even though chairs find it more difficult to create the committee coalition necessary to report out major policy initiatives, their support is an even more crucial determinant of committee success.

House and Senate Differences

The distinctive history, culture, and rules governing the two chambers of Congress raise the possibility of significant variation in the two bodies' treatment of legislation within committees. For example, Polsby (1969: 62–64) has described the House as a "highly specialized instrument for processing legislation," but suggests that passing legislation is a less important matter in the Senate, which views itself as a forum for policy debate. That difference may be reflected in the behavior of committees and their chairs in the two chambers and in their policy interactions with the president.

One of the most interesting similarities in the chambers is the chairs' relatively high rates of success in getting their own bills reported out of committee, with Senate chairs at a slightly higher rate (36%) than their House counterparts (32.5%). The two chambers diverged significantly on the rates achieved by other legislators, with the Senate far more likely than the House to allow legislation to be sent to the floor. Senate committee members succeeded in getting 17.8% of their bills favorably reported out, as opposed to only 7.3% in the House, and non-committee members succeeded only 10.4% of the time in the Senate and 7.5% in the House.

At least part of the reason for the higher rates of non-chair legislation reported out of the Senate committees is the famous senatorial norm of collegial courtesy. Chairs in the Senate are more likely than House chairs to provide their opponents with a forum to consider their legislation.[22] However, the biggest factor is probably the much higher workload in House. Even though the House reported out a far lower percentage of bills, the overall number of bills (353) going to the floor from the House banking committee is still greater than the number of Senate bills (292) going to the floor from its banking committee. If the House committees did not exercise their "gatekeeping" power in a fairly ruthless manner, the House as a whole would be completely overwhelmed by the sheer quantity of legislation reaching the floor.

Figure 4.2. **Banking Bills Reported Out: Differences Between House and Senate**

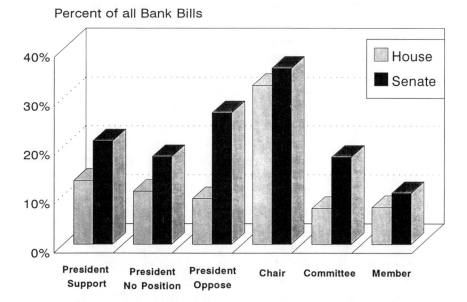

Percent of all Bank Bills

Bills on which presidents took a position are treated differently by House and Senate committees. As might be expected, given their workload, House committees report out a relatively low percentage of all bills, including those supported by presidents. Overall, the House banking committees reported out only 13% of bills that had presidential support, only slightly higher than the 10.8% rate for bills on which presidents took no public position and the 9.3% on bills that presidents opposed. Consistent with its lighter workload, the Senate's willingness to report out a higher proportion of bills carried over to those on which presidents staked a position. The independence of the Senate is demonstrated by its reporting out a remarkable 26.9% of bills that presidents explicitly opposed, compared to only 21.1% of bills with presidential support and 17.9% of those on which they took no position. These results clearly indicate that Senate committees are less susceptible to presidential influence. These differences are summarized in Figure 4.2.

Baseline Comparisons

The quantitative data presented thus far do not distinguish between policies with or without presidential support and the backing of chairs.

Nor do they show what percentage of policies favored by neither presidents nor chairs are reported out. Only 8.4% of all non-duplicate bills without presidential or chair support are favorably reported out of committee. This percentage represents a baseline that can be used to measure the success of presidential and chair-sponsored legislation.

Presidential support alone improved only slightly the chances that a bill would be favorably reported out of committee. Out of the 132 bills that presidents supported but which were not sponsored by chairs, only twelve (9.1%) were favorably reported out of committee, or less than 2% of all bills reported out. More important, the presidential bills without the support of committee chairs were only slightly more likely than the baseline bills to be reported out. These bills were also less likely than the average bill, on which presidents took no position, to be reported out.

In contrast, legislation sponsored by chairs, but which did not have the support of presidents, were reported out of committee at a very high rate. More than one-third (33.9%) of these 744 bills were favorably acted on by committees, more than three times the baseline figure for bills with neither presidential nor chair support. The 252 bills that chairs managed to get reported out of committee without the help of presidents constituted 41% of all bills favorably reported out of committee.

Presidential support increased only marginally the chances that chair-sponsored legislation would be favorably reported out of committee. Fifteen out of the forty bills (37.5%) with joint support were favorably reported out of committee, indicating that the support of presidents has, at best, a small effect on a bill's chances to get past committee "gatekeepers" and that the support of chairs is the critical determinant of success at this stage. See Table 4.2 for a comparison of the different rates of bills being reported out of committee.

Political Parties and Committee Actions

Political parties have often been described as the "glue" uniting the legislative and executive branches, and they certainly were a factor in the enactment of deposit insurance and the Federal Reserve System.[23] It is, therefore, important to consider what, if any, impact party has on committee decisionmaking. The most obvious effect of party on the likelihood of legislation being reported out of committee is through the affiliation of the prime sponsor. However, with the exception of mem-

Table 4.2

The Impact of Different Support Patterns on Bills Being Reported Out of Committee

	Neither President nor Chair	President only	Chair only	Both Chair and President
Number	336	12	252	15
Percent of category	8.4	9.1	33.9	37.5
Percent of all bills	54.6	2.0	41.0	2.4

Note: The percent of category row shows the percentages of all bills within that category that are favorably reported out of committee. For example, the 8.4% under the neither President nor Chair heading means that only 8.4% of all banking bills without their support were reported out of committee. The percent of all bills shows what percentage each of the various categories contribute to the overall total number of bills favorably reported out of committee.

bership in third parties, partisan affiliation did not affect whether a bill was favorably reported out of committee. Republicans and Democrats were equally proficient in getting legislation out of committee.

The degree of party control over the House, Senate, and the White House is often posited as having a significant impact on whether legislation is reported out of committee. However, the chances that a bill would be reported out of committee were only marginally affected by institutional differences in partisan control. When the same party controlled the presidency and had a majority of the members in one chamber of Congress, only 11% of all banking bills were favorably reported out of committee. Success increased to 13.5% when one party had a majority in both the House and the Senate but another party controlled the White House, and was only 14.2% when the same party controlled both Congress and the White House. In some ways these results are surprising. Given the recent outcry over the ills of divided government, one would expect extensions in party control to yield far greater policy success when there were united governments. However, this line of reasoning contains one major flaw. Since one party always has a majority within congressional committees, an increase in the percentage of bills favorably reported out of committee should not be expected whether the government is united or divided.

Party control may also indirectly influence committee decision-making by changing the effectiveness of different actors within the system. Within Congress, only committee chairs experienced increases in the percentage of bills reported out as partisan control was extended to additional institutions. Non-committee members were actually less successful when party control increased: they were able to get 9.6% of their bills out when Congress was divided, 8.3% when Congress and the presidency were held by different parties, and 7.7% when party control was unified. Ordinary committee members got 10.5% of their bills out when Congress was divided, 11.9% when Congress was united against the president, and 10% when both branches were controlled by the same party. However, committee chairs' success was positively related to increases in party control. They only got 21% of their bills out when Congress was divided, but that increased to 31.3% when Congress and the presidency were controlled by opposing parties, and 37.9% when a single party controlled both branches.

One of the most inexplicable findings is the strong negative correlation between party control and presidents' ability to get favorable committee action on their bills. Presidents experienced their greatest success when both chambers of Congress were controlled by different parties; a whopping 30.6% of bills with presidential support were favorably reported out of committee. The figure drops to 18.2% when Congress was controlled by one party and the presidency by another, and to 11.2% when the president, the House, and the Senate were in the hands of the same political party.

Legislation and Adverse Economic Conditions

Within the last twenty years a considerable literature has developed seeking to explain the relationship between politics and economics. While some scholars (Cameron 1978) try to explain the causes of long-term government growth, most (Hibbs 1982; Nordhaus 1975; Peretz 1983; Tufte 1978) test various aspects of the political business cycle theory, which holds that before elections incumbents use fiscal and monetary tools to stimulate the economy and create favorable economic conditions. These activities are motivated by the politicians' belief that the voters will punish or reward incumbents on the basis of short-term economic performance.

The underlying assumption of political responsiveness to the economy is intuitively appealing. Politicians, whether driven by self-interested electoral motives or simply by a desire to advance the financial well-being of their constituencies, are concerned about economic conditions. In particular, they are likely to be especially sensitive to adverse economic performance. Since there is a difference between desiring to advance the economic well-being of one's constituency and successfully doing so, the introduction of banking legislation, committee behavior, and passage will be treated separately. Distinctly different economic stimuli might be responsible for changes in bill introductions, bills reported out of committee, and the passage of legislation. This chapter examines the relationship among the changes in the economy and bill introductions and bills reported out of committee; bill passage will be taken up in the next chapter.

To answer these questions, bill introductions and bills reported out of committee are correlated with a wide range of economic indicators, which are described in the Appendix. Generally, the economic variables that performed best are deflated wheat, wool, and cotton prices, and the number of bank failures. The agricultural prices are available for the entire time period, but records of the number of bank failures go back to only 1864. A lack of long-term economic data prevented the use of many of the more conventional indicators of economic performance.

Bill Introduction

The simple correlations show a strong negative correlation between the deflated agricultural prices and bill introduction, which infers that whenever the agricultural sector is depressed, legislators from farm states tried to assist undercapitalized agricultural banks and aid farmers by loosening credit. Whether these bill introductions represent serious attempts to enact change or mere credit claiming is unclear at this point.

Deflated agricultural prices are negatively correlated with bill introductions, meaning that as the prices of agricultural products declined banking bill introductions increased. For example, deflated wool prices have a negative correlation of −.6228 and deflated wheat prices a −.4496 correlation with the introduction of banking bills into Congress.[24] The slightly weaker correlation between deflated cotton prices and bill introduction could be the result of cotton's geographic concentration in the South. Wheat and wool are produced in a wider geographic area. The correlations are stronger in the Senate for wheat and cotton but stronger in the House for wool. A logical explanation for such Senate responsiveness is the per capita overrepresentation of rural interests in the Senate.[25]

Reported Out of Committee

The simple correlations between the economic variables and the total number of bills reported out of committee are quite weak. Only the bank failure variable is significantly correlated with the total number of banking bills favorably acted on by the committees. The bank failure variable has a positive correlation of .4117 with bills reported out of committee; as the number of banking failures increased, the number of banking bills reported out of committee also increased.

Even though the agricultural variables are not correlated with all the bills reported out of committee, they are negatively correlated with routine and major bills reported out of committee. As the deflated prices of agricultural products increased, the number of non-minor banking bills reported out of committee declined. For example, deflated wool prices have a negative correlation of −.4042 with routine bills and −.5279 with important bills reported out of committee.[26]

The well-being of the agricultural sector of the economy and the behavior of legislators seem to be related. Not surprisingly, legislators introduced more banking bills and the committees favorably acted on more non-minor banking bills when the agricultural parts of the country were in distress. In contrast, banking failures did not trigger an increase in the number of bill introductions, but were positively related to the number of banking bills reported out of committee.

Modeling Bills Reported Out of Committee

The material presented thus far suggests that certain actors and social conditions have an impact on the likelihood that legislation will be reported out of committee, but it does not identify causality, allow predictions about future outcomes, or permit conclusions about the relative influence of various predictors. Fully fleshed-out models including all variables that might have an impact over such a long period of time cannot be constructed, but models with variables that have already been identified as likely to have an effect can be built. In addition to measures of congressional sponsorship and presidential position, other variables likely to have an effect include those measuring bill importance, degree of party control, agricultural prices, bank failures, and the number of banking committee staff. The latter, a measure of the institutional capability of Congress as a whole, is described in the Appendix. The length of time, changes in the surrounding socioeconomic and political environment, and the very high number of bills (many of which were either not serious attempts to enact policies or measures that needed a longer time to build support) make it unlikely that any model could explain a large amount of the variance in the probability that bills will or will not be reported out of committee. Instead, the model provides a realistic context for understanding the relative influence of the president and Congress on legislation.

Since the dependent variable in the model is dichotomous rather than continuous, ordinary least squares provide an inappropriate methodology because the error terms are not normally distributed and they are heteroskedastic.[27] Logit analysis, which uses the logarithm of the odds that a particular outcome will occur, is a superior statistical technique under these circumstances because the probabilities of the dependent variable fall within the (0,1) interval (Kennedy 1979: 36). Specifically, the choice is reported or not reported out of committee, given the values of the independent variables.

In general, the logit models of committee behavior were consistent with the results of the earlier descriptive statistics. Most variables, which had been found to be related to whether bills were reported out of committee, were found to be significant in the logit model. Not surprisingly, presidential position on legislation was a poor predictor of committee action, consistent with the earlier analysis showing only a tenuous relationship between presidential support and committee decisionmaking. However, because the major concern in this research is to understand better the roles played by the president and Congress in policymaking, the presidential position variable was kept in the model.

Furthermore, none of the economic variables was significant when combined with other predictor variables in a general model; their explanatory power is picked up by one of the other variables in Model 1. However, the banking staff variable, designed to capture the overall capacity of the system to cope with changes in committee workload, contributes significantly to an explanation of committee decisionmaking. This variable is described in more detail in the Appendix.

The logit equation is:

$$\text{Log} \frac{1}{1-P} (\text{REPORT}) = B_0 + B_1\text{PRES} + B_2\text{CHAIR} + B_3\text{PARTY}$$
$$+ B_4\text{BANKSTAFF} + B_5\text{IMPORTANCE} \qquad (1)$$

In this model all variables are significant, except the measure of presidential position, and even it is positive. Not surprisingly, the most powerful independent predictor of whether committees vote to favorably report legislation out is whether the chair is the primary sponsor, with a coefficient of 1.71, significant at the 0.00005 level.[28] The next strongest independent variable is the measure of bill importance, which has an inverse relationship to whether legislation is acted on favorably by the committees. Its −0.26 coefficient, significant at .00005, indicates that as the importance of legislation increases, it becomes more difficult for it to be acted on favorably by the committee. The degree of party control is negatively related to whether bills are reported out of committee, but its −.11 coefficient is only significant at the .05 level. This somewhat counterintuitive finding has many possible explanations. It may be a function of the relative number of bills introduced during the different periods or a result of partisan committee behavior during times of divided control. During periods of divided control, a committee controlled by one party may wish to exert pressure or embarrass institutional actors from another party by reporting out bills that they do not favor.

Finally, the new bank staff variable, designed to measure the overall institutional capacity of congressional committees, also is highly significant. The −0.01199 coefficient is significant at the 0.00005 level. The negative value implies a paradox: as the number of banking staff increases, it becomes more difficult for individual bills to be reported favorably out of committee. Although more staff should make it easier for committees to handle their workload, increased committee efficiency does not necessarily lead to higher productivity as measured by reporting more legislation onto the floor. To the contrary, with additional professional staff, committees might find it easier to reject bills that are not well conceived. Moreover, the expansion in committee staff coincided with a dramatic increase in the number of omnibus bills reported out of committees. In the past two and a half decades, the number of these "megabills," which are hundreds or thousands of

Table 4.3

Reasons Why Banking Bills Are Reported Out of Committee (Model 1)

Variable	Estimated coefficient	Standard error	t-score	Probability
Constant (B_0)	−0.11	0.50	−0.23	0.817
President	0.18	0.15	1.15	0.252
Chair	1.71	0.10	17.20	0.000
Party control	−0.11	0.06	−1.98	0.047
Bank staff	−0.012	0.0015	−8.03	0.000
Bill importance	−0.26	0.02	−11.01	0.000

Number of Observations: 4,916
Chi-Square: 547.07
Chi-Square Probability: 0.00005
Pseudo R-Square: 0.14
Correct predictions: 87%

pages in length (Oleszek 1989: 42), has increased, and greater staff size may facilitate the formulation of such complex legislative packages.

One of the main differences between conventional regression analysis and qualitative response models, such as logit, is the absence of an equivalent to the R-square statistic. Econometricians have developed many goodness-of-fit measures, including a pseudo R-square measure, yet none of them provides a natural interpretation of how well the overall model explains the results.[29] In this model the pseudo R-square statistic of .14 is not the equivalent of the R-square statistic generated by regression analysis and is not intuitively understandable. However, the pseudo R-square must be weighed against the other more generally accepted measures of the performance of qualitative response models. In this case, the model's chi-square has less than a .00005 probability of occurring randomly. But an even better indication of the model's performance can be derived from its success in predicting which bills are reported out of committee and which are not. If the probability of a bill being reported out of committee was less than .5, then the prediction was that the bill was not reported out of committee; a probability greater than .5 predicted that the bill would be reported out of committee. This model correctly predicted the committee's actions on 87% of all banking bills. Given both the number of bills and the time period studied, that is a high success rate. See the summary table (Table 4.3) for Model 1.

The Pattern over Time

The likelihood of legislation being reported out of committee has varied enormously over time. Since records of committee activities were poorly kept before creation of the *Congressional Record* in 1873, only subsequent years will be covered.

Presidential Influence

During most of this period, bills that presidents opposed actually had a greater likelihood of being favorably reported out of committee than did legislation supported by presidents. Between 1873 and 1912, the time period associated with the rise of big business, presidents supported fifty-three bills, but only five (8.6%) were actually reported out of committee. Out of the fifty-four bills that they opposed, seven (13.0%) were favorably reported out of committee. During the short interlude stretching from the 1913 inauguration of President Woodrow Wilson to the 1932 election of President Franklin Roosevelt, presidents experienced their greatest success. Seven out of the fifteen bills with presidential support were reported out of committee; the 46.7% rate of bills reported out is the highest achieved during any period, and presidents were able to keep three out of the four bills that they opposed bottled up in committee.

In one sense, this degree of presidential effectiveness is surprising, because it predates the advent of the modern presidency, commonly associated with presidential dominance of the legislative arena. But the Progressive Era was a time when the discipline of public administration, with its emphasis on hierarchical and executive-dominated leadership, first became fashionable (Straussman 1985: 178).[30]

During the period covering the presidencies of Franklin Roosevelt through Dwight Eisenhower (1933–60), the ability of presidents to move desired legislation out of committee declined sharply. Only three out of the twelve banking bills endorsed by presidents were reported out, compared with two out of eight that they opposed. This means that bills presidents favored were no more likely to get a favorable committee recommendation than those they opposed.

In the final period (1961–86), presidential activism dramatically increased. Instead of supporting an average of one banking bill every two or three years, presidents supported three to four banking bills every year, leading to a sharp decline in their success with committees; only twelve out of eighty-seven bills (13.3%) were favorably reported out. Of the fourteen bills opposed by presidents, two (14.3%) were reported out of committee.

Congressional Influence

The ability of the different groups of legislators to get bills reported out of committee was much more consistent over time. With one exception, legislators who were not on the banking committees had about half the success of regular committee members in generating favorable dispositions for their bills. Their success was the highest (12.1%) in the earliest period (1873–1912) and the lowest (5.3%) in the most recent period (1961–86). The pattern for ordinary committee members was similar; they were most successful (22.5%) in the earliest period and the least successful (5%) in the most recent several decades. Most interestingly, since the 1960s ordinary committee members have experienced a slightly lower, but statistically insignificant, rate than non-committee members.

Overall, committee chairs have successfully moved almost half the bills that they sponsored out of committee, but since 1960 their success rate dropped to 21.4%. This decline can be explained several ways. The most obvious is that the reforms of the 1970s, which modified the seniority system, created secret ballot elections of chairs and gave subcommittees more autonomy while reducing the relative power and leverage of chairs.[31] Another is that perhaps to offset this loss of influence occasioned by such reforms, committee chairs, like presidents, became much more legislatively active in the last several decades. Rather than sponsoring five to eight bills per year, chairs increased their average to fifteen bills per year, thereby diluting their ability to shepherd a high percentage of legislation through committee in any year.

Three critical generalizations must be kept in mind when comparing the effectiveness of committee chairs and presidents. First, throughout every period committee chairs have sponsored far more bills than have presidents. Second, in every period chairs have been able to successfully report out a higher number and percentage of bills than have presidents. And finally, the difference between those rates has nar-

Figure 4.3. **Banking Bills Reported Out: Success of Presidents and Chairs**

Number of Bills Reported Out of Committee

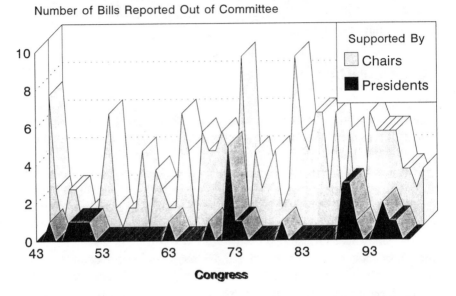

rowed dramatically in the most recent period. See Figure 4.3 for a comparison of the effectiveness of committee chairs and presidents across time.

Modeling Committee Action over Time

In the construction of models predicting changes in the behavior of the banking committees over time, insights gained in the preceding sections were incorporated. In these time-series models, the dependent variable is the number of bills reported out of the committees during each Congress. By focusing on the overall output of the committees rather than the fate of individual bills, many of which were attempts to garner constituency support rather than to enact policies, the time-series models probably better indicate the relative influence of the institutional actors than the logit models.

The unit of analysis is the number of bills reported out of individual Congresses rather than the year. The cyclical nature of congressional decisionmaking is skewed because bills tend to be introduced in the first year of a Congress and passed in the second. A year-by-year analysis would be distorted by these fluctuations, so the more natural congressional cycle is used.[32]

Since all government economic statistics are kept by the year rather than by the Congress, figures from the first year of the cycle were used in the time-series models. This worked better than either the mean of the two years or the second-year figure. Because consideration of most bills extends into the second session of a Congress, this provides an automatic lag factor in the equations. More traditional types of lagged variables performed poorly in all of the models.

The primary institutional variables were also changed to accommodate the shift from measuring support for individual bills to measuring the number of bills they supported in each Congress. The construction of a suitable measure of legislative importance was more problematic. Since the composite measure of importance used in the previous analysis had measured the importance of individual bills, a means of extending that to the entire legislative workload of a Congress had to be derived. The mean importance of all the banking bills introduced into a Congress was used as a measure of the overall significance of the legislation under consideration during those two years. Since earlier findings showed a decrease in the percentage of individual bills reported out as the importance increased, one would expect to find an inverse relationship between the level of importance and the number of bills passed in a Congress. All other variables used in the time-series models are identical to those used in the logit models. Variables such as those measuring party control and the number of bank failures did not have to be adapted for use in time-series analysis.[33] See the Appendix for a more detailed discussion of the creation of the time-series variables.

None of the general models used to predict the number of bills reported out of Congress over time was improved by the inclusion of a variable measuring presidential support or opposition. In fact, the goodness-of-fit measures were significantly worse when the variable was included. However, since this is an exposition of executive-congressional relations, the presidential support variable needed to be included in the equations. The equation for Model 2 includes as predictors the number of bills with presidential support, the number of bills sponsored by committee chairs, the number of banking committee staff, the total number of banking bills introduced, the number of bank failures, and the mean level of legislative importance.

$$REPORTB_t = B_t + B_1PRES_t + B_2CHAIR_t + B_3BANKSTAFF_t +$$
$$B_4BILLS_t + B_5BANKFAIL_t + B_6IMPORTANCE_t \qquad (2)$$

With the exception of presidential support, all the variables in this model have coefficients that are significant or at least very close to significant at the .05 level customarily used in social science research. As expected, presidential support had no measurable impact on committee decisionmaking. In contrast, the chair sponsorship variable has an estimated coefficient of .24 that is significant at the .003 level. Increases in the number of bills sponsored by committee chairs have a positive effect on the total number of bills treated favorably by banking committees. As was the case with the logit model, the banking staff variable is negative, −.14, and highly significant, which indicates that growth in committee staff contributes to a decline in the number of bills reported out. The other system capability variable, the total number of banking bills introduced, has a .12 coefficient that is significant at the .0001 level. The total number of bills reported out of committee is probably largely determined by the total committee workload. Similarly, when the committees confront the more important pieces of legislation, overall output will be lower than when they address less sweeping initiatives. The coefficient of the importance variable is −3.60, significant at the .001 level. Economic distress in the broader society as measured by the number of bank failures has the anticipated positive impact on the number of bills favorably reported out, but the relationship is relatively weak, perhaps a function of the wide range of bills included in this model. Banking failures probably do not have much affect on the number of minor bills, such as those seeking name changes for nationally chartered banks.

Overall, this model explains approximately 59% of the variance in the number of bills reported out over the past 120 years, impressive given the time period and the range of legislation included. The Durbin-Watson score of 1.907 indicates that there is no serial autocorrelation in the model, so the adjusted R-square provides a good measure of fit. See Table 4.4, a summary of Model 2.

Time-Series Models by Importance Levels

Since much of the previous work indicates that presidents and members of Congress behave in systematically different ways depending on

Table 4.4

Reasons Why Banking Bills Are Reported Out of Committee (Model 2)

Variable	Estimated coefficient	Standard error	t-score	Probability
Constant (B_0)	33.27	8.83	3.77	0.000
President	−0.04	0.14	−0.28	0.778
Chair	0.24	0.75	3.18	0.003
Bank staff	−0.14	0.04	−3.44	0.001
Bank bills	0.12	0.02	4.93	0.000
Bank failures	0.002	0.001	1.88	0.065
Bill importance	−3.60	0.99	−3.63	0.001

Number of Observations: 60
R-Square: 0.63
Adjusted R-Square: 0.59
Durbin-Watson D: 1.907
1st Order Autocorrelation: 0.026

the importance of the legislation, the data were divided into the same three levels of importance utilized previously. The upper quartile of all bills is included in the important data set. The next 50% is included in the routine data set, and the lower quartile comprises the minor data set.

Minor Bills

As one would expect, the factors influencing committee decisions on whether to report out minor bills appear rather idiosyncratic. None of the institutional variables had coefficients that even approached significance, and the only variable with any apparent impact on the number of minor bills reported out of committee over time was party control. While not significant at the .05 level, the sign of the coefficient was in the expected direction and at least approached significance. Because these variables performed so poorly, including a model predicting the number of minor bills reported out of committee over time would not be worthwhile. Because one-quarter of the bills are minor and difficult to predict, much of the unexplained variance in the general models can probably be attributed to their presence in the larger data set.

Routine Bills

Designing a model with all the factors that influence committee deliberations would be difficult, but modeling committee decisionmaking on routine bills would not be. After all, by their very nature routine bills are exactly that—routine (i.e., normal bills likely to be considered in the normal way and influenced by ordinary considerations). The very routineness of these bills increases the chances of explaining their treatment by a normal set of variables. In contrast, the idiosyncrasies that affect minor bills and the extraordinary circumstances that affect important bills make them much more difficult to model.

The models explaining committee behavior on routine bills performed noticeably better than those dealing with either minor or important legislation, yet some of the institutional variables were unexpectedly strong. Again, as anticipated, the presidential support variable did not exert significant influence on the committees' treatment of routine bills. This stands in stark contrast to the very strong impact of committee chairs. The equation for Model 3 predicting the number of routine bills reported out of committee over time included as independent variables the number of bills supported by presidents, the number of bills sponsored by committee chairs, and the number of bank failures.

$$\text{REPORTB}_t = B_t + B_1\text{PRES}_t + B_2\text{CHAIR}_t + B_3\text{BANKFAILURES}_t \qquad (3)$$

Not surprisingly, the chair variable is the strongest predictor of the number of routine banking bills reported out of committee. The .23 coefficient for the chair variable is significant at the .0005 level. Although positive, the presidential support variable has a coefficient that is far from significant. The final variable in the model, the number of bank failures, is also positively related to the number of bills favorably considered by the committees. Unlike the quite weak relationship found in the model, which included all the bills, the relationship on routine bills is rather robust. The bank failure variable has a .0019 coefficient, significant at the .002 level.

The model's goodness-of-fit, as measured by its adjusted R-square and Durbin-Watson, is quite good. This model explains 60% of the variance, and serial correlation has not seriously affected the adjusted R-square. See Table 4.5, which summarizes Model 3.

Table 4.5

Reasons Why Routine Banking Bills Are Reported Out of Committee
(Model 3)

Variable	Estimated coefficient	Standard error	t-score	Probability
Constant (B_0)	1.65	0.56	2.97	0.005
President	0.08	0.08	1.07	0.288
Chair	0.23	0.03	6.63	0.000
Bank failures	0.002	0.0006	3.18	0.002

Number of Observations: 56
R-Square: 0.62
Adjusted R-Square: 0.60
Durbin-Watson D: 1.746
1st Order Autocorrelation: 0.076

Important Bills

The most notable difference between modeling the determinants of committee action on important and routine bills is that for the first time presidential support became a factor, as did the degree of party control across institutions, also for the first time. The main predictors in Model 4 (summarized in Table 4.6) are the number of important bills supported by presidents, the number sponsored by committee chairs, the degree of party control, and bank failures.

$$REPORTB_t = B_t + B_1PRES_t + B_2CHAIR_t + B_3PARTY_t + B_4BANKFAIL_t \qquad (4)$$

Only when the data set is limited to the most important category of bills does the support of presidents exert a measurable influence on the number of bills that committees dispose of favorably within a Congress. The coefficient of the presidential support variable is .09, which approaches the minimum significance for social science research. However, even on these important bills Congress has had a much greater impact than presidents. The support of chairs, as measured by the number of bills they sponsor within a Congress, is a more powerful determinant of the number reported out. The .05 coefficient nearly reaches the .01 degree of significance.

Table 4.6

Reasons Why Important Banking Bills Are Reported Out of Committee
(Model 4)

Variable	Estimated coefficient	Standard error	t-score	Probability
Constant (B_0)	3.00	0.53	5.64	0.000
President	0.09	0.05	2.04	0.049
Chair	0.05	0.02	2.64	0.013
Party control	−0.91	0.28	−3.30	0.003
Bank failures	0.0007	0.0003	2.30	0.029

Number of Observations: 36
R-Square: 0.54
Adjusted R-Square: 0.48
Durbin-Watson D: 2.441
1st Order Autocorrelation: −0.375

The negative coefficient associated with the party control variable when all bills were included in the data set can be attributed to the impact of the important bills, because it is strongly indicated in this model. The degree of party control, which was not negatively related to committee actions on either minor or routine bills, is strongly significant when only important bills are considered. The inverse relationship between party control and the number of bills reported out is present only on the most important category of bills, supporting the notion that the members of the banking committees take positions contrary to the institution(s) controlled by the opposing party. Not surprisingly, the number of bills that passed was also positively related to increases in the number of bank failures, which had a .00066 coefficient.

The adjusted R-square indicates that approximately half the variance in the number of important bills reported out of committee is explained by the model. Given the time period and the multitude of factors affecting decisionmaking on major bills, that is certainly respectable. The Durbin-Watson score of 2.441 indicates that some serial autocorrelation is present, but not enough to reject the findings. Parenthetically, observations were included from only thirty-six Congresses, because no important banking bills were introduced during the other years in the study.

Conclusion

This exercise in tracing Polsby's "river of bills-becoming-and-not-becoming laws back to its sources" has provided new insights into the policymaking process, such as the different and often complementary roles played by chairs and presidents, the unique functions performed by the two legislative chambers, the distinct patterns of committee decisionmaking associated with bills of differing degrees of importance, and the minimal impact of unified party control on committee behavior.

The data analyzed in this chapter support the position that constitutional differences between the legislative functions assigned to the president and to Congress indeed have measurable impacts on the actions of individuals within the two branches. As predicted by the theory of dynamic constitutionalism, presidents take positions on only a small percentage of all bills, and a far higher than expected proportion of the bills are drawn from the most important category. The timing of presidential involvement can also be traced back to those same constitutional provisions. Because of the need to husband relatively limited legislative resources, presidents become involved in legislation only after it has been incubated within congressional committees. While the support of both chairs and presidents does appear to aid in reporting legislation out of committee, the former has a far greater impact. Chairs support many more initiatives, those of both moderate and high levels of importance.

The characterization of the House of Representatives as a "highly specialized instrument for processing legislation" appears to be accurate. The Senate seems to see its function more in terms of encouraging a wide-ranging debate than in passing legislation. Chairs in the Senate are more willing to allow legislation they did not sponsor to be reported out of committee even if the policies are unlikely to pass.

The logit model corroborated some of the earlier findings and added additional insights into the relative influence of the president and different congressional actors on the treatment of legislation within the committees. The logit model, which predicted committee decisions on whether to report individual bills out of committee, supported the earlier findings that committee chairs exercise a great deal of influence over their committees. It also showed that presidential support did not significantly affect the decisionmaking within committees. The inverse relationship between bill importance and the chances of being reported out of committee was also consistent with the earlier results. Several of the findings were a bit more paradoxical, most notably the negative signs of the party control and banking staff variables. Perhaps the party controlling a committee will report out a higher proportion of bills during times of divided party control in an attempt to pressure or embarrass the opposing party. The negative sign of the banking staff coefficient may reflect a role in which staff weeds out poorly conceived bills and crafts omnibus legislation. An overall indication of the effectiveness of the model is its 87% accuracy in predicting whether the committees would favorably report out bills.

The time-series models strongly supported the idea that Congress is the branch predominantly responsible for policy incubation. Presidential support was not found to be significantly related to the number of bills reported out of committee over time. Only on the most important bills did presidential support even come close to being a significant predictor. However, variables designed to measure the impact of congressional actors were significant predictors in all the models. Even though none of the economic variables showed up in the logit models, increases in the number of bank failures did have a positive effect on the number of banking bills reported out of committee.

Notes

1. Sundquist (1968) provides one of the best case studies of different areas of policymaking across administrations. Most of the other case studies focus on the development of a single policy. See Birnbaum and Murray (1987); Derthick (1979); Light (1985); and Marmor (1970).

2. In order to understand the development of health and transportation policies during the late 1970s, Kingdon conducted 247 interviews with congressional staff, members of the executive branch, and important non-governmental actors (Kingdon 1984).

3. The Library of Congress contains copies of all bills ever introduced into the House and Senate. No comparable records exist of policy positions taken by executive branch agencies and interest groups.

4. On extremely rare occasions the sponsor of a bill may ask that it not be referred to committee and instead be passed by the unanimous consent of the chamber.

5. Within the House of Representatives, the "Era of Boss Rule" stretched from the 1890 adoption of "Reed Rules," which gave the Speaker sole authority to assign legislation to committees and to prevent bills from being considered on the floor, until the overthrow of Speaker Cannon in 1910. This era constituted the

nadir of independent committee power. However, even during this period the chairs of the major committees functioned as the Speaker's "cabinet" and exercised significant control over their committees (Cooper 1960: 13; Swenson 1982: 13).

6. See, for example, Jack L. Walker's study of agenda setting within the Senate for a discussion of how Senator Warren Magnuson played just such a role in the passage of the 1966 Highway Safety Act (Walker 1977: 435).

7. Huitt (1954), in an early behavioralist study of the 1946 hearings held by the Senate Banking and Currency Committee on extending wartime price controls, described them as "public platforms for opposing groups."

8. Fenno classifies congressional committees as either "corporate" or "permeable." Committees of the latter type are less oriented toward institutional prestige, have more activist members, and are more open to outside influences—all of which contribute to a higher likelihood that they will develop new policy initiatives without executive branch involvement (Fenno 1973: 278–79).

9. All permanent committees except the four joint House and Senate committees—Economic, Taxation, Library, and Printing—have legislative authority. See Smith and Deering (1990: 2–5) for an explanation of the differences among standing committees, ad hoc committees, select committees, and conference committees and their respective powers.

10. Some scholars have classified the ability of committees to resist change as a negative power that can completely halt change. Committees can also limit the choices available to the parent chamber to those alternatives that are least threatening to the status quo. The ability of committees to press successfully for changes in the status quo has been labeled a positive committee power. See Krehbiel (1988); Smith (1989: 168–96); and Smith and Deering (1990: 9–14).

11. Because of its size and the huge volume of legislation it must consider, the House's "gatekeeping" power is stronger than the Senate's. The germaneness rule governing floor amendments to House bills is the linchpin supporting the "gatekeeping" power within House committees. While special rules, discharge petitions, and a suspension of the rules provide means for majorities within the House to circumvent the committees and bring legislation up on the floor, these procedures are rarely used. Because the Senate has no rule requiring that amendments be germane, senators can more easily overcome committee obstructions and bring legislation up on the floor. The House's adoption of procedures allowing bills to be referred to multiple committees is also thought to have strengthened the power of the Speaker and undercut that of committees and their chairs. See Davidson, Oleszek, and Kephart (1988).

12. See Smith and Deering (1990: 24–56) for a concise history of the development of standing committees in the House and the Senate. Skladony (1985) shows how some of the early select committees were actually predecessors to many subsequent standing committees. Gamm and Shepsle (1989) attempt to reconcile organizational and rational choice accounts of the development of standing committees.

13. The 1880 passage of a House rule requiring that legislation be referred to a committee before consideration on the floor reified what had already become the accepted practice.

14. Joseph G. Cannon (R, Illinois), who served as Speaker of House from 1903 until 1911, is generally considered the most powerful of all Speakers in the

history of the House of Representatives. The roots of Cannon's 1910 overthrow, which led to a diminution of the Speaker's power, can be traced to his failure to recognize the link between "substantive" and "procedural" majorities in the House, a mistake that no subsequent Speaker has repeated (Jones 1968).

15. While all modern legislatures organize their workload through the use of committee systems that effectively divide labor, these various committees operate very differently. Among parliamentary systems, committees within the British House of Commons are considered extraordinarily weak. These committees are completely dominated by the majority party, and their membership composition changes according to the bill under consideration. British standing committees do not specialize in particular policy areas and are designated by the letters of the alphabet. In contrast, while still dominated by the party caucus, the standing committees of the German Bundestag specialize in certain policy areas and retain some autonomy. However, no observer of any parliamentary system would describe their standing committees as "little legislatures." For a comparative analysis of legislative committee systems, see Loewenberg and Patterson (1979); Mezey (1979); and Thaysen, Davidson, and Livingston (1990).

16. But, as Steven S. Smith succinctly pointed out, "committees are nothing but agents of their parent chambers. All congressional committees are creations of, and may be restructured or abolished by their parent chambers. Committees exist because they are performing valued service for the chambers and individual members. . . . In this light, committees are never truly autonomous decision-making units, but rather they normally must operate in a procedural fashion and with a substantive effect that is consistent with the interests of their parent chamber" (Smith 1989: 168).

17. In the last twenty-five years, duplicate bills have often been introduced during a Congress. If each of these bills is counted separately, the effectiveness of support from key actors such as presidents can be underestimated. Because of this problem, only the results of statistical analyses performed on a data set with the duplicate bills removed are given in the text. See the Appendix for a more detailed discussion of the reasons for removing the duplicate bills from the analysis.

18. Case studies probably provide the only means of gauging a chair's use of discretionary power to shape legislative outcomes. A particularly good example of the use of the case study methodology to provide a window on the type of committee leadership exercised by chairs is Fenno's (1991) description of Pete Domenici's leadership of the Senate Budget Committee.

19. Polsby discovered that in 1967 and 1968 less than 7% of all House bills were reported out of committee (Polsby 1971: 90).

20. Because no reliable records were kept of committee decisions on reporting legislation out to the larger chambers before the *Congressional Record* was begun in 1873, only the bills introduced into Congress between 1873 and 1986 will be used in any measurements of the rates of bills reported out of committee.

21. However, when the smaller set of 312 policies is used in the analysis, the ability of presidents to move their policies past committee "gatekeepers" is far higher. They were able to get two-thirds (66.7%), or eighteen policies, reported out of committee, representing 14.4% of all the policies so reported. Even though presidential success appears significantly greater when the legislative chaff is excluded from the analysis, more than 85% of the bills that moved onto

the formal agenda by being reported out of committee did so without involvement of presidents. Policies sponsored by chairs have a 67.9% chance of being reported out, and these bills constitute almost 60% of the total policies reported out of committee. Clearly, having the support of committee chairs is a major advantage in getting legislation reported out of committee. When both committee chairs and presidents support the policy, it has a 75% chance of being favorably reported out of committee. The results from the smaller policy subset also yield interesting, but not entirely surprising, results. That approximately two-thirds of the policies that eventually win support from presidents or committee chairs are reported out is to be expected because these are powerful individuals whose support can be influential. More intriguing is the still relatively limited involvement of presidents.

22. Ripley gives an example of this occurring when Senator James Eastland (D, Mississippi) allowed Senator Edward Kennedy (D, Massachusetts) to take his place as chair of a subcommittee so Kennedy could preside over discussions on a bill that Eastland opposed (Ripley 1969: 119–20).

23. Much of the early behavioralist research touted the importance of "responsible" parties as a means of overcoming institutional, geographic, and demographic divisions within the polity. See American Political Science Association Committee on Political Parties (1950); Ranney (1954); and Schattschnieder (1942).

24. The correlation between deflated wool prices and bill introductions is significant at the .00005 level, while the correlations involving all the other agricultural products are significant at the .001 level.

25. Even though surprisingly little scholarly attention has been paid to the representational significance of having non-proportional representation in the Senate, both practical politicians and academics have been aware of the overrepresentation of rural interests within that body. In 1959 Senator Paul Douglas (D, Illinois) professed, "The people of industrial states, which have an overwhelming proportion of the population who pay the overwhelming proportion of the taxes are left out in the cold, with no attention paid to them." This speech was reprinted in Andrews (1960). Many academics have also found that the non-proportional representation within the Senate leads to an overrepresentation of rural areas and small towns. See Barker and Friedelbaum (1966: 177) and Ripley (1984: 42).

26. The correlation between deflated wool prices and routine bills is significant at the .03 level, and with important bills is significant at the .004 level. The negative correlations with the other agricultural products were significant at the .0005 to .08 level.

27. Several different statistical techniques are available for estimating models with a dichotomous dependent variable, all of which give roughly equivalent results. Logit and probit are the best known of these techniques. See Pindyck and Rubinfeld (1981: 275–300) and Wonnacott and Wonnacott (1979: 131–34) for an explanation of logit analysis.

28. The coefficients in a logit analysis are Maximum Likelihood Estimates of predictor variables on the log linear probability that an event will occur. The sign of the coefficient and its relative size in relation to the standard error are interpreted in the same way as they are in regression analysis.

29. For a summary of the econometric literature on goodness-of-fit measures for qualitative response models, see Ameniya (1981) and Greene (1983: 651–53).

30. The best known example of the influence of public administration on executive-congressional relations was the 1921 Budget and Accounting Act that created the Bureau of the Budget. It was an attempt to replace a series of uncoordinated appropriations bill with one unified federal budget under the direction of the president.

31. Even though the recent shift of power to the subcommittees has diminished the power of chairs, they still have formidable power and "remain crucial figures in the legislative process" (Oleszek 1989: 97). See Oleszek (1989: 94–97) for an excellent, concise summary of the impact of the 1970s reforms on the power of committee chairs.

32. Using Congresses instead of years also avoids the potential problem of party variables changing in the middle of a year, an especially acute problem until the sessions of Congress were standardized.

33. Because data on bank failures are available only from 1864 onward, only that period will be covered in the time-series models.

5

Passing Legislation

Background

More than a hundred years ago Woodrow Wilson expressed the conventional view of Congress when he wrote, "It is not far from the truth to say that Congress in session is Congress on public exhibition, whilst Congress in committee-rooms is Congress at work" (Wilson 1956: 69). While few observers then or now would argue that what occurs within committees is not very important, minimizing the significance of the policymaking that occurs on the floors of the House and the Senate would be a mistake. The strongest committee recommendation is worth nothing unless legislation is brought up and passed on the floor.[1]

For those trying to promote legislative change, the genesis of much of their frustration lies in the Constitution. In their attempt to guard against both tyranny and popular passions, the Founders created a government in which the self-interest of one institution could be used to check that of others. The Constitution was explicitly designed to set various interests against one another. The House of Representatives, designed to be more responsive to the common people, would be set against the Senate. The power of the executive would be checked by the power of the Congress. And so it went in a system designed more to frustrate than to legislate, a system that reflected Founders' ambivalence toward democracy and their somewhat pessimistic view of human nature. As Madison said:

> Ambition must be made to counteract ambition. The interest of the man must be connected with the constitutional rights of the place. It may be

a reflection on human nature that such devices should be necessary to control the abuses of government. But what is government itself but the greatest of all reflections on human nature? If men were angels, no government would be necessary. (Madison, Hamilton, and Jay, 1987 edition: 319)

Effective government requires the cooperation of institutions that are structurally positioned against one another, and the American system is explicitly designed to slow rather than accelerate change. Despite these difficulties, politicians have managed to find ways to make the system work. Every year hundreds of bills are passed into law.[2] This chapter discusses the patterns of support necessary for legislation to pass successfully through this seemingly intractable system.[3]

The central concern of this chapter is the effect of such support on the passage of bills. Presidents may have a greater impact, and chairs less, on floor decisions than they did on committee decisions. The differences in the constituencies, internal structures, and time frameworks that diminished a presidential role in the early stages of policy development and on a wide range of legislation probably have their greatest impacts on decisionmaking within committees. Once legislation has ascended onto the formal agenda by being reported out of committee, it may have generated enough momentum for a president to consider spending some of his limited time and resources to push the initiative through to passage. Hence, the relative influence of presidents vis-à-vis chairs will probably increase on legislation that is considered on the floor.

The analysis of the passage of legislation will be divided into three parts. The first part examines the impact of presidential and committee support on the passage of only those 651 banking bills that were favorably reported out of committee. This allows their impact on the floor to be measured separately from their influence within committee. The second part uses all the non-duplicate banking bills to measure quantitatively the extent to which different support patterns help or hinder a bill's chances of getting through both the committee and floor stages. Their cumulative influence over the entire legislative process will be assessed. Conditions and actors that may alter the typical pattern are examined. For example, political parties and economic distress might help sponsors to overcome common institutional impediments to bill passage. The last part of the chapter analyzes historical patterns. Particularly intriguing is the effect the modern presidency has on the patterns of interaction within committees and on the floor. The growth in White House staff and the entire executive branch of government may have transformed the pattern of interaction. One possibility is that the increase in staff made it feasible for presidents to exert earlier influence on more bills. Alternatively, staff may have had different agendas than the president and paradoxically diminished his legislative influence.[4]

In a sense, the approach used to analyze the passage of banking bills in this research combines aspects of both pre-behavioralist studies that emphasized collective decisionmaking and the more recent focus on the behavior of individual legislators.[5] This research retains a collective orientation, in that what is being measured is whether legislation is or is not passed into law without an analysis of individual legislators' votes. However, the emphasis on the impact of support from key actors, such as presidents and committee chairs, distinguishes this research from most of the collective voting studies emphasizing partisan and ideological alignments.

Floor Success

By analyzing only the bills that have been reported out of committee, the effectiveness of different actors on floor decisionmaking can be assessed separately from overall measures of bill passage. This, in turn, will allow separate evaluations to be made of the different actors' success within committees, on the floor, and cumulatively from bill introduction through passage. Since 1873, the banking committees have reported out 651 bills, of which 264 were passed into law. No records were kept of the primary sponsors of 6 of the bills reported out of committee, so only 645 bills will be used in the analysis of the influence of the different congressional actors, compared to the 651 bills used in the analysis of presidential influence.

The General Pattern

As anticipated, presidents were far more able to influence floor action on bills that had already gained committee approval than they were able to determine committee behavior.[6] Of the bills that had already been reported, 55.6% of those that presidents favored, 40.2% of those on which they took no position, and 25% of the measures they opposed became law. Presidents were far more successful in achieving their aims on the floor than they had been within committee. Bills with presidential support were about three and a half times more likely to succeed on the floor than all the presidential bills considered within committee. However, legislation that presidents opposed also did better on the floor than within committee.

Although these figures superficially appear quite impressive, the actual number of bills that passed was quite low. Fifteen out of the twenty-seven bills with presidential support passed, as opposed to three out of the twelve bills that were opposed. Bills supported by presidents constituted less than 6% of the banking bills passed into law during the past century and a half, but even that limited success cannot be attributed solely to presidential influence. Eleven of the fifteen were sponsored by committee chairs, and the remaining four had other committee members as their primary sponsors. Because presidents have so few formal positive legislative powers, they have a strong incentive to nurture working relationships with powerful congressional actors in order to achieve their policy goals. This reciprocity, however, only applies to a relatively small portion of the bills. While presidents need congressional help to succeed on the floor, members of Congress generally do not require presidential support. Since 94.3% of the banking laws were passed without the support of presidents, little doubt can remain as to which branch is responsible for most legislation.

In percentage terms, committee chairs were slightly less effective than presidents in getting their legislation passed, but in sheer numbers of bills committee chairs were responsible for more than ten times as many bills, getting 126 out of the 267 bills (47.2%) that they sponsored passed into law. Overall, chairs were responsible for introducing almost half (48.8%) of all the banking bills that passed. Most of these laws were enacted without presidential support, and some were enacted over presidential opposition. One indication of committee chairs' independence and power is their sponsorship of two-thirds of the laws opposed by presidents.[7] Two very plausible circumstances can explain this chair success. First, there is a long tradition of floor deference toward committees' expertise on legislation within their jurisdiction; although that tendency has declined somewhat in the recent past (Smith 1989: 23), it is especially important when chairs sponsor the bills under consideration.[8] Kingdon (1989) discovered that party leaders in the House of Representatives were particularly likely to vote with the ranking committee members from their own party. He quoted one Democrat as saying, "They [party leaders] let party policy be made by the committee chairman. Whatever the chairman says, that becomes the policy" (Kingdon 1989: 111). Second, the work of committee chairs on behalf of legislation does not cease when bills are reported out of committee. Until recently chairs were routinely asked to act as floor managers for committee bills (Smith 1989: 21). Even though subcommittee chairs have assumed some of the responsibility for floor management, chairs still act as managers for a large percentage of their committees' legislation.

One of the more interesting and perplexing findings is that banking committee members other than the chair are less effective on the floor than are non-committee members; the former succeeded only 28.1% of the time, as opposed to 39.9% for the latter. The eighty-seven laws with non-committee sponsors comprised 33.7% of the total number of banking laws enacted, while ordinary banking committee members were responsible for forty-five banking laws, 17.5% of the total. Given the strength of committee "gatekeeping," it would be fair to assume that these non-committee bills were generally non-controversial measures. Therefore, one would expect these measures to do well on the floor.

Non-committee members' success is surprising because it defies the conventional wisdom regarding committee expertise and deference. One possible explanation, which will be explored in the next section, is that committee members and non-members sponsor different types of legislation, and the discrepancies between their rates of success are really a result of substantive differences between the bills. In particular, the higher rate of bill passage achieved by those not serving on the banking committees could be a function of their sponsorship of a far higher proportion of minor bills than committee members. See Table 5.1 for a comparison of presidential and congressional passage rates on legislation reported out of committee.

Adjusting for Importance

The preceding chapter included indications that the dynamics associated with reporting out bills varied systematically according to the degree of legislative importance and from actor to actor. Even though the likelihood that legislation would be reported out of committee was

Table 5.1

Impact of Congress and President on Floor Decisions

	Congress			President		
	Non-committee	Committee	Chair	Oppose	Neutral	Support
Number	87	45	126	3	246	15
Percent of category	39.9	28.1	47.2	25.0	40.2	55.6
Percent of all bills	33.7	17.5	48.8	1.1	93.2	5.7

Note: These figures are calculated using only the bills already reported out of committee. The percent of category row shows the percentages of all bills within that category that are passed. The percent of all bills shows what percentage each of the various categories contribute to the overall total number of bills passed.

inversely related to the level of importance, presidents had only minimal success with bills of the lowest level of importance and their highest success with routine bills. In contrast, members of Congress experienced a declining chance of their legislation being reported out of committee as the level of bill importance increased.

The probabilities of a bill getting out of committee and passed on the floor differ in two respects. First, the relationship between the probability of passage on the floor and the degree of legislative importance is bell-shaped, unlike the inverse relationship between bill importance and the likelihood of the committee reporting the bill out. The highest rate (43.9%) of bill passage was for routine bills, the next highest (38.9%) was for minor bills, and the lowest (35.0%) for important bills. Perhaps the unexpectedly low passage rate on minor bills is a function of the difficulties that insignificant measures face in getting onto the floor calendar. Second, the highest and the lowest rates of bill passage achieved by the different groups of congressional sponsors differ by less than nine percentage points, compared with a spread of almost seventeen percentage points between the extremes within the committees, indicating that after a banking bill has been reported onto the floor, it matters less whether its sponsor is the chair or even a member of the banking committee.

The pattern of presidential success was different from the general one, but the small number of cases make generalization difficult. Only one minor bill with presidential support was reported out of committee, so its passage gave presidents an inconclusive "perfect" score on minor bills. The second-highest presidential bill passage rate occurred on the most important bills, with six out of ten bills enacted, and the least success was on routine bills, where eight out of sixteen passed. Congressional opponents were able to pass 20% of routine bills and 50% of important bills that presidents publicly tried to stop, but again the very small numbers—two routine bills and one important bill—make generalizations risky.

Committee chairs had success rates that conformed to the normal distribution of passage, with a significantly higher success rate on routine bills and lower rates on the minor and important bills. As expected, chairs were far more successful on all categories than were any of the other legislators: 53.1% of routine bills, 42.3% of minor bills, and 40% of important bills. The other members of the banking committees were far less successful on the floor than the committee chairs or non-committee members with routine and minor legislation.

Much, but not all, of the overall success of non-committee members can be traced to the large number of minor bills they sponsored that passed into law. Non-committee members sponsored fifty-six minor laws, compared to thirteen minor laws from ordinary committee members. Even excluding such bills, ordinary committee sponsors still had a lower rate of bill passage than did non-committee members (31.4% versus 36.4%). One possible explanation is traceable to the internal committee dynamics that lead chairs to replace junior committee members as the primary sponsors of promising legislation. If this is the case, the role of ordinary committee members would be systematically understated, because they would get no credit for legislation they nurtured but that chairs eventually guided to passage. Another possibly related reason lies in the historical role of chairs as floor managers of all committee legislation. Chairs may devote their energies to the passage of their own pet bills and give other committee bills only limited attention. This, however, would only lead to higher rates on non-committee members' bills if the chairs chose to give them more attention than the bills sponsored by ordinary committee members. While this might occur as a result of intercommittee bargaining and log-rolling, detection of a bona fide pattern would need to be investigated.

House and Senate Differences

Based on this study, perceptions of the House as more committed to the passage of legislation and the Senate as a forum for policy debate are borne out. Although the Senate was more likely than the House to report bills out of committee, those Senate bills were more likely to fail on the floor. House bills reported out of committee had a 45.1% and Senate bills a 34.9% chance of being enacted. Not only were representatives able to get a higher proportion of their sponsored legislation passed, the total number of new laws originating in the House was far higher than that originating in the upper chamber. The House's higher probability of bill passage carried over to all groups of legislators. For example, chairs in the House succeeded in getting 51.1% of their bills passed, while their counterparts in the Senate were able to get only 43% enacted. House chairs were the primary sponsors of seventy-one of the new laws, as opposed to the fifty-five new laws that were sponsored by Senate chairs.

While the Senate passed a lower percentage of the bills reported out of committee, in some ways it was more receptive to committee power than was the House. Chairs and committee members in the Senate were responsible for a much higher percentage of the total number of that chamber's bills enacted into law than were House chairs and committee members. Chairs sponsored 53.9% and committee members 20.6% of the Senate bills that were passed, but only 45.5% of the House total was sponsored by chairs and 15.4% by committee members. This is unexpected because senators are traditionally viewed as more independent in their voting than House members.

Presidents also were able to get more legislation they supported passed in the House than in the more autonomous Senate. Ten out of the fifteen House bills (66.6%) and only five out of twelve Senate bills (41.7%) with presidential support were enacted into law. The Senate also demonstrated its independence by passing two out of seven bills (28.6%) that presidents opposed. Only one House bill out of five with public presidential opposition was passed.

Baseline Comparisons

None of the preceding analysis assesses the chances of legislative success without the support of chairs or presidents, nor does it examine chair success without presidential support and vice versa. The 128 banking laws enacted without the support of presidents or committee chairs constituted almost half (49.6%) of the all new banking laws. A bill favorably reported but without the support of the president or a committee chair has a 35% chance of being passed into law, a useful benchmark for measuring the impact of support from presidents and chairs.

Bills backed only by presidents fared slightly worse than bills that neither presidents nor chairs supported. Four out of twelve (33.3%) of these bills were enacted into law, accounting for only 1.5% of all banking bills enacted. Almost half (45.6%) of the bills sponsored by chairs but not backed by presidents were enacted into law, and these 115 laws accounted for 44.6% of all bills passed. Although not definitive, these results suggest that the impact of presidential influence alone is limited, but that committee chairs are independently influential. Combined support makes a dramatic difference. Eleven of the fifteen bills (73.3%) backed by both were enacted, more than twice the rate on bills that were not actively supported and were markedly different from what occurred on bills with joint support within committees, where the chances of success only improved slightly when presidential support augmented the sole support of chairs. Despite the relatively small numbers, the joint support of chairs and presidents can heavily affect the odds for bill enactment. However, these bills only account for 4.3% of all the laws enacted.

Summary

In some ways the results of this assessment of the influence of presidents and key legislative actors on the floor were predictable. When only bills that have already been favorably reported out of committee are analyzed, presidential support initially appears to play a much bigger role than it did in committee decisionmaking. This is somewhat misleading for two reasons. First, so few bills with presidential support actually become law that it is difficult to attribute much overall influence to presidential support. Second, presidential support by itself may not be particularly advantageous—it only appears efficacious when combined with the support from committee chairs. However, this does not imply that these bills would necessarily pass if they lacked presidential support. Perhaps presidents influenced the decisions of committee chairs to sponsor the legislation in the first place. As anticipated, the committee chairs were still far more effective than presidents in getting bills enacted into law. They also continued to be more influential than ordinary committee members and non-committee members in determining the fate of bills. In addition, as expected, the chairs in the House of Representatives were more successful than their counterparts in the Senate in getting their bills enacted into law, but legislation sponsored by Senate chairs comprised a larger portion of enacted bills in their chamber than did legislation sponsored by House chairs.

The Overall Pattern of Bill Enactment

The material presented in Chapter 4 and in the preceding section divides the process of enacting legislation into two parts: the committee stage and the floor stage. During the first stage, presidents have very little influence on the legislative outcomes, while the committee chairs have a large impact. Once bills move onto the formal agenda by being reported out of committee, presidential support appears to increase significantly the likelihood of floor success, but, again, not as much as does that of committee chairs. The combined support of chairs and presidents, which minimally increased the likelihood of success at the committee level, makes a much more dramatic impact at the floor level.

Measuring Effectiveness

This section measures the effectiveness of the different actors at the committee and floor stages and develops overall measures of effectiveness. Since 1823, 5,138 non-duplicate banking bills have been introduced into Congress,[9] of which only 299, or less than 6%, were enacted. One banking bill was passed on an average of every five months. A worthwhile gauge of legislative effectiveness is a comparison of actors' actual success in moving bills through the committee and floor stages and their hypothetical achievements if the chance of success is randomly distributed.

For example, committee chairs were able to move 34.1% of their bills out of committee, and, since an average of only 14.4% of all banking bills were reported out, they were almost two and a half times more effective than the hypothetical average legislator in getting their bills through the first stage. At the next stage, committee chairs were about 12% more effective than the 40.6% mean passage rate of all bills reaching the floor. In contrast, bills sponsored by ordinary committee members were significantly disadvantaged at both the committee and the floor levels. Their bills were more than one-third less likely than the average bill to be reported out of committee, and, even if successful at that stage, they suffered an additional 30.8% disadvantage on the floor. Chairs exercise such overwhelming dominance of committee deliberations that the ordinary member is actually more effective on the floor than within committee. As expected, non-committee members have less success at the first stage, where their bills are 41.7% less likely than the hypothetical average bill to be reported out of committee, but on the floor their bills are only 1% less likely to be passed. Perhaps these non-specialists are able to combine their own networks of non-banking committee members with the committee coalitions that got the bills favorably reported out, thereby achieving greater success on the floor than can be achieved by the ordinary committee members.

As was already shown, presidential support is of little help in getting legislation past committee "gatekeepers." Bills endorsed by presidents are only 1.1% more likely than the average to be reported out of committee, while bills that they oppose also have a 1% advantage. However, after bills endorsed by presidents are out of committee, they are 13.7% more likely than the average to be enacted into law, while those they oppose are 37.5% less likely to become law. Although this suggests that presidential support is an advantage, these figures do not measure the independent impact of presidential support. However, what is clear is that presidential opposition can be a serious handicap when bills are considered on the floor.

Overall Effectiveness

Although ascertaining the effectiveness of different support patterns at the committee and the floor stages is important, overall measures of the likelihood of passage may provide a broader notion of presidential and congressional clout in the legislative arena. Only 5.8% of all bills introduced into Congress were enacted into law, a figure that can be used as a benchmark to assess the cumulative influence of the different actors in getting bills passed. Since chairs managed successfully to shepherd 16.3% of their bills through the committee and floor stages, their support roughly tripled the average bill's chance of passage. In contrast, bills sponsored by either ordinary committee members or non-committee members had less than a 4% chance—one-third less likely than the hypothetical average—of enactment.

Figure 5.1. **Success at Different Stages: Effectiveness of President, Chair, Committee, and Members**

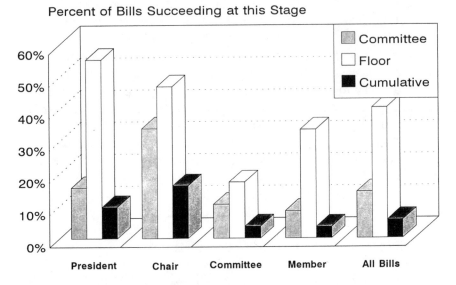

Percent of Bills Succeeding at this Stage

Using the same approach for bills that presidents publicly endorsed or opposed showed that presidential involvement significantly affects passage. Fewer than 10% of the bills supported by presidents and 4.4% of those that they opposed became law. Hence, presidential support increased the probability of passage 67.2% above the average, while bills that presidents opposed were 24.2% less likely to be passed. Any assessment of overall influence on policymaking must also consider the numbers. For example, almost half (46.7%) of all the banking bills enacted into law had chairs as their primary sponsors, but only 6.4% were endorsed by presidents. Figure 5.1 compares the effectiveness of presidents and members of Congress within committee and on the floor, and then combines those two indicators into an overall measure of effectiveness.

By treating the committee and floor stages separately, the research has been able to demonstrate that presidential support does not move legislation out of committee, but it does help a few bills at the floor stage. In contrast, the support of committee chairs dramatically aids at both the committee and the floor stages, especially the former. Other senators and representatives are markedly disadvantaged at both stages of the process. Presidential involvement affects the likelihood of passage, but because they remain neutral on most bills before Congress, the president's effect overall, is relatively small. The same cannot be said about committee chairs. Legislation they sponsored is almost three times as likely to be passed as the average, and they sponsored almost half the banking bills enacted over the past century and a half.

Political Parties and Bill Passage

Political parties might affect passage in many ways. For example, bills sponsored by members of one party may, at the most rudimentary level, be enacted at a consistently higher rate than those of another party. However, this is not usually the case, since there is little difference between the enactments of the two major parties: neither Democratic nor Republican sponsors have significantly higher rates of bill passage. The results are strikingly different if the sponsor of legislation belonged to one of the many minor parties that drifted in and out of American politics over the past century and a half. Even though third-party legislators play an important role in pushing policy proposals onto the political agenda and keeping them alive until mainstream support can be built, they were unable to enact a single banking measure that they sponsored.

Party Control

The degree of party control over the two congressional chambers and the presidency in each two-year Congress is an alternative means for partisanship to affect bill passage rates. As Hinckley reminds us, "The physical structure of the House and Senate reflects the political. Aisles divide the two parties. Cloakrooms, office space, and softball teams are partisan" (Hinckley 1971: 108). More recently, those influenced by critical realignment theory have shown that shifts in party dominance of the federal government are associated with major policy changes (Brady 1985, 1988). In one sense, the impact of party control is weaker than expected. During 63.4% of the time studied, when one party controlled the House, Senate, and presidency, the legislative output was only minimally greater than might be randomly expected—66.9% of all new banking laws. Although a partisan split between the executive and legislative branches of government is the classic example of divided government,[10] less policy "gridlock" occurs during such times than when Congress itself is divided.

When the House and the Senate were controlled by different parties only 3.9% of the bills introduced during those years passed, but when one party controlled both chambers of Congress and a different party controlled the presidency, 5.5% of them passed. The decrease in gridlock may result from the relatively limited role that the president actually plays in the enactment of banking policy. When the same party controlled both branches of government, 6.8% of the bills introduced passed. Superficially, an increase from 3.9% to 6.8% does not appear to be much of an improvement, yet those few percentage points represent an improvement of 81.5%. The increase also illustrates that divided congressional control is more damaging than a partisan division between the White House and Congress. This point is consistent with the view that Congress is the branch of government with primary responsibility for legislation.

Impact on Key Actors

The degree to which one party controls both branches of government may alter the effectiveness of key actors within the system. Although all actors may experience greater legislative success when their party controls both branches of government, there is no particular reason to assume that the degree of party control has the same effect on passage rates of the different members of Congress as it does on the chief executive.

Although bill passage generally increased as the degree of party control increased, this pattern was not duplicated for all membership groups in Congress. Committee chairs performed as expected, with passage rates of 10.1% when the Senate and House were controlled by different parties, 16.7% when different parties controlled Congress and the White House, and 17.5% under unified party government. Most noticeable about the effect of partisanship on committee chairs' success was the big jump that occurred when Congress became united, and the very small increase when the presidency was controlled by the same party. This also illustrates the relatively marginal involvement of presidents in the development of most banking policies. Ordinary committee members only got 2.3% of their bills passed when Congress was divided, but 4.2% when there was a partisan split between Congress and the White House and when the House, the Senate, and the presidency were controlled by the same party. More success may have been anticipated when one party controlled both houses of Congress and the presidency, but because presidents chose to support only a handful of bills sponsored by ordinary committee members, their support did not alter the overall pattern. The moral of this story for an ordinary committee member is that if he wants to get legislation passed, his best chance is to bide his time until he builds up enough seniority to become chair, because until then his chances of success are low unless he persuades the chair to sponsor the bill. The pattern for non-committee members most strongly deviated from the general trend. They were able to get 3.7% of their bills passed during periods of either partisan splits within Congress or unified governance, and only 2.5% when Congress and the presidency were controlled by different parties. However, even at their best, non-members had a minuscule chance of getting their bills passed.

The degree of party control has a different effect on the success of presidents than it does on members of Congress. Paradoxically, presidents appear to experience their greatest success when the two branches are controlled by opposing parties. Presidents got 11.1% of their bills passed when Congress was divided, 18.2% when Congress and the presidency were controlled by different parties, and 8.8% when the same party controlled both branches of government. This may be a function of the number of bills that presidents supported under the different party control scenarios. Presidents backed a total of only eleven banking bills when the two branches were controlled by two different parties, and only two such bills (18.2%) were enacted. In contrast, when the same party controlled the entire government, presidents pushed many more policy initiatives than they did during any other period. They supported 148 bills during periods of unified control, or 20% more than might be expected by chance.

Economic Conditions and Bill Passage

The data presented in the preceding chapter and the case studies in Chapter 3 showed that legislators are responsive to economic distress. The total number of bill introductions was found to be inversely related to deflated agricultural prices. Declining agricultural prices also corresponded to spurts in the number of routine and important bills reported out of the banking committees. Increases in the bank failure rate did not cause the number of bill introductions to increase, but they were related to increases in the overall number of banking bills favorably acted on by the committees. Still undetermined is whether these relationships extend to bill passage. Many reasons might account for why the link between the economy and bill passage might be different. Possibly, legislators are more concerned with position taking than bill passage, or agricultural downturns by themselves may not be sufficiently important to the rest of the country to spawn new laws designed to aid that sector.

The deflated agricultural prices were much less strongly correlated to bill passage than to bill introduction. The strongest correlation, $-.2492$ between deflated wool prices and bill passage, was significant only at the .06 level. However, bank failures, not at all correlated to bill introductions, had a .2886 correlation with the passage of new banking legislation, and the correlation increased to .5258 when only the most important bills were used in the analysis.[11] With respect to the passage of legislation rather than introduction of bills, the number of bank failures is a better indicator than any of the deflated agricultural prices. This might be because of the more pervasive influence of, and interest in, the health of the banking community compared to the agricultural sector.

Modeling Bill Passage

As expected, Model 5, the logit model of bill passage, includes the basic variables designed to measure the impact of presidential and congressional support on bill passage. A new institutional variable, the number of sustained vetoes per Congress, was also included to provide an indication of the degree of interbranch conflict. Not surprisingly, several variables that had already been shown to be related to bill passage were significant predictors of passage. These variables included the degree of party control, the number of bank failures, and bill importance.

The logit equation is:

$$\text{Log} \frac{1}{1-P} (\text{PASSAGE}) = B_0 + B_1\text{PRES} + B_2\text{CHAIR} + B_3\text{VETO}$$
$$+ B_4\text{PARTY} + B_5\text{BANKFAIL} + B_6\text{IMPORTANCE} \qquad (5)$$

This model provides generally strong additional support that the relationships identified in the preceding sections are correct. All coefficients are at least close to the .05 cutoff for statistical significance. Unlike in the models of committee behavior, the 0.80 coefficient of the presidential position variable is highly significant, illustrating the differences between the roles the two branches played in the formulation of policy. Presidential support has an impact on bill passage, but not on committee deliberations. The coefficient of the chair variable, significant at the .0005 level in models of both reporting legislation out of committee and final passage, indicates that the role of chairs encompasses both stages. The new veto variable, which assesses presidential behavior only at the very end of the legislation process, is also highly significant at the .0005 level. The positive sign of the variable was unexpected, since a higher number of sustained vetoes seemingly indicates an adversarial relationship between the branches. However, it could also provide an incentive for the two branches to reach accommodations on other pieces of legislation or to force a reconsideration of some of the provisions of the bills in question.

Unlike in the models of committee decisionmaking, the party control variable is positive; as the degree of party control increased, the chances of bill passage also increased. This difference between the signs in the models supports the argument in the preceding chapter that the increase in bills reported out during periods of divided government was a result of committees' partisan political behavior. The 0.15 coefficient of the party control variable is almost significant at the .05 level; it had a relatively weak, but positive impact on bill passage, consistent with the earlier findings. As anticipated, the measure of bill importance is highly significant and inversely related to bill passage, and its −0.26 coefficient is significant at the .0005 level. The bank failure variable also performed as expected, with a 0.00021 coefficient positively related to bill passage but only significant at the .016 level.

Assessments of goodness-of-fit, such as the pseudo R-square, chi-square probability, and the ability of the model to predict passage correctly, provide different results. The pseudo R-square statistic is only .112, which would usually indicate that the model does not perform very well. However, because none of the methods that attempt to replicate an R-square equivalent for logit analysis reliably indicate the model's fit, they must be considered in conjunction with other indicators of the model's performance. In this case, the other indicators show that the model accurately predicts outcomes. The probability of the chi-square occurring randomly is less than .00005, and the variables in

Table 5.2

Reasons Why Banking Bills Are Passed (Model 5)

Variable	Estimated coefficient	Standard error	t-score	Probability
Constant (B_0)	−3.69	0.63	−5.83	0.000
President	0.80	0.96	3.95	0.000
Chair	1.60	0.13	12.20	0.000
Veto	3.51	0.96	3.65	0.000
Party control	0.15	0.08	1.83	0.067
Bank failures	0.0002	0.0001	2.42	0.016
Bill importance	−0.26	0.03	−7.63	0.000

Number of Observations: 4,945
Chi-Square: 251.85
Chi-Square Probability: 0.00005
Pseudo R-Square: 0.11
Correct predictions: 94%

the model are able to predict correctly the fate of 94% of all banking bills. See Table 5.2, which summarizes Model 5.

Bill Passage over Time

At the beginning of the period studied, American society was primarily agricultural. Canals, which provided a transportation network that led to a national market, were just beginning to be built (Lee and Passell 1979: 72–78). Businesses were small and primarily family owned and operated (Porter 1973: 11). However, the situation had changed enormously by 1910, when almost all the large corporations that continue to dominate society had come into existence (Porter 1973: 78–79). These changes in the broader society were reflected in new social, economic, and regulatory demands being made on government. Political institutions faced mounting difficulties in responding to the needs of an industrial and commercial nation. The New York Bureau of Municipal Research and President Taft's Commission on Economy and Efficiency typified early attempts to apply business management techniques to government. Before the Budgeting and Accounting Act of 1921, there was no unified federal budget. The government was funded through a series of uncoordinated appropriations bills. According to Straussman, a primary concern of good government Progressives was efficiency.

> When the reformers railed against political bosses like Plunkett, it was not only about their corrupt practices and overall moral laxness. Reformers also criticized their overall incompetence. Good administration was supposed to be not only politically neutral but also *efficient*. This concept, the mainstay of many municipal reforms during the progressive era, became an overriding concern in the practice of public administration for a large part of this century. (Straussman 1985: 178)

These demands led to changes in the organization of political institutions and to shifting expectations about the roles that Congress and the president should play in society. Throughout the twentieth century, as American society has moved from an industrial to a postindustrial society and to become the pre-eminent world power, the public has continued to demand an increasingly activist government to redress social ills. Given these enormous social changes, the interaction between Congress and the president could not be expected to remain constant. The individuals who occupied government offices during that time were as much products of their society as people are today. Their world views were shaped by the prevailing ideologies and intellectual currents of the period, and they responded to the demands of their constituencies in a manner deemed appropriate at the time. Over the past 160 years, the number of banking bills introduced into Congress and the degree of legislative activism exhibited by key policy actors have both increased enormously. Among the five time periods studied, in only one, between 1933 and 1960, did the level of banking bill introductions decrease.

1823–1860: Minimal Leadership

Legislative leadership cannot be easily attributed to any policy actors during the antebellum period (1823–60) because only three banking laws were enacted during those years. In 1840, after three years of lobbying by President Martin Van Buren, Congress passed the Independent Treasury Act, which was designed to establish a subtreasury system within the Treasury Department for the maintenance of government funds. One year later, when the Whigs regained a majority within Congress, they passed a second banking act, which repealed the Independent Treasury Act. The emboldened Whigs then passed a bill to incorporate a "fiscal bank of the United States," which closely resembled the Second Bank of the United States. This bill was vetoed by President John Tyler. The only other banking legislation that was enacted during this period was a very minor piece of legislation to extend the national bank charter of a Washington, D.C., bank.

An average of fewer than three banking bills were introduced into Congress every year in this period. Presidents endorsed eighteen bills, or approximately one bill every 4.7 years, but only one was passed into law. Presidents apparently did not try to preserve their legislative influence through support of only the most important policy initiatives; they supported five minor, six routine, and eight important bills. Perhaps because their actual legislative influence was so limited, presidents did not feel constrained to limit themselves to only working on behalf of major bills. Committee chairs were somewhat more active; they introduced a total of twenty-seven bills, or one bill every 1.4 years, but were no more successful than presidents in actually seeing their legislation through to passage. Their bills were almost equally distributed among the three levels of legislative importance. Presidents and chairs sometimes attempted to cooperate, but because eight of the nine bills with their combined support failed to pass, it is fair to assume that any interbranch cooperation was singularly ineffective. The only exception was the previously mentioned Independent Treasury Bill, which had the support of President Van Buren and was sponsored by Senate Finance Committee Chair Silas Wright, Jr. (D, New York).

This lack of legislative accomplishment in the area of banking policy is a bit surprising because financial issues figured so prominently on the country's policy agenda in the years leading up to the Civil War. The best-known legislative action, President Andrew Jackson's veto of the renewal of the Bank of the United States's charter, was an example of a president's use of a negative legislative power and as such did not add to the agenda. Jackson's other actions regarding the Bank of the United States involved the exercise of administrative rather than legislative power. Even though banking policy continued to be debated throughout the period, no group was able to muster the majorities necessary to enact their desired policies.

1861–1912: Congressional Leadership

In the half century after the Civil War, almost twice as many banking bills were introduced annually as in the preceding period, and sixty-nine of these bills actually became law. Unlike the antebellum period, when neither branch forged much positive policy leadership, Congress was clearly responsible for the bulk of legislation. Presidents publicly endorsed four routine bills and one important bill, but none of them was enacted.[12] Even the National Bank Act of 1863, at the time the most significant piece of banking legislation since the creation of the Bank of the United States, was not publicly endorsed by President Lincoln, but instead was strongly supported by his Treasury secretary, Chase. However, President Lincoln is reputed to have lobbied behind the scenes on behalf of the bill.

The years after the Civil War were unusual because the sponsors of two-thirds of the new laws were not members of the committees with jurisdiction over banking legislation. Non-committee members got a remarkable total of forty-one, or 33.6%, of their bills passed into law, far higher than the 14.3% achieved by ordinary committee members and the 27.1% of committee chairs. At least part of the success of the non-committee members can be traced to the type of legislation they sponsored. More than 85% of the bills sponsored by non-committee members made very minor changes in the country's banking laws, such as changes in name or location of particular national banks. Another reason for the greater proportional success of non-committee members is institutional developments in the House and Senate. By the late 1890s congressional party leaders had become extremely powerful and aggressively used their control over committee assignments and floor procedures to limit the type of legislation considered by the entire chamber. This unprecedented power is probably responsible for the relative success of non-committee members. Bills with the support of party leaders did not need the additional sponsorship of committee chairs in order to be enacted, and when chairs pushed legislation opposed by the party leaders it usually died. For example, Speaker Joseph Cannon (R, Illinois) prevented Banking and Currency Committee Chair Charles Fowler (R, New Jersey) from getting his bill to create deposit insurance considered by the entire House in 1908.

Given the limited presidential activism and the limited power of committee chairs in the period, the fact that only one attempt was made to get a bill enacted using the support of both the president and a committee chair is not surprising. In 1873 Representative Horace Maynard (R, Tennessee) introduced a bill to create a postal savings system, and as was discussed in Chapter 3, Maynard was unable even to get the legislation reported out of his own committee.

1913–1932: A New Pattern Emerges

As industrialization prompted greater demands on government, pressure for governmental reform, principally in the form of greater governmental efficiency, also increased. The change in the executive branch was gradual, at least in part prompted by a perceptual shift in views about presidential roles that was dramatically captured in the great Roosevelt-Taft debates. Other suggested changes, such as those proposed by Taft's Commission on Economy and Efficiency, were concrete attempts to restructure the government apparatus. Even though many of these proposals were not accepted at the time, they were indicative of this shift toward a hierarchical business model of government. Woodrow Wilson, who succeeded Taft as president, was explicitly committed to the goal of active presidential leadership in legislation. Wilson's assistant secretary of the Navy, Franklin Roosevelt, was greatly influenced by the spirit of the times and told friends it was crucial to make government as efficient as private business (Schlesinger 1957: 358). This sentiment was echoed a few years later by President Calvin Coolidge when he said, "This is a business country . . . and it wants a business government" (Schlesinger 1957: 61).

Within Congress, two reform periods are noteworthy. The overthrow of Speaker Cannon in 1910 and the retirement of Senator Aldrich (R, Rhode Island) two years later led directly to an increase in the power of committee chairs at the expense of the House Speaker and Senate Majority Leader (Sundquist 1981: 177). Normally a reform that dispersed power in this fashion would be seen as decreasing efficiency, but this was unusual for two reasons. First, by the time Speaker Cannon was overthrown, his leadership had already been almost completely discredited, so that the reform was expected.[13] Second, the reform enhanced the power of the chairs because it centralized power within committees rather than within the chambers and led to the development of legislative leadership by policy area.

The pattern of legislative behavior during this period was radically different from that of the nineteenth century, and nowhere more so than in the sharp increase in legislative activism among all participants. An average of more than thirty-seven banking bills were introduced each year into Congress, nearly four times the annual rate of the preceding period and nearly fourteen times the antebellum rate. Presidents on the average supported 1.3 bills and chairs sponsored 8.5 bills per year. Nearly 90% of the bills with presidential support fell into the most important category, and the remainder were routine bills. In contrast, chairs sponsored a wide range of legislation (33.1% minor, 50.3% routine, and 16.6% important). Another notable difference between this period and those preceding was that the institutionalization of committee power increased the ability of committee chairs to dominate the legislative process. Unlike the nineteenth century, in this period committee chairs were the legislative leaders, getting 17.2% of their bills passed as compared with 3.5% for non-committee members and 5% for ordinary committee members. Moreover, chairs were responsible for more than half the fifty-two banking laws that were enacted. At least part of the reason for the success of committee chairs in this period relates to the type of bills that had their support. As was noted above, most of the legislation sponsored by chairs was of either routine or minor significance.

Furthermore, for the first time, the banking legislation publicly endorsed by presidents did better than that which they opposed. In fact, none of the eight banking bills that presidents lobbied against were enacted. The extent of presidents' influence is difficult to determine, because all four of the bills they supported were also sponsored by committee chairs. Three out of the four bills with joint support were enacted, including those creating the Federal Reserve System and the Reconstruction Finance Corporation. The only unsuccessful bill ostensibly backed by both was a bill to make minor changes in the Agricultural Credits Act, and neither likely worked very hard for its enactment.

1933–1960: The Pattern Continues

As was mentioned earlier, the decision to treat the years from 1933 to 1960 as a separate period was based on two factors. First was the massive expansion in government activities initiated during the New

Deal years. One way to measure government expansion is to look at the increase in government agencies regulating banks, the stock market, transportation, labor and management relations, and welfare. Executive agencies were established to administer unemployment compensation, Social Security, and agricultural price supports. The resultant growth in the number of federal employees was even more dramatic: between 1932 and 1941, that number mushroomed from 600,000 to more than 1.4 million (Burnham 1986: 359). The second reason to treat the period as distinct relies on the conventional wisdom by which Franklin Roosevelt is regarded as the first of the modern presidents. All post-Roosevelt presidents have been measured against his presidency.[14] Although Roosevelt may have only continued and reinforced the tendencies already extant for two decades, the sheer scope of government was so much larger after his administrations that the same criteria cannot be used to evaluate presidencies before and after his tenure.

While the New Deal and its aftermath are usually considered a period of executive dominance, the legislative pattern resembles that of the Progressive Era. Although legislative activism in the banking area abated somewhat, the level of bill introductions was still much greater than in the nineteenth century, with 715 banking bills introduced during the period, or an average of nearly twenty-six bills annually. Presidents supported only twelve of these bills, four of which were enacted, and two banking bills were passed into law over presidential opposition.

Within Congress, chairs continued to control and dominate the legislative agenda. Smith and Deering (1990: 45) describe committee chairs as the "chief brokers of many competing interests in their committees' broad jurisdiction," and an analysis of the legislative histories of banking bills certainly supports that characterization. No other congressional actors came close to the success of the chairs in producing legislation that garnered both committee and floor support. Committee chairs were able to get more than a quarter (27.4%) of their initiatives enacted into law, compared with 4.4% for non-committee members and 5.4% for ordinary committee members. Chairs sponsored almost 60% of the sixty-seven new banking laws. Committee chairs also sponsored three of the four laws that had presidential support. All of these laws, enacted during Roosevelt's first term, dealt with the collapse of the country's banking system during the Great

Depression. On 9 March 1933, Congress passed the "Emergency Banking Act," sponsored by House Banking and Currency Committee Chair Henry Steagall (D, Alabama). The main effect of this law was to remove any doubts about President Roosevelt's authority to issue the executive order closing the banks.[15] Three months later, a second Steagall-sponsored bill, the 1933 Banking Act, further centralized the Federal Reserve System and created the Federal Deposit Insurance Corporation. Two years later many of its provisions were supplanted by the third bill with joint support, the Banking Act of 1935, which concentrated more authority in the White House and gave the president the power to appoint and remove all members of the Federal Reserve Board.

1961–1986: Renewed Activism

Around 1960, legislative behavior abruptly changed, as the activism of senators, representatives, and presidents sharply increased. The 2,128 banking bills in the period represent a threefold increase in the average number of bill introductions. Presidential support grew from an average of one bill every 2.3 years to more than three bills per year. However, a larger portion of the bills supported by presidents were of minor or routine significance. Of the bills with presidential support, 11% were minor, 54% were routine, and 34.5% were important. Instead of sponsoring five bills a year, committee chairs sponsored fourteen, and similar increases were recorded for other legislators. Chairs continued to sponsor bills of differing degrees of importance (17.6% minor, 61.2% routine, and 21.1% important). Two explanations for this abrupt shift deserve consideration. The first is simply that the transition from the low-key leadership style of Dwight Eisenhower to the more activist John Kennedy brought a new spirit to Washington. The other explanation involves a longer-term institutional reason for change. The staff of both branches of government expanded enormously during the 1960s (King and Ragsdale 1988: 205; Ornstein, Mann, and Malbin 1992: 126–30), which made it easier for presidents to push more initiatives and members of Congress to sponsor more legislation.

This period also witnessed a large increase in the annual number of banking laws passed. This increase was, however, far smaller than the increase in bill introductions. Although bill introductions were approximately three times more numerous than in the preceding period, the number of enactments grew by only about a third. The passage rate of each of the different groups of legislators declined by approximately one-half: the rate for non-committee members dropped from 4.4% to 2.2%, for ordinary committee members from 5.4% to 2.3%, and for committee chairs from 27.4% to 13.8%. The effectiveness of presidential support declined even more precipitously from a 33.3% passage rate in the preceding period to a 9.2% rate. This downward trend in the passage rates of legislators and presidents might be traceable to the even sharper increase in their legislative activism. Committee chairs lack the time, energy, and clout to guide fourteen bills a year through to passage; perhaps their activism was a means of gaining credit with increasingly activist constituency groups. The new laws, which had been sponsored by committee chairs, differed in their policy significance. Nearly 10% were from the most important category, 62.7% were of routine significance, and 27.5% were of only minor importance.

Committee chairs sponsored a majority (56%) of the ninety-one new laws, and presidents continued to be involved in the passage of only a small portion—eight (8.8%) of the laws had presidential support before enactment, and nearly two-thirds of those were of routine significance. Here, too, credit for passage cannot be allocated solely to presidential influence, because committee chairs sponsored six of the new laws. None of these laws in any way rivaled the significance of those passed during the New Deal era. For example, on 3 March 1965 a law was enacted with the support of President Lyndon Johnson and House Banking and Currency Committee Chair Wright Patman (D, Texas) to eliminate the requirement that Federal Reserve Banks hold 25% of their reserves in gold, thus providing the government with access to additional gold to help pay its international balance of payments. While certainly a significant piece of legislation, it lacks the scope of those enacted during Franklin Roosevelt's presidency. See Figure 5.2 for a comparison of the legislative achievements of the presidents and committee chairs across time.

Modeling Bill Passage over Time

To understand further how the pattern of executive-congressional interaction on banking legislation has changed over the past century and a half, time-series models were constructed to predict the number of

Figure 5.2. **Passage of Banking Bills: Success of Presidents and Chairs**

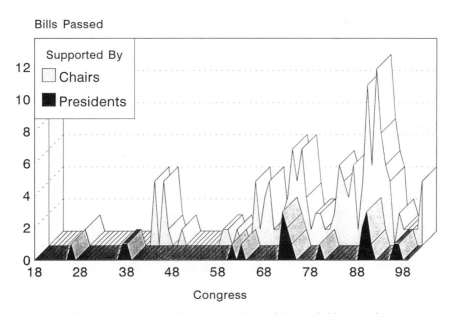

Bills Passed

banking bills passed in each Congress. Most of the variables are the same as those created for use in the time-series models in Chapter 4. One difference is that a dummy variable designed to measure the effect of New Deal reforms was significant in one model.

Although presidential position and sustained vetoes affected bill passage in the logit models, neither presidential support nor opposition measurably influenced the number of bills enacted in the Congresses under consideration, but the presidential support variable was included in Model 6 because of its importance to the analysis. Much of the effect of the congressional variables was captured by system capability measures, such as the number of bill introductions and banking committee staff, rather than by the chair variable. The bank failure variable was about equally important in this model as it was in the model predicting the number of bills reported out of committee.

$$\text{PASSAGEB}_t = B_t + B_1\text{PRES}_t + B_2\text{CHAIR}_t + B_3\text{BANKSTAFF}t$$
$$+ B_4\text{BILLS}_t + B_5\text{BANKFAIL}_t + B_6\text{IMPORTANCE}_t \qquad (6)$$

With the exception of the presidential support, all the variables in this model have coefficients that exert a measurable impact on the

Table 5.3

Reasons Why Banking Bills Are Passed (Model 6)

Variable	Estimated coefficient	Standard error	t-score	Probability
Constant (B_0)	17.50	4.34	4.03	0.000
President	0.02	0.07	0.36	0.720
Chair	0.16	0.04	4.23	0.000
Bank staff	−0.03	0.02	−1.68	0.098
Bank bills	0.03	0.01	2.17	0.034
Bank failures	0.001	0.0006	1.72	0.092
Bill importance	−1.82	0.48	−3.76	0.000

Number of Observations: 61
R-Square: 0.56
Adjusted R-Square: 0.51
Durbin-Watson D: 1.745
1st Order Autocorrelation: 0.127

number of bills passed in each Congress. Although presidential support has the expected positive sign, it does not even approach significance. The other major institutional variable, chair support, is highly significant. The 0.16 chair coefficient is significant at the .0001 level. Some of the variance in this model is captured by the system capability variables. The number of banking committee staff, like in the models of bills reported out of committee, had a negative impact, −0.03, which was significant at the .10 level. The total number of bill introductions had a positive effect on the number of bills passed. Its 0.03 coefficient is also significant at the .03 level. As anticipated, bill importance was negatively related to passage, with a −1.82 coefficient significant at the .0004 level. Bank failures also provided an impetus for bill enactments, but it was not a strong predictor. Its coefficient failed to reach the .05 cutoff for significance, but it was close.

The model has an adjusted R-square of .51, which indicates that it explains half the variance in the number of banking bills enacted into law over the last twelve decades. The Durbin-Watson score shows that serial autocorrelation is not a serious problem in the model. Given the number of bills and the length of time analyzed, that is remarkable. See Table 5.3, which summarizes Model 6.

Time-Series Models by Importance Levels

Because of strong indications that the pattern of interaction varied systematically according to the level of bill importance, the data were divided into the following three subsets: minor bills, routine bills, and important bills. This is the same grouping as was used in the analysis of committee behavior by importance levels.

Minor Bills

As was mentioned in the preceding chapter, patterns of behavior on minor bills are difficult to identify because so many idiosyncratic factors disrupt the normal patterns of interaction. This description applies equally well to floor actions. None of the normal institutional variables are significant, and the model explains very little of the total variance.

Routine Bills

Unlike the idiosyncratic influences on the fate of minor and important bills, the factors that govern the passage of routine bills are primarily the stuff of day-to-day politics, which are more easily captured by the normal set of institutional variables. In Model 7 the number of bills with presidential support, the number of chair-sponsored bills, party control, the number of bank failures, and a dummy variable designed to measure the impact of the New Deal era are used to predict the number of routine bill enactments over time.

$$PASSAGEB_t = B_t + B_1PRES_t + B_2CHAIR_t + B_3PARTY_t + B_4BANKFAIL_t + B_51933_t \qquad (7)$$

The most noticeable fact about this model is that presidential support was a strong predictor of the number of routine bill enactments across time. The .10 presidential support coefficient is significant at the .01 level. As expected, however, the support of committee chairs has a greater impact than presidential support. Its coefficient is significant at the .0005 level. The degree of party control was also significant, but just barely. As party control expanded across the governing

Table 5.4

Reasons Why Routine Banking Bills Are Passed (Model 7)

Variable	Estimated coefficient	Standard error	t-score	Probability
Constant (B_0)	−0.49	0.40	−1.22	0.227
President	0.10	0.04	2.66	0.010
Chair	0.09	0.02	4.57	0.000
Party control	0.45	0.22	2.07	0.043
Bank failures	0.0009	0.0003	3.01	0.004
1933 dummy	−1.13	0.39	−2.90	0.005

Number of Observations: 61
R-Square: .68
Adjusted R-Square: .65
Durbin-Watson D: 1.869
1st Order Autocorrelation: 0.055

institutions, the number of routine bill enactments increased. Bank failure was also strongly related to the passage of routine bills. The .00088 bank failure coefficient is significant at the .004 level. The 1933 dummy variable also exerted an upward influence on the number of routine laws passed. Its 1.13 coefficient is significant at the .005 level, which gives credence to the view that Roosevelt's election ushered in a distinctly different type of governance.

As was the case with the models predicting committee decisions on whether to report out legislation, those dealing with routine bills explain more of the variance than any of the others. Model 7 accounts for two-thirds of the variance in the number of routine bill enactments. Its adjusted R-square is .65. The Durbin-Watson score of 1.869 indicates the absence of serial autocorrelation. See Table 5.4, which summarizes Model 7.

Important Bills

Unlike the passage of routine bills, primarily affected by day-to-day political interactions that are easily modeled, the determinants of the number of important bills passed over time are more difficult to identify. In Model 8 (see Table 5.5) the number of bills supported by presidents, the number sponsored by committee chairs, and the number

Table 5.5

Reasons Why Important Banking Bills Are Passed (Model 8)

Variable	Estimated coefficient	Standard error	t-score	Probability
Constant (B_0)	0.12	0.13	0.88	0.383
President	−0.03	0.02	−1.58	0.190
Chair	0.03	0.01	3.48	0.0001
Bank failures	0.0007	0.0002	4.60	0.000

Number of Observations: 61
R-Square: .40
Adjusted R-Square: .37
Durbin-Watson D: 1.886
1st Order Autocorrelation: −0.026

of bank failures are used to predict the number of important bills passed in each Congress.

$$PASSAGEB_t = B_t + B_1 PRES_t + B_2 CHAIR_t + B_3 BANKFAIL_t \quad (8)$$

The negative sign associated with the presidential support variable indicates an inverse relationship between the number of banking bills with presidential support and the number of important bills passed, but the coefficient is not significant at the .05 level. Perhaps when presidents divide their support by focusing on too many initiatives, the efficacy of their support diminishes for the most important category of bills, which need strong, coordinated backing from all sectors to be enacted. Not surprisingly, the chair sponsorship variable was strongly positive. The .03 coefficient for the number of bills sponsored by committee chairs was significant at the .001 level. Moreover, as expected, the number of bank failures exerted a strong positive impact on the number of important banking bills passed into law, with a .00070 coefficient, significant at the .0005 level.

This model explains only about a third of the variance in the number of important bills passed over time. Given the length of time covered and the difficulties in predicting the influences on important legislation, the adjusted R-square of .37 is not unexpected. The Durbin-Watson score of 1.886 indicates that serial autocorrelation is not a problem.

Conclusion

This analysis of bill passage strongly supports the view that Congress is indeed the "first branch" of government and the dominant influence on policymaking. Many interesting findings emerged from this study. Presidents and chairs play distinctly different roles in bill passage. Those roles are largely determined by the importance of the legislation. Surprisingly, parties have only limited impact on bill passage. In addition, the only economic variable with a consistently strong relationship to passage is the number of bank failures. As was the case within committees, chairs are major actors on a wide range of legislation, but presidents put the bulk of their energies into the passage of more important legislation. Once again, measures supported by both presidents and chairs do far better than other bills. These jointly supported measures contribute much more to the passage rates of presidents than of chairs. More than two-thirds of the laws supported by presidents were also sponsored by chairs. In contrast, these cooperative measures constitute only a small portion of the laws with chair support.

The logit model of bill passage provided additional evidence that Congress and the president fulfill very different roles in policymaking. When passage is modeled, rather than committee decisions to report or not report out legislation, the position that presidents take on the bills is actually an important determinant of whether the legislation passes. Although not as strongly predictive as the position of committee chairs, it is still important. System capability variables that are linked directly to committee performance do not affect passage in the same manner as they do committee decisionmaking. The degree of party control, bill importance, and bank failures exert similar amounts of influence in both models. The logit model of bill passage correctly predicted whether 94% of the bills would pass or die.

The time-series models provide general support for the notion that Congress is the predominant legislative power and that the president plays a different and far more limited role in the policymaking process. In fact, presidential support was significantly related only to the passage of routine bills. On important legislation, an inverse relationship existed between the number of important bills endorsed by presidents and the number of important bills enacted into law, but it was not significant. In all the models predicting the number of bills passed over time, the number of bills supported by committee chairs had a large effect. The passage of minor and important bills was strongly affected by idiosyncratic events, while the passage of routine bills was determined mostly by normal everyday politics. For this reason, the latter were far easier to model. The time-series model predicting the number of routine bill passages explained two-thirds of the variance on these bills.

Notes

1. Even though most bills reported out of committee are considered on the floor, not all standing committees are equally successful in getting floor action on their bills (Lewis 1978: 465). Also, the political predispositions of those in "gatekeeping" roles, such as the chair of the House Rules Committee, can profoundly affect a bill's chances of consideration. For example, every Congress between 1955 and 1960 the House Rules Committee, under its conservative chair, Howard Smith (D, Virginia), bottled up approximately thirty bills that were favorably reported out of committee (Matsunaga and Chen 1976: 139).

2. In the postwar period the number of bills passed per Congress by the House of Representatives ranged from a low of 704 bills in the Ninety-seventh Congress to a high of 2,482 bills in the Eighty-first Congress. In the same period the ratio of House bills passed to bills introduced also varied a great deal, ranging from 0.049 in the Ninety-third Congress to 0.236 in the Eighty-first Congress. Within the Senate the number of bill enactments ranged from the low of 803 bills in the Ninety-seventh Congress to the high of 2,550 bills passed by the Eighty-fourth Congress. The ratio of Senate bill introductions to bill passage varied from 0.235 in the Ninety-second Congress to 0.564 in the Eighty-fourth Congress (Ornstein, Mann, and Malbin 1992: 151–53).

3. The sheer size of this undertaking mitigates against consideration of the actual floor politics associated with bill passage. Rather the emphasis will be on the general patterns of support that facilitate passage. See Sinclair (1989) and Smith (1989).

4. The political power school of presidential research, which originated with Neustadt (1960) deals with the relative weakness of presidents, particularly their inability to get their ostensible subordinates to carry out their policy wishes. A president must persuade individuals who have different bases of support, different constituencies, and possibly different policy aims to do his bidding.

5. See Collie's (1985) review of the collective and individual approaches to the study of legislative voting.

6. The term "floor" is used in this context as a synonym for the stage in the legislative process when bills move out of committee and are considered by the larger collectivity or its representatives. See Smith (1989: 4) for an explanation of the alternative definitions of the term.

7. This willingness of committee chairs to go against the wishes of presidents, even those of their own party, has been documented by much of the previous research comparing the level of support among party leaders and committee chairs for presidential initiatives. See Bond and Fleisher (1990: 131–40).

8. Other scholars have argued that the committee chairs are often adept at anticipating what policies will and will not gain floor acceptance, and they often

act within these constraints. See Fenno (1973) and Manley (1970). Kingdon distinguishes between the "normal pattern" of interaction, where committee leaders balanced what they would like to accomplish against what could be passed on the floor, and the more extraordinary situations, where the committee "got rolled" on the floor and lost badly. But Kingdon argues that the House as a whole tends to defer to committees on minor legislation and on the details of major legislation, which gives committees a great deal of legislative latitude (1989: 134–39).

9. The sponsors of twenty of these bills are unknown. For this reason all the material involving congressional sponsors will be analyzed using the 5,118 non-duplicate bills with recorded sponsors.

10. For example, Fiorina, in a chapter entitled "The Consequences of Divided Government," described the likelihood that the Tom Foleys, George Mitchells, and George Bushes would put aside their differences and work for the good of the country as "the stuff of fairy tales," because divided government gives the leaders of both Congress and the White House political incentives to run against the other branch (Fiorina 1992: 87).

11. The correlation with the passage of all banking bills is significant at the .03 level, while that involving only the most important bills is significant at the .0005 level.

12. Unlike recent presidents, whose statements of support for legislation tend to be very specific, most nineteenth-century presidents spoke in only the most general terms. For example, President James Buchanan in his 8 December 1857 "First Annual Message" made the following legislative recommendation: "Congress, in my opinion, possesses the power to pass a uniform bankrupt law applicable to all banking institutions throughout the United States, and I strongly recommend its exercise. This would make it the irreversible organic law of each bank's existence that suspension of specie payments shall produce its civil death. The instinct of self preservation would then compel it to perform its duties in such a manner as to escape the penalty and preserve its life." See U.S. President, *Messages and Papers of the Presidents,* Vol. 7, p. 2972.

13. Jones (1968) argues that a Speaker in the House of Representatives must be able to maintain two different types of majorities (procedural and substantive) if he wants to govern. According to Jones, Cannon's insistence on using all the powers of his office to "force" members to go along with his extremely conservative viewpoint eroded his support and caused policy stalemate in Congress. Cannon was able to use his power to block legislation that progressives wanted, but he found it increasingly difficult to push through his own initiatives. Republican Insurgents eventually joined with Democrats, causing him to lose both his procedural and substantive majorities.

14. An example of this tendency to treat Franklin Roosevelt as the first modern president can be seen in the title *In the Shadow of FDR,* which Leuchtenburg gave to his 1983 book on the Truman through Reagan presidencies.

15. Upon taking office, Roosevelt had issued a series of executive orders, based on powers granted by the 1917 Trading with the Enemy Act, to declare a bank holiday and take the country off the gold standard. Since the United States was not in a state of war as required by the Act, some questioned Roosevelt's authority to take these unilateral actions.

6

A Comparison of Theories

Theoretical Framework

The purpose of this chapter is to test the utility of alternative conceptions of the underlying patterns of legislative leadership over time. Providing clear legislative leadership is more difficult in the United States than in parliamentary democracies, because government in this country lacks an organic link between its legislative and executive functions. Separately elected legislative and executive branches of government are expected to share the responsibility for policymaking.

At different times scholars have used different analytic lenses to study the problem of policymaking in the United States. The three most important approaches employ the lenses of constitutional law, modernization, and political time to analyze the relative power of the branches. In the past only modernization and political time were thought to have predictive power. Those using the modernization school predict that the passage of time will witness a linear increase in the relative power of presidents and a commensurate decline in congressional power.[1] In contrast, the political time approach predicts that the underlying pattern is cyclical in nature.[2] Unlike these diachronic theories, the constitutional law approach, with its emphasis on the enduring nature of the Constitution, has been seen as more suitable for normative theory than for generating testable hypotheses about future interbranch behavior.[3]

The basic theoretical argument of this work is that the Constitution has played a major part in determining the existence and extent of changes in the balance of power between Congress and the president.

Those who wish to explain change do not typically look to the Constitution, because constitutions are regarded as static documents that seek to enforce a universal balance of power. However, constitutions are typically unbalanced, and those who design them wish to keep some things unchanged while allowing others to change over time. This chapter tests the predictive power of the modernization and political time approaches and then uses dynamic constitutionalism to explain some of the results found anomalous under the first two approaches.

The Modernization Lens

By the middle of the twentieth century, changes within government and the broader society convinced political scientists of the need for a more dynamic analytic lens than that provided by the traditional constitutional law approach, which emphasized the formal powers of each branch. Many scholars contributed to the development the modernization thesis, which holds that although Congress provided most of the policy leadership in the nineteenth century, the presidency is better suited to the demands of the twentieth century. In contrast to the stability of the constitutional approach, the modernization thesis argues that the movement from an agricultural to an industrial society created new social, economic, and regulatory demands on government.

The intellectual roots of this theory can be traced to scholars' fascination with Franklin Roosevelt and the New Deal. The Roosevelt administration was considered the first modern presidency, and Roosevelt's success in pushing legislation through Congress in his administration's first hundred days became the standard against which all subsequent presidents were measured. With Roosevelt as the model, scholars (Corwin 1957; Rossiter 1960) in the early postwar years developed the concept of the "president as chief legislator."

This conception of executive power created a no-win situation for Congress. If Congress refused to pass legislation favored by a president, it was damned for being obstructionist. If Congress passed the measures, it was criticized for being too acquiescent. This dilemma was summarized by Huntington when he wrote, "Congress can defend its autonomy only by refusing to legislate and it can legislate only by surrendering its autonomy" (Huntington 1973: 306). Huntington extrapolated from these observations to derive a theory explaining the decline of congressional leadership in the twentieth century. He argued that centralization enables the presidency to respond to the complex, modern world better than Congress. Hampered by its insulation, diffuse structure, and preoccupation with its oversight function, Congress, according to Huntington, is unable to respond to rapidly changing social forces (Huntington 1973: 308). This view of the relationship between Congress and the president was consistent with common perceptions of reality. Although the bulk of New Deal legislation underwent a long incubation in Congress before President Roosevelt took up the gauntlet, most observers believed that Congress was little more than a rubber stamp, simply passing or rejecting the president's program. In a similar vein, Congress in the 1950s and 1960s was considered an obstructionist institution that thwarted the liberal agendas of presidents.[4]

The Political Time Lens

The string of ineffective or repudiated presidencies from Lyndon Johnson through Jimmy Carter raised serious doubts about the validity of the modernization thesis. Another decade would pass before new institutionalists turned their attention to executive-congressional relations.[5] Probably the most provocative attempt to apply historical "new institutionalism" to the interaction between the president and Congress on legislation is the work of Stephen Skowronek (1986, 1984).

Building on critical realignment theory, Skowronek argues that presidential leadership evinces a pattern of decline and resurgence, and is largely determined by "political time" (i.e., the point in a regime sequence when a president is in office):

> A broad view of American political development reveals patterned sequences of political change with corresponding patterns in presidential performance. Presidential history in this reading has been episodic rather than evolutionary, with leadership opportunities gradually dissipating after an initial upheaval in political control over government. Presidents intervene in—and their leadership is mediated by—the generation and degeneration of political orders. The clock at work in presidential leadership keeps political rather than historical time. (Skowronek 1984: 156)

Skowronek divides presidents according to their location at the beginning, middle, or end of a political regime. A new political regime begins with a powerful and united governing coalition, which gradually erodes as conflicts develop among its members and new social groups emerge. This evolutionary process makes it ever more difficult for presidents to exercise effective leadership until eventually the governing political regime is replaced by a new one. Skowronek identifies the powerful presidents (Washington, Jefferson, Jackson, Lincoln, Wilson, and Franklin Roosevelt) as men who started new political regimes. He also identifies some mid-regime and late-regime presidents, but many are unclassified. The strength of this theory is its ability to explain strong presidents of the nineteenth century, as well as repudiated ones in the twentieth century.

But Skowronek's theory has one important, internal inconsistency. Although Wilson was a powerful and effective leader, at least during his first term, he was not a regime builder but a Democratic anomaly during a strongly Republican era. Preceded by three Republican presidents and followed by three additional Republicans, Wilson was able to squeak into office in 1912 with less than 42% of the popular vote because the Republicans split their votes between William Taft and Theodore Roosevelt. If these men do not share the common characteristic of being regime builders, then they are united only by their common designation as powerful presidents, and Skowronek's theory, at least as applied in this case, is tautological (i.e., powerful presidents are indeed powerful). Because Wilson may be either an anomaly or a misclassification, the entire theory cannot be rejected simply on the basis of his placement.

The Dynamic Constitutionalism Lens

The central thesis of this research is that throughout our country's history the Constitution has been a major determinant of legislative leadership provided by Congress and the president. On the most fundamental level, the Constitution assigns to Congress a broad range of formal legislative powers while it confers to the president very modest ones, ensuring that Congress will always be the branch with principal responsibility for legislation. The Founders' assignment of specific formal legislative powers to each branch created a bounded system of governance in which all subsequent developments are forced to occur within the parameters established by them in the Constitution. In particular, the potential for presidential aggrandizement is checked by the paucity of formal legislative powers granted the president. Unlike parliamentary systems, where the chief executive is also a member in good standing of the legislature, in the United States the president has fewer legislative powers than the most junior member of the House of Representatives. Since the president cannot even introduce bills in his own name, he must convince a representative or senator to do so. Although presidents can use informal methods to expand their legislative role, the overall growth of that role will be constrained in accordance with the congressional prerogatives established by the Constitution. This view was expressed by Keller, who asserts that the Constitution defines the boundaries of political debate within the United States (Keller 1988: 15).

Policy formation within the constitutional framework is not a zero-sum game, in which leadership by one branch necessarily diminishes the other's role, but a mechanism for an impetus for an implicit division of labor and interbranch cooperation. In addition to the boundary-setting stipulations of the Constitution, other, less stringent provisions encourage the president to defer to Congress on a wide range of legislation. The constitutionally mandated differences in electoral constituencies and electoral cycles, as well as the internal structures of each institution, increase the likelihood that presidents will limit the breadth and depth of their policymaking role. Unlike members of Congress, who must be responsive to the policy demands of many relatively small constituency groups, the need for presidents to build a broad, national electoral coalition in order to be (re)elected forces them to focus on issues of national concern. In fact, if a president becomes too concerned with mundane day-to-day legislative issues, he will be criticized, as President Jimmy Carter was, for "micro-managing" and losing his focus on the overall picture. The hierarchical structure of the White House reinforces this constitutionally based presidential tendency to concentrate attention on issues of national importance, while the decentralized and relatively egalitarian structure of Congress provides senators and representatives with the means to pursue their more parochial policy concerns. Similarly, the statutory limitations on the length of time presidents may serve in office discourages them from taking on more policy goals than they can achieve in the allotted time. The dynamic constitutionalism framework does not posit that the balance of legislative power has remained constant over time, merely that the Constitution has constrained the manner of its development.

Tests of the Modernization Thesis

To test Huntington's thesis that the presidency has adapted better to the demands of the twentieth century than has Congress, the data set was divided into two parts, with 1900 as the breakpoint. There were 1,305 bills introduced into the House and Senate before 1900, and 3,833 from 1900 to 1986. Separate comparisons of the effectiveness of presidents and Congress in the nineteenth and twentieth centuries were used to assess Huntington's view of modern presidential ascendancy and congressional decline.

Presidents in the Nineteenth and Twentieth Centuries

Huntington correctly concluded that presidents in the nineteenth century provided ineffective policy leadership. Of the seventy-five banking bills supported by presidents between 1823 and 1899, only two (2.7%) were passed into law. Since the overall passage rate for banking bills in the nineteenth century was 5.4%, measures supported by presidents performed well below the norm. In fact, during the nineteenth century a bill had a better chance of passage if the president was neutral (5.8%) or even opposed (2.9%) than if the president was a supporter.[6]

If Huntington's theory is correct, performance of presidents should have markedly improved during the twentieth century, and the post-1900 data do show some improvement in presidential effectiveness. Presidential support appeared to help rather than hinder the passage of bills. More than 14% of the banking bills supported by presidents passed, as opposed to 5.7% of those on which they did not take a position. One of the most striking indications of presidential involvement in the passage of banking legislation is the increase in the percentage of new laws that were enacted with the support of presidents. In the nineteenth century, only 2.8% of the new laws had presidential support, but in the twentieth century 7.5% had public support from presidents before passage. Congress, however, continued to succeed occasionally in overcoming presidential opposition. Almost 7% of the bills opposed by presidents were passed into law.[7] A comparison between nineteenth- and twentieth-century presidential effectiveness is presented in Table 6.1.

Table 6.1

Presidential Effectiveness in the Nineteenth and Twentieth Centuries

	Nineteenth Century				Twentieth Century			
	Op-posed	Neutral	Favor	Total	Op-posed	Neutral	Favor	Total
Bills intro-duced	68	1,162	75	1,305	45	3,668	120	3,833
Number passed	2	67	2	71	3	208	17	228
Percentage passed	2.9	5.8	2.7	5.4	6.7	5.7	14.2	5.9

Congress in the Nineteenth and Twentieth Centuries

According to Huntington, a highly centralized nineteenth-century Congress exercised the leadership that the president was unable or unwilling to provide. Since presidents publicly supported the passage of only two out of the seventy-one banking laws enacted during the nineteenth century, Congress, if only by default, was the legislative leader. Beyond this broad institutional dichotomy, however, the question then becomes whether certain members of Congress were responsible for providing this leadership because of their position or whether it was randomly dispersed throughout the membership. To answer this question, the initial plan was to divide the legislators into four categories: those occupying House or Senate party leadership positions, committee chairs, ordinary committee members, and non-committee members. However, none of the banking bills were sponsored by individuals occupying leadership positions within the entire chamber. Whatever actions they took on behalf of legislation were informal and not amenable to this type of quantitative analysis.[8]

The data from the nineteenth century show the expected pattern of increasing effectiveness as one moves closer to the formal loci of congressional power over banking policy. Only 3.9% of the initiatives sponsored by those not on the relevant committees passed, compared with 5.6% for ordinary committee members and 8.3% for chairs. However, this apparent effectiveness of chairs is mitigated by the small number of bills involved, an average of one chair-sponsored bill passed every 7.7 years. Thus any legislative leadership exercised by

Congress in the creation of banking policy during the nineteenth century was the result of a power leadership vacuum rather than of a centralized and effective leadership structure.

Because many observers consider the period between 1890 and 1910—when Speakers Reed and Cannon were in charge of the House—to be the height of congressional leadership, that period was analyzed separately. During the turn-of-the century "golden age," committee chairs were only marginally more effective than in the earlier period. While Speakers and other leaders may have been powerful during this period, they primarily used their power negatively, at least in banking policy, to halt reform and preserve the status quo. For example, when House Banking Chair Charles Fowler (R, New Jersey) refused to acquiesce in an attempt to derail reform efforts and instead promoted a comprehensive reform bill, he was stripped of his chairmanship. Given the extreme turmoil in the banking sector during much of the nineteenth century, the negative use of power to halt reform cannot be equated with policy leadership. Neither branch was providing much positive leadership during this period. Huntington accurately conveyed the ineffectiveness of presidents but failed to realize that Congress was only marginally better in the nineteenth century.

According to Huntington, the effectiveness of Congress has declined during the twentieth century because it is unable to cope with demands of modern society that point toward institutional specialization and centralization (Huntington 1973: 318–19). However, at least at the committee level, both specialization and centralization have increased during the twentieth century. Unlike the nineteenth century, in which 61% of the bills that passed were introduced by members who were not on the relevant committees, in this century almost three-quarters originated within the banking committees. Furthermore, the data show that the role and the effectiveness of chairs have increased significantly. Chairs alone were responsible for over half of all enacted legislation, guiding 124 bills, or 17.7% of the ones they sponsored, to passage. Instead of the nineteenth-century average of one every 7.7 years, chairs were able to get their bills passed at the rate of approximately one every nine months.[9] The passage rate of the other committee members (3.5%) was roughly comparable to that of non-committee members (3.3%), both lower than the rates from the nineteenth century. This implies that institutional adaptations have occurred in Congress as well as in the presidency. Congressional leadership centralized by policy areas and within the committee structure. See Table 6.2 for a summary of these results, as well as those from the nineteenth century.

Alternative Interpretations

Huntington explicitly compares the nineteenth and twentieth centuries, but a division of the data into two parts, separated by the turn of the century, could be criticized as simplistic. Two alternative strategies can be adopted if a literal interpretation of Huntington is rejected. The first is that his theory is essentially correct, but he defined the time periods too rigidly. Because Huntington describes the overthrow of Speaker Cannon in 1910 as an important cause of congressional decline, the first decade of this century should be included with the nineteenth century. To provide uniformity between the chambers, 1912, rather than 1910, was chosen as the end of the first period because Senator Nelson Aldrich's retirement from the Senate that year marked the end of arbitrary and autocratic rule in that body, just as the overthrow of Speaker Joseph Cannon signified the end of an era in the House. Although intuitively appealing and historically valid, the use of a different dividing line did not produce markedly different results. Huntington's theory still cannot explain the increasing congressional effectiveness in the modern era. As demonstrated, an increase in the scope and effectiveness of chief executives does not necessarily imply a decrease in the activities of congressional leaders.

Those seeking to explain the balance of power between Congress and the president have often mistakenly analyzed the issue as a two-person zero-sum game. Thus in observing the growth of presidential power they have reflexively concluded that the relative power of Congress is declining. This approach suffers from two problems. First, the game has more than two players. Others, such as the judiciary, state governments, and local governments, also seek power in the American system. Second, it is not a zero-sum game. The power of all these governmental actors can grow at the expense of the residual power of the people. Furthermore, the growth in the size, population, and economy of the United States has led to a larger pie, with more power opportunities for all. A more fruitful strategy recognizes that both institutions have adapted to the changes in the broader society. In the nineteenth century the range of problems confronting society was much smaller, and so was the need for specialization. The increasingly

Table 6.2

Congressional Effectiveness in the Nineteenth and Twentieth Centuries

	Nineteenth Century				Twentieth Century			
	Non mem-ber	Com-mittee mem-ber	Chair	Total	Non mem-ber	Com-mittee mem-ber	Chair	Total
Bills intro-duced	931	233	121	1,285	1,798	1,273	702	3,773
Number passed	36	13	10	59	59	45	124	228
Percentage passed	3.9	5.6	8.3	4.6	3.3	3.5	17.7	6.0

complex modern world has led to institutional adaptation. Huntington was correct in his analysis of the developments within the executive branch, but erred in equating specialization within Congress with a lack of policy leadership. A pattern of leadership has developed within different policy areas that takes into account the need for greater specialization required by contemporary society.

Tests of the Political Time Thesis

To test the political time thesis, the data were initially divided according to Skowronek's identification of presidents at the beginning, middle, or end of a political regime. His classification scheme excluded nineteen presidents and resulted in a far smaller number of cases in each category than in much of the previous work. For this reason, and after consulting with Skowronek, the administrations that he omitted were also classified according to regime time. The resultant data set then consisted of 825 regime change bills, 3,118 mid-regime bills, and 1,195 late-regime bills.[10]

Comparisons among the three regime periods must be adjusted to take into account their different lengths of time. The regime change periods comprised thirty-nine years (23.8% of the time), as opposed to ninety-six years (58.5% of the time) for the mid-regime periods and twenty-nine years (17.7% of the time) for the late-regime periods. A comparison of the absolute numbers of bills passed during each period would be misleading. For example, the regime change period constitutes less than a quarter of the total number of years studied, so one cannot learn anything by directly comparing its output (i.e., the number of bills passed) with that of the much longer mid-regime period.

Based on the political time theory, presidential effectiveness should show a pattern of decline as the age of the political regime increases. Presidents at the beginning of a regime sequence should have the greatest ability to make changes, especially important ones. Mid-regime presidents should be less effective and primarily concerned with more routine regime maintenance issues. By the end of the sequence, the regime should have become discredited and its presidents unable to provide leadership. (Skowronek's definition of presidential leadership includes the administrative side of the presidency, while this analysis includes only legislative leadership.)

Change in Political Time

The overall pattern of bill passage during each of the three regime periods was compared to get a general sense of the relationship between change and political time. As Skowronek's theory predicted, the highest percentage of total bills was passed during the regime change period. Of the 825 banking bills introduced during the regime change period, fifty-six, or 6.8%, were passed. However, the difference between the percentage passed during the regime change period and the mid-regime period, when 205, or 6.6%, of the 3,118 bills passed, was small. These two periods differed significantly from the late regime period, when only thirty-eight, or 3.2%, of the 1,195 bills were passed. This is consistent with Skowronek's conception of the late regime period as one of political incapacity.

However, when the comparative output of bills is adjusted for the different lengths of time in each period, the results look quite different. The total number of bills passed in the regime change period was 5.1% lower than would be randomly predicted. In contrast, the mid-regime period appears far more productive than the theory would predict. Mid-regime period Congresses passed 10.1% more bills than would have been expected. In the late regime period, 5% fewer bills passed than the length of time would be expected to generate.

Political Time and Passage Rates

Of course, not all bills are of equal magnitude. The greater success of the mid-regime period can be attributed to the passage of a disproportionately high number of minor bills, which is consistent with its characterization as a time of regime maintenance. The highest passage rate of important bills—bills most likely to be associated with the major changes that Skowronek discusses—occurred in the regime change period. The regime change period, which accounted for only 23.8% of the total time studied, produced 30.6% of all successful important bills. However, the late regime period also accounted for an unexpectedly high percentage of all the enacted important bills. Even though the late regime period spanned only 17.7% of the time period studied, it accounted for 22.2% of the important bills that passed. This implies a cyclical pattern to the passage of important bills, but not one consistent with Skowronek's theory that opportunities for leadership have dissipated by the late regime period. The late regime and regime change periods should be considered a single entity. The turmoil and conflict that ultimately culminates in a regime change provide an impetus throughout the two periods for major legislative enactments. In contrast, the mid-regime period is relatively calm and its legislative enactments are disproportionately of a routine nature. See Table 6.3 for a comparison of the types of bills passed during each regime period.

Presidents and Political Time

While helpful in understanding the general patterns of change, the research thus far does not address Skowronek's central concern—presidential leadership. Because his theory is fundamentally about presidential leadership, simply knowing when the most important changes occur is insufficient. One must determine whether the effectiveness of presidents as policy leaders was greatest at the beginning of a regime and declined thereafter. Therefore, the overall effectiveness of presidents needs to be examined and measured by the degree of importance of the legislation.

When bills of all levels of importance were used in the analysis, presidents were clearly most effective during the regime change period. They were able to pass 20% of the bills they favored during that period, compared with 7% during mid-regime and 10% during the late

Table 6.3

Bill Passage by Significance Level and Regime Time

	Regime change	Mid-regime	Late regime	Total
Minor bills	12 (9.5%)	108 (85.0%)	7 (5.5%)	127 (100%)
Routine bills	33 (24.3%)	80 (58.8%)	23 (16.9%)	136 (100%)
Important bills	11 (30.6%)	17 (47.2%)	8 (22.2%)	36 (100%)
Total	56	205	38	299

Note: The top figures are the actual numbers of passing bills and the bottom figures are the overall percentages of passing minor, routine, and important bills. These percentages should be compared with the total amount of time in each period (i.e., 23.8% in the regime change period, 53.8% in the mid-regime period, and 17.7% in the late regime period).

regime. When presidential outputs for the three periods are compared, taking into account the differing lengths of time in each period, both the regime change and late regime periods are more productive than would be randomly predicted. The regime change period, which accounted for 23.8% of the total time period, produced 31.6% of the bills passed with presidential support. The late regime period, 17.7% of the years, produced 26.3% of the bills enacted with presidential support. The mid-regime period, which comprised 58.5% of the time studied, was less productive than would have been randomly predicted, with only 42.1% of the presidentially supported bills that passed.

Although these figures suggest that presidents are more effective in the late regime period than in the mid-regime period, these results could be skewed by the degree of importance of the legislation. Because different types of initiatives could be supported by presidents during different periods, presidential support patterns were examined by regime time, controlling for the degree of legislative importance. Presidents during the regime change and late regime periods are disproportionately concerned with important legislation. Two-thirds of the legislation supported by presidents during the regime change period, and 64% during the late regime period, was important. However, in the mid-regime period most legislation supported by presidents was routine, and only 33% of the bills they supported were classified as important. The actual numbers of important enacted bills with presidential support follow these percentages. Only one such bill passed during the mid-regime period, compared with five during the regime change period and four in the late regime period. Thus presidents were far more effective in enacting major changes during the late period than during the mid-regime period. According to Skowronek, the late regime period was a time of complete disarray and collapse on the part of the governing political coalition. Presidents supposedly had great difficulty getting any legislation, much less important initiatives, through Congress.[11]

Excluding the Wilson presidency, because, as previously discussed, it was misplaced as a regime change presidency, adds to the decline in the relative effectiveness of regime change presidents vis-à-vis the presidents in the other two periods. For example, the deletion of the Wilson presidency decreases from 20% to 17.2% the passage rate of regime change presidents for all bills they supported, and equalizes the number of presidentially supported important bills passed in the slightly shorter late regime period and in the longer regime change period. While not definitive, these data reinforce the perception that the greatest distinction was between the relatively routine politics of the mid-regime period and the more turbulent and far-reaching politics of the late regime/regime change period.

Adding in the Constitution

Both the modernization and the political time theses have added greatly to our understanding of the ways in which the legislative process has changed over time, but, as with all theories, by emphasizing some aspects of the process, they have obscured others. Nonetheless, they focus our attention on the ways in which legislative leadership has changed as a result of economic and political changes within the country. In some other very tangible ways, which neither theory is able to explain, the process has been relatively stable and continuous. The modernization thesis, for example, cannot explain why Congress has continued to be the primary legislative actor. To argue that the theory remains viable because Congress is subject to the same universal forces of modernization begs the question. Only through a recognition of the constitutional constraints on the legislative leadership of presidents can the impetus for continuing development within Congress be fully understood. Likewise, the political time thesis cannot account for the upsurge in the passage of important legislation at the end of regimes. An understanding of both the broader changes in society and the constitutional factors that facilitate a division of labor and interbranch cooperation are necessary to comprehend this development. In short, a holistic approach that combines both the dynamism of the modernization and political time theories with the boundary setting of the Constitution is needed.

Adapting the Modernization View

As was discussed earlier, the Founding Fathers clearly intended that in the legislative arena Congress was to be the dominant actor, with the president playing a much smaller role. After all, Congress is by definition the legislative branch of government, and constitutional provisions purposefully limit the ability of presidents to usurp this function. The evidence supports the contention that Congress continues to play the dominant role in enacting legislation. Overall, presidents took positions on less than 6% of all the legislation studied, and only 6.4% of the bills that passed were supported by presidents. Congressional dominance, when adjusted for the much larger legislative workload, has continued unabated in the twentieth century. In fact, nineteenth-century presidents took positions on a higher percentage of bills than their counterparts in the twentieth century; in the nineteenth century, presidents took a public stance on 11% of the bills before Congress, in contrast to the 4.3% presidents supported or opposed in the twentieth century. Presidential support did play a greater role in the enactment of legislation in the current century. During the nineteenth century Congress was solely responsible for the enactment of more than 97% of all new banking laws, but only slightly under 93% after 1900. These figures indicate that Congress has indeed remained the "first branch," as anticipated by the Founders.

Much of the legislative success of presidents is also attributable to their ability to work with powerful committee chairs. Because the Constitution gives them limited legislative powers, presidents hoping to enact policies must work with Congress. Even when a president proposes a policy change, he still must rely on members of Congress to introduce and guide the bill through the legislative labyrinth. While having veto power allows the president some influence over ongoing legislation, this authority is obviously ineffective with respect to the introduction of new legislation. Thus a president who wishes to advance his own platform has much to gain from a cooperative stance.

To ascertain the importance of cooperation between presidents and committee chairs, legislation with joint support was examined separately from other legislation. Not only does this permit measurement of the extent of cooperation, it allows the effectiveness of presidents and chairs to be measured separately. The 20% overall passage rate for initiatives supported by presidents is misleading because of the enormous difference between the passage rate on those bills supported solely by presidents and those with the additional sponsorship of committee chairs. Presidents had only a 7.3% passage rate on the former, as compared with a 44.8% passage rate on the latter.

The division of legislative responsibilities delineated in the Constitution certainly propels presidents toward, but does not compel them to take, a more cooperative approach with Congress. If a president has little interest in providing legislative leadership, he has scant reason to develop this type of a relationship with Congress. As Barber (1977) has noted, almost all modern presidents have been legislative activists, but nineteenth-century presidents took fewer positions on legislation, and even their infrequent proposals for change were couched in the most general terms. Before 1900 most presidents accepted the view that legislation was primarily a congressional responsibility. In the entire century only two banking bills had the support of both the president and the relevant committee chairs, and neither of these bills passed. However, as modernization brought increased demands on government, presidential activism and cooperative efforts with congressional leaders also increased. During the twentieth century more than two-thirds of all enacted presidential legislative initiatives were also sponsored by committee chairs.

Adapting the Political Time View

In a similar vein, the surprising upsurge in presidential effectiveness on important legislation at the end of regimes can be understood by examining constitutional and economic factors. Two constitutional provisions impel presidents toward a greater focus on important legislation. First, because presidents are elected by voters from the entire country, they are less likely to devote attention to legislation that is more parochial. Second, the Constitution also statutorily limits the length of time that presidents may serve, requiring them to, as Paul Light succinctly put it, "move it or lose it" (Light 1982: 218). Presidents are thus much more likely to devote their attention to more important policies. The data at least indirectly support the view that presidents expend a disproportionate amount of their energy on the passage of the most important bills. Despite the generally inverse relationship between passage and bill importance, on bills backed by presidents the correlation was positive. Moreover, their greatest success occurred on legislation that was also sponsored by committee chairs. Interbranch cooperation seems to exert a strong countervailing pressure on the normal pattern of bill enactments.

Economic factors also appear to affect the degree of interbranch cooperation on important legislation. As was seen in Chapter 5, increases in the number of bank failures strongly influence the number of important banking bills passed into law. Economic crisis, which is often a contributory factor in the overthrow of a dominant political regime, also provides an incentive for cooperation on important bills. For example, President Hoover and the hostile Seventy-second Congress produced legislation creating the Reconstruction Finance Corporation and the Federal Home Loan Bank System—important institutional changes that appear insignificant only when juxtaposed against the sweeping reforms of Roosevelt and the Seventy-third Congress.[12] President Roosevelt had the "advantage" of the continuing economic crisis, which helped foster interbranch cooperation, and Democratic control of both chambers of Congress.

Additional Insights

A new theory should not only explain the anomalies in existing theories, but should also be able to provide new insights into areas that the preceding theories have not considered. Probably the most important new theoretical insight provided by dynamic constitutionalism is its explanation of the continuing division of labor between Congress and the president. The differences in electoral constituencies, internal structures, and time framework all foster an implicit functional distinction between the branches. Congress and the president play discretely different roles in the legislative process. As was seen in Chapter 4,

Congress was primarily responsible for the early stages of policy development and presidents became involved only after initiatives had gone through a period of congressional incubation. In general, more than three years passed from the time a policy was introduced into Congress until a president decided to support it. As was seen in Chapters 4 and 5, senators and representatives play consequential roles in shepherding legislation of all degrees of importance through the various stages, while presidents are disproportionately concerned with the outcomes of the most important bills.

The dynamic constitutionalism framework by itself cannot explain all the changes in executive-congressional policy interaction over the past century and a half. Understanding historical trends, particularly differences between centuries, requires the insights provided by modernization theory and political time, as well as the Constitution's assignment of primary legislative responsibility to Congress. Rather than supplanting either of the existing theories, the dynamic constitutionalism framework works in conjunction with them.

Conclusion

This chapter has tried to demonstrate the strengths and limitations of the two major diachronic theories of legislative leadership and to show how dynamic constitutionalism provides additional explanatory power. Generally, modernization theory correctly posited a relationship between economic development within society and concomitant changes within government. Huntington was also accurate in asserting that presidential effectiveness increased enormously during the twentieth century, but he incorrectly maintained that it was accompanied by a decline in the effectiveness of Congress. The theory failed to acknowledge that the Founding Fathers' assignment of primary legislative responsibility to Congress necessarily meant that adaptation would occur on Capitol Hill as well as in the White House. In a similar vein, Skowronek is to be commended for linking legislative leadership to political time. Skowronek is the first to extend previous notions of intra-administration cycles across presidencies. The theory, however, fails to take into account adequately the secular evolution of the state. As the scope of governmental responsibilities expanded in the twentieth century, presidents, even those at the end of a regime cycle, were held accountable for the economic well-being of the entire society and made serious efforts to address those concerns. Together with the constitutional provisions, this pushed presidents to cooperate and focus on the most important legislation, and helps explain the effectiveness of presidents during the late regime period.

The modernization and political time theories failed to acknowledge that all three analytic lenses are needed to understand fully the development of legislative leadership over time. Therefore policymaking should be regarded as occurring within a bounded system, the parameters of which are defined by the Constitution. If the formal separation of powers set forth in the Constitution was the sole determinant of the functional division between Congress and the president, one would expect a static equilibrium system to prevail. But that is not the case. Economic development exerts pressure on government to modernize in a linear fashion. If economic modernization were the only dynamic, hierarchical business forms would be replicated within government, creating the presidentially dominated system described by Huntington. This tendency, however, is constrained by the constitutional division of powers and political time. The dynamic of party decline and renewal described by critical realignment theorists and applied by Skowronek to the role of the president introduces a cyclical dimension missing from the other two approaches. The end result is a much more complex and interrelated system than any of the theories, by themselves, would predict.

Notes

1. Even though the modernization thesis had been an implicit part of most early postwar scholarship on the presidency, Huntington (1973) is generally considered the definitive spokesman of this view. Michael Mezey's (1989, 1991) representational model of Congress's role in policymaking is a contemporary articulation of the view that the presidency is better adapted to providing policy leadership in the modern world than is Congress.

2. The "political time" theory of presidential leadership is a version of the critical realignment theory put forth by Skowronek (1986, 1984), who argues that a cyclical pattern of decline and resurgence occurs in presidential leadership. Presidents who assume office at the beginning of a political regime period, such as the New Deal regime, have a great deal of success in enacting sweeping policy change, while those at the end of a regime sequence have little latitude.

3. Even though constitutional scholars (Fisher 1975, 1987; Ford 1898; Pious 1979; Stanwood 1898; Wilson 1911, 1956; Woodward 1825) from the beginning have been concerned primarily with the formal powers of the two branches rather than with generating theoretical propositions, it is possible to do so.

4. Even Neustadt (1960) generally falls within the presidential dominance school, because he focuses on what a president must do to pass his program rather than on how the two branches work together in formulating policy.

5. There are two groups of scholars who claim the title of "new institutionalist." Because this research seeks to explain developments over time, only the work of the historical branch (rather than the rational choice branch) of "new institutionalism" will be examined. A major difference between the historical and rational choice variants is that the former does not accept the assumption that tastes and preferences of political actors are fixed and exogenous. Instead, those using the historical approach maintain that political preferences are shaped at least partly by endogenous institutional factors. For a summary of the differences between the two variants of "new institutionalism," see Smith (1990).

6. But Congress's success in passing legislation opposed by the president did not extend to success in overriding presidential vetoes. All four of the nineteenth-century banking bill vetoes were subsequently upheld by Congress.

7. The most recent of these was the 1983 repeal of the Withholding Tax on Interest and Dividends Act, which was strongly opposed by President Reagan.

8. A hidden role, if any, played by party leaders in the House and the Senate in the passage of banking legislation would be impossible to gauge over this period, because no comprehensive records of their activities were kept. In the contemporary period, information can be obtained about the roles played by the Speaker, Majority Leader, and other party leaders, on a limited number of bills. One useful approach to gauge the behind-the-scenes activities of party leaders would be an extension of Rundquist and Strom's analysis of preferences incorporated during the bill construction stage. See Rundquist and Strom (1987).

9. The data do not allow a determination of whether this success is the result of chairs persuading other members to adopt their position or of their ability to forge consensus that accommodates different members' needs. Both, however, are part of an effective leadership style.

10. All the statistical tests were also run on the smaller data set, and the results were similar in all cases.

11. The only two successful overrides of presidential vetoes occurred during the regime change period. In 1937, Congress voted to override President Roosevelt's veto of HR6763, and a year later they overrode his veto of HR10530. Both bills provided for preferential interest rates for farmers victimized by the agricultural downturn of the Great Depression.

12. Over the past thirty years revisionist historians have spearheaded a widespread re-evaluation of the Hoover presidency and its policies. The recent work shows that Hoover, rather than an obstacle to political change, was actually quite open to political innovation (Degler 1963; Romasco 1975; Wilson 1975).

7

Concluding Thoughts

The Theory Revisited

The central purpose of this research has been to develop and test an alternative theory of legislative leadership, based on the premise that a government composed of constitutionally "separated institutions sharing powers" over time will replicate certain characteristic patterns of interaction. The separation between the executive and legislative functions, fundamental to the American system, sets the country apart from most other democracies. Yet, aside from the many discussions of policy "gridlock," scholars have devoted relatively little attention to its significance. Political scientists have tended to ignore the mundane, yet critically important, policymaking implications of the constitutional separation of powers.

Rather than ignoring the implications of the institutional fragmentation, the underlying theoretical premise of this book is that this peculiar governing structure has important policy consequences, and that throughout our nation's history it has heavily influenced legislative outcomes. As was discussed in Chapter 1, the most significant constitutional provisions are those defining the boundaries of subsequent institutional development, primarily through the Constitution's assignment of specific formal legislative powers to the president and to Congress. These formal legislative powers are not divided equally among the branches. Most notably, the Constitution gives the president weak legislative powers (i.e., the power to make suggestions and to veto legislation), especially compared to those of Congress. The historical pattern of interaction has favored Congress, unlike the pattern in parliamentary systems, where the executive heads the legislative assembly. The fundamental disparity in the assignment of formal legislative powers constrained presidential aggrandizement of the legislative role and has perpetuated Congress's status as the "first branch" of government.

The Constitution also affects policymaking through provisions that encourage, but do not require, certain patterns of interbranch interaction. Constitutional definitions of the electoral constituencies, internal structures, and terms in office provide incentives for presidents with legislative agendas explicitly to cooperate with Congress in the formulation of policy initiatives, and implicitly to defer to Congress within its sphere of interest. This deferral may occur on specific types of policies (i.e., minor and routine bills) or at a particular point in the legislative process (i.e., within committee).

In this study, these constitutional provisions led to the formation of four testable propositions about which patterns of legislative interaction between Congress and the president are most likely to occur, and recur over time. The argument is not that Congress and the president play policymaking roles in the twentieth century identical to those of the nineteenth century. That would be absurd, given the transformations in socioeconomic conditions and demands on government. Instead, the argument is that, despite these contextual changes, the interbranch relationships that developed were predictable and within the framework established by the Constitution. The four propositions, discussed in Chapter 1, dealt with the allocation of primary responsibility for legislation, the roles of Congress and the president in the early stages of policy incubation, the types of policies handled by each, and the need for presidents to gain congressional support for their policy initiatives.

The next step, in Chapter 2, was to devise an appropriate empirical means to test the validity of these propositions, avoiding the biases inherent in either "presidency-centered" or "Congress-centered" perspectives. Approaches limited in scope to a consideration of only parts of presidential legislative agendas or key votes systematically overstate the role of the White House. Since presidents take no position on the vast majority of bills, limiting research to only those bills with presidential involvement leads to biased outcomes. A co-institutional perspective required the consideration of legislative initiatives on which presidents took no position and those that they explicitly opposed, as well as those that they supported. To avoid implicit institutional bias, all House and Senate bill introductions in a single policy area were used to construct the basic data set. The area chosen, banking policy, was distinctive as one of the few issue domains that figured prominently on the country's legislative agenda since the Revolutionary War. Thus it could be used to study how the pattern of interaction and roles of each branch have changed over time.

This particular exploration of executive-congressional relations is unique not only for its emphasis on the Constitution, but because the approach is co-institutional and diachronic. None of the previous studies of executive-congressional relations have utilized a data set of this size or historic scope. But, as explained in Chapter 2, a project of this sort necessarily required some real methodological trade-offs, primarily involving limitations in the data that could be incorporated into the models. In some cases the bills were relatively obscure and records were never kept, and in others the information was lost over the years.

Major Findings

Different aspects of the propositions were addressed in the various chapters, and a general assessment of how well the theoretical propositions were answered requires combining elements from throughout the book.

First Proposition

The first proposition—that Congress will continue to be primarily responsible for the development of most legislative initiatives—was strongly supported by the data. The vast majority of all bills introduced into Congress never receive any attention from the president. Overall, only 3.5% of the bills were supported publicly by presidents and 1.6% were opposed by them. Presidents supported a greater percentage of legislation in the nineteenth century (5.7%) than in the twentieth century (3.1%).

However, bill introductions are only a small part of the story. What really matters is whether Congress or the president is primarily responsible for the enactment of bills into laws. The large number of nonserious bill introductions, especially in the twentieth century, necessitates an assessment of the involvement of senators and representatives on the basis of their legislative success, not their sponsorship of bills.

Throughout the period studied, 6.4% of all bills enacted had presidential support, and an additional 1.7% were passed by Congress over presidential opposition. In other words, 92% of all new banking laws were passed without presidential involvement. There are, however, some fairly significant differences between the nineteenth and twentieth centuries. During the nineteenth century, enactments with presidential support comprised 2.8% of the total, compared with 7.5% in the twentieth century. The growth in absolute numbers of new laws with presidential support is visually illustrated in Figure 5.2 (page 147). Despite a significant increase in the presidential role, Congress continues to bear the primary responsibility for most new legislative enactments. Barring a major revision of the Constitution, this is unlikely to change.

Second Proposition

The second proposition asserted that Congress will be responsible for the early development and political incubation of most policies and that presidents will be only minimally involved in the early stages. As was argued in Chapter 4, although congressional committees are not even mentioned in the Constitution, the high degree of independent judgment and policy initiative exercised by congressional committees is a result of the institutional separation between the executive and legislative functions. The genesis, development, and structure of legislative committees in this country differ radically from those in parliamentary systems. For more than 150 years, standing committees have been a forum through which the parent chambers develop new policy initiatives and weed out the chaff. Thus any investigation into the early stages of American policy initiation must focus on the activities of congressional committees.

Although the influence of different actors on committee decision-making can be analyzed in many different ways, all approaches clearly demonstrate that presidents had little impact on committee outcomes, and that chairs were by far more influential. The most straightforward approach, identifying which actors principally developed most of the legislation reported out to the parent chambers, showed that less than 5% of the bills reported out were endorsed by presidents, and most of these were also sponsored by the committee chairs. Within Congress, committee chairs were by far the most important actors. They were primary sponsors of more than 40% of the bills favorably reported out of committee. A shortcoming of this approach is its measurement of only the total number of bills supported by each actor; it does not determine rates of success on bills that members of Congress specifically supported.

In order to determine and compare the success of different actors in getting bills they supported out of committee, the first step was to calculate the average bill's chance of being favorably reported, and then to make comparisons among the actors' ability to influence committee decisions. Since approximately 14% of all bills were reported out of committee, the 15.7% success rate of presidents is a clear indication of their weakness within committees. In fact, bills that presidents explicitly opposed were almost as likely to be reported out as those that they endorsed. In stark contrast is the ability of committee chairs, who succeeded in getting more than 34% of their sponsored bills reported out. As was illustrated by Figure 4.3 (page 107), the pattern has been consistent over the last century and a half. Although the number of presidentially supported bills reported out of committee has increased somewhat over time, this increase is primarily a function of increased legislative workload rather than growth in the relative influence of the president.

Both the logit model predicting committee decisionmaking on individual bills and the various time-series models predicting the numbers of bills reported out over time showed that presidents have little effect on committee decisions. Not surprisingly, the only model with a presidential support coefficient that was close to significant was the time-series model predicting the number of important bills reported out. This is consistent with the notion that constitutional incentives compel presidents primarily to limit their involvement to the most important legislation. In contrast, variables measuring the impact of congressional actors were among the strongest predictors in the logit model and all the time-series models on committee decisionmaking.

The timing of involvement is another criterion for assessing differences in the roles played by different actors. Those who become involved at an early stage are important to the shaping of policy initiatives. The postal savings, Federal Reserve System, and deposit insurance case studies presented in Chapter 3 showed the absence of presidential involvement during the early stages of policy incubation, although presidents were crucial in the final push toward passage. To test whether this late presidential participation was part of a general pattern or simply the idiosyncratic result of those individual cases, the legislative histories of 312 policies were traced over time. Policies, rather than bills, were chosen because the latter die at the close of each Congress. The slowness of presidential support in the case studies was not anomalous but consistent with a general pattern. On average, presidents took 3.33 years after the initial introduction of legislation to support it publicly. In contrast, the mean time for committee chairs to sponsor similar legislation was roughly ten months. Both these findings further support the view that Congress, rather than the president, is primarily responsible for the early stages of policy development.

In short, the results were similar regardless of the approach used to study the impact of presidents and different congressional actors on committee decisionmaking. All the data strongly indicated that presidential involvement during the early stages of policy formation is minimal, that Congress is the principal incubator for policies, and that within Congress, chairs dominate committee deliberations.

Third Proposition

The validity of the third proposition—that presidents are most attentive to the important policy initiatives while members of Congress are responsible for a far wider range of policies—was also supported by this research. Although they took positions on a relatively few bills, presidents supported almost twice as many important bills as would have been expected if their support were randomly dispersed among all banking bills. While important bills comprised less than a quarter of all banking bills, nearly half the bills publicly endorsed by presidents were important. Moreover, most of the remaining bills with presidential support were routine bills. Presidential support of minor bills was two-thirds lower than the rate for randomly distributed support. Presidents supported roughly the same proportion of minor, routine, and important bills in the nineteenth and twentieth centuries. Given the enormous changes in the composition of the executive branch and the massive increase in the number of White House staff, the constancy in the bill support pattern was unexpected. One question that cannot be answered by this research and would be difficult for any scholar to answer definitively, because the records have been lost, is whether the type of bills supported by other influential executive branch actors has changed over time.

Unlike presidents, congressional actors generally split their support (as measured by bill sponsorship) in accordance with the proportion of bills in each category. For example, bill introductions by committee chairs roughly equaled the overall proportion of each category in the total sample: 26.9% minor, 53.7% routine, and 19.4% important. However, the type of bills sponsored by committee chairs changed dramatically over time. In the nineteenth century roughly half, and after 1900 less than a quarter, of the chair-sponsored bills were minor in character. The decline in minor bills was offset by a sharp increase in routine bills and a more modest jump in important bills. These changes further support the point, made in Chapter 6, that Congress has undergone transformations that have centralized the leadership by policy area and within committees.

The depth of presidential concern for the most important category of bills was further indicated by these bills' unusually high rate of success as they moved through the legislative process. The typically inverse relationship between the importance of a bill and its chances of being favorably reported out of committee was missing in bills supported by presidents. Presidents got 7.1% of minor bills, 20% of routine bills, and 12.8% of important bills they supported favorably reported out of committee. Compared with the average rates of committee success, minor bills with presidential support are only a third as likely to be reported out, routine bills are twice as likely, and important bills are nearly two times as likely as the average to be reported out. Although these figures do not directly measure the effort expended by presidents on different categories of bills, it can be inferred that presidents worked harder on behalf of routine and important bills than on minor ones. In contrast, all members of Congress experienced declining rates of committee success as the level of bill importance increased. For example, committee chairs got 46% of minor bills, 30.9% of routine bills, and 26.3% of important bills reported favorably out of committee. The rates of presidentially supported and chair-sponsored bills reported out of committee varied somewhat over time. As pointed out in Chapter 4, presidential efforts were particularly futile in the nineteenth century, and, after a sharp increase in success during the Progressive Era, lost effectiveness again after 1960. The rate for committee chairs hovered around 50% for all periods except the most recent, when it dropped, probably because of the sharp increase in bill in-troductions; such an increase creates a legislative logjam, which makes it difficult to shepherd a high percentage through the process. Only the time-series model predicting the number of important bills reported out over time was improved by the inclusion of the presidential support variable. Congressional support variables were significant predictors in all the logit and time-series models dealing with bills reported out of committee.

Because few bills with presidential support were actually considered on the floor, presidential effectiveness cannot be generalized at this stage. Only one minor bill with presidential support was considered on the floor, and it passed. Sixty percent of important bills and 50% of routine bills that reached the floor with presidential support passed, but the small numbers make generalization untenable. Nonetheless, the results strongly suggest that presidents devote little attention to minor bills and quite a bit more to routine and important bills. In the twentieth century presidents supported some routine and minor bills that were enacted, whereas in the preceding century all the new laws with presidential support fell into the important category. In contrast, congressional actors were most successful on the floor with routine bills, followed by minor and important bills. For example, the floor passage rates for chair-sponsored bills were 53.1% for routine bills, 42.3% for minor bills, and 40% for important bills. Somewhat higher rates of chair-sponsored bills were reported out in the twentieth century than in the nineteenth century, but the general pattern—greatest success on routine bills and least on important bills—was unchanged.

The results are ambiguous for the logit and time-series models, which assess the cumulative impact of different actors on the passage of individual bills and the number of bills passed over time. All models show that congressional support variables are powerful predictors of passage. The logit model also shows that presidential support is positively related to the passage of individual bills, but this finding is replicated only in the time-series model predicting the number of routine bills passed in each Congress. The time-series model using only important bills found an inverse relationship between the number of bills with presidential support and the number of bills passed over time, but it was not statistically significant.

Fourth Proposition

The final proposition—that presidents need the support of key congressional actors to get their initiatives enacted—was unequivocally supported by this research. Bills without the support of presidents and committee chairs were seldom reported out of committee and passed. Bills supported by presidents but not chairs were only marginally more likely (9.1%) to be reported out of committee than bills without the support of presidents and committee chairs (8.4%). Committee chairs were much more effective, with 33.9% of bills they championed without presidential support reported out. The addition of presidential support to chair-sponsored bills increased this percentage only slightly (3.6%). The relationship between presidents and committee chairs was asymmetrical: presidents needed chairs far more than chairs needed presidents. Of all the presidentially supported banking bills reported out of committee, 55% were sponsored by committee chairs, while only 5% of the chair-sponsored bills reported out of committee were supported by presidents. Furthermore, almost all other presidentially supported bills that were reported out were sponsored by other members of the banking committees. Presidents in this century were much more likely than their nineteenth-century counterparts to support chair-sponsored bills. The chances of passage on chair-sponsored bills have been far greater in this century than in the preceding one. But regardless of the time period, these results clearly indicate that presidents who want to succeed at the committee level would be wise to enlist the support of committee chairs, or, at least, other members of the committee.

In some ways the interbranch interaction on the floor resembles that which occurred within committee, while in other ways the two are dissimilar. The most notable similarity is the extremely low rate of success on bills with presidential support but without the sponsorship of committee chairs. Thirty-five percent of bills favorably reported out of committee passed with neither presidential nor chair support, but the rate for bills with only presidential support is actually lower (33.3%), indicating that presidential support alone does not improve the chances of passage. Chair-sponsored bills without presidential support fare better (45.6%), consistent with the results achieved within committees. The big difference between the floor and the committee is what happened on bills sponsored by chairs and supported by presidents. Within committees the addition of presidential support made little difference to the outcome, but on the floor it had a fairly large effect. More than 73% of bills supported by both chairs and presidents passed. Although both chairs and presidents are well served on the floor by cooperative efforts, here too, presidents need the support of chairs more than vice versa. Of the new laws sponsored by chairs, 91% had no presidential support, but only 26.6% of the new laws with presidential support were sponsored by non-chairs.

Dynamic constitutionalism has provided new insights into the patterns of executive-congressional interaction on policymaking. These patterns are not immutable, but they are evolutionary—the product of constitutional provisions that assign to each branch different powers and responsibilities. Expansion in the role of the president in the modern era has been mitigated by the continuing pre-eminence of Congress in the legislative arena. In fact, the congressional innovations designed to deal with the complexities of the modern world are at least as interesting as those that have occurred at the opposite end of Pennsylvania Avenue.

Additional Findings

While much of this research has centered on the development of a predictive theory of legislative leadership derived from the Constitution's assignment of formal powers to Congress and the president, it has also touched on other aspects of the policymaking process, such as the different legislative roles played by the House of Representatives and Senate, the impact of political parties on legislative outcomes, and the relationship between economic distress and bill passage.

House and Senate Differences

The commonly held view of the House as the "legislative" chamber and the Senate as the world's foremost debating society was generally supported by this study. The differences in each chamber's approach to its legislative responsibility can be traced to the differences in their respective sizes. Because of the House's far larger size, committees in the House were more rigorous in the exercise of their "gatekeeping" function. In the House only 10.8% of all bills are favorably reported out of committee, compared with 18.2% in the Senate. As was seen in Figure 4.2 (page 97), this reluctance of House committees to report bills out occurred on bills with every possible mix of support and sponsorship. The greater willingness of the Senate to report out bills that presidents opposed demonstrated its greater independence and autonomy, consistent with the chamber's reputation as a forum for policy debate. In fact, the Senate reported out a higher percentage of bills opposed by presidents than bills with presidential support. The Senate's autonomous tendency also meant that a larger proportion of Senate bills than House bills were defeated on the floor; on the average, House bills reported out of committee had a 45.1% chance of passage, compared with a 34.9% chance for Senate bills. The lower number of bills reported out of the Senate, coupled with their higher failure rate on the floor, meant that the upper chamber initiated significantly fewer new banking laws than the House. Nearly two-thirds of the new banking laws originated in the House of Representatives, further supporting the view that the House is the greater processor of legislation.

Political Parties

Although many scholars have blamed policy gridlock on divided party control of the White House and Capitol Hill, this study concurs with Mayhew's finding that "unified as opposed to divided control has not made an important difference . . ." (Mayhew 1991: 4). Increases in the degree of party control brought about a jump of only 11% to 14.2% in the number of banking bills favorably reported out of committee. Although it could be argued that, because one party necessarily always has a committee majority, there is no particular reason to associate a significant increase in committee output with an expansion in party control across institutions, bill passage grew from 3.9% to 6.8% with the shift from divided to united party control. In all cases, the largest increase occurred when the two congressional chambers moved from divided party control to united party control. The subsequent extension of party control to the White House resulted in only a small additional boost in the passage rate—all of which indicates that presidents are only marginally involved in the development of most banking bills. Interestingly, the party control variable is only significant at the .05 level in the logit model that predicts whether individual bills are reported out of committee and the time-series model that predicts the numbers of important bills reported out over time. While not definitive, these results suggest that party control is most effective within committees and on the most important category of bills.

Economic Distress

The results of this study also show that Congress responded to declining economic conditions, but that the response varied with the type of economic distress. A decline in deflated agricultural prices triggered a sharp increase in the number of banking bill introductions, but there was no concomitant increase in banking bills reported out of committee or passed into law. In contrast, increases in the number of bank failures triggered increases in the number of bills reported out and passed into law, but not in bill introductions. The relationship was most pronounced when the passage of only the most important bills was considered. The logit and time-series models also indicate that the relationship between banking failures and legislative outcomes became stronger as the level of bill importance increased. The only models where banking failures did not significantly improve the predictive power were those dealing solely with minor bills.

Political responsiveness varied systematically according to the type of economic distress, as none of the deflated agricultural prices contributed to the overall predictive power of the models. Downturns in the agricultural sector generated more bill introductions, but no noticeable change in legislative output, whereas a decline in the health of the banking sector generated no noticeable increase in bill introductions, but resulted in more routine and major bills reported out of committee and passed into law. Perhaps this differential response reflects the relative importance of the agricultural and financial sectors within our society. However, an analysis of the relative influence of different economic sectors on policymaking is beyond the scope of this research.

Thoughts About the Future

In some ways this project has raised as many questions as it has answered. Although it certainly demonstrates the continuing impact of the Constitution on policymaking, much has yet to be explored. In particular, subsequent research should focus on the extent to which the bureaucracy's role has changed and is separate from the president's. Moreover, because this research dealt with only a single policy domain, the pattern of executive-congressional interaction on banking policy needs to be considered in the context of other domestic policies; in turn, domestic policy should be compared to defense and foreign policies.

Although crystal ball gazing is hardly within the realm of political science, political scientists are occasionally tempted to make predictions about the future. Whatever else the future may bring, it will not include a return to the simpler agrarian society of the nineteenth century. Instead, we will continue to live in an increasingly complex world, where demands on government will escalate, prompting calls for greater efficiency and pressures for presidents to assume larger legislative roles. So long as the Constitution's provisions assigning legislative responsibilities remain intact, the tendency of the president to become a super-legislator will continue to be constrained by congressional prerogatives. The truly interesting question for the future is how Congress, rather than the executive, will respond to these pressures.

Appendix: The Primary Data Set and Variables

Primary Data Collection

Before identifying and cataloguing the banking bills, I had to establish clear parameters about which bills to include in the data set. In keeping with my primary interest in legislation dealing with the behavior of domestic commercial banks, I decided to include only bills concerned with activities within the United States or involving domestic banks. Bills dealing with foreign banks operating in the United States and foreign activities of domestic banks would be included, but bills dealing with international institutions, such as the Export-Import Bank, would not.

In addition, domestic commercial banks operate in a universe inhabited by many other financial institutions, so I had to make decisions about whether to include bills involving other financial institutions, and if so, which ones. I decided to limit my interest to their major competitors, the other financial intermediaries. Bills dealing with these institutions were included because changes in their operations profoundly affect the competitive position of commercial banks. Financial intermediaries are institutions that acquire IOUs issued by borrowers and at the same time sell their own IOUs to savers (Rose and Fraser 1985: 4). Bills dealing exclusively with non-intermediary financial institutions, such as security brokers and dealers, mortgage bankers, and investment bankers, were not part of the data set. While important in their own right, these institutions have different concerns from the financial intermediaries.

After the parameters of the data set were established, I next identified the relevant bills. Because bills introduced into the House of Representatives and Senate before the start of the *Congressional Record* in 1873 are not indexed, I went through copies of all bill introductions for the first fifty years studied. These are available on microfilm from the Library of Congress. For the remaining years I used the *Congressional Record* indexes to identify bills and then read copies of the bills in the Library of Congress. There were 6,579 House and Senate bills involving state and nationally chartered commercial banks, credit unions, mutual savings banks, and savings and loan associations. Sometimes the conflicts among these institutions were attempts to restructure the financial community through the passage of wide-ranging "financial institutions bills." At other times, the conflicts centered on fights to change the tax code with what were nominally tax bills; these cases were included because of their importance to the financial intermediaries. Changes in the tax code, which appeared to modify rates only slightly, were often written in such a way as to seriously disadvantage one type of financial institution in its turf battles with other intermediaries. Tax bills that were minimally important to these institutions were not included.

Bill Classification

For each bill I recorded a brief summary of its contents, the date it was introduced, and its sponsor. I then devised a measure of its importance. This was more problematic, because definitions of importance are often subjective. For example, is a bill that creates credit unions more important than one that allows commercial banks to branch across state lines? Although a bill establishing a new type of a financial institution is important, credit unions are relatively insignificant financial institutions based on assets while commercial banks are clearly the most significant. I addressed this problem by creating a fourfold ordinal coding scheme designed to measure the different dimensions of a bill's importance: scope, salience to the universe affected, effect on balance of power within the financial community, and impact on actors outside the financial community. The higher the numerical score assigned, the greater the importance within the particular dimension. I coded these four characteristics in the following manner:

Scope (i.e., size of the universe):
1 = specific individual banks by name

2 = other financial institutions
3 = state banks only
4 = national banks only
5 = state and national banks (including central banks)
6 = banks and other financial institutions

Salience to universe affected:
1 = zero/low
2 = medium
3 = high
4 = new institutions

Effect on balance of power within the financial community:
1 = zero/low
2 = medium
3 = high
4 = new institutions

Impact on actors outside the financial community:
1 = zero/low
2 = medium
3 = high

Scope

The difficulties presented in coding this system varied from category to category. The category of scope (i.e., size of the universe) did not present any problems. It was clear in all cases where the bill belonged. The lower the numerical code assigned to a bill, the smaller its impact on the universe of financial institutions. A code of 1 was given to all bills that referred to specific individual banks (other than the Bank of the United States) by name. An example of this type of bill is one that requested a tax refund for the Dover National Bank. If parts of a bill applied to a general class of institutions and other parts applied only to an individual bank, the bill was given the higher numerical code. A code of 2 was given to bills that apply to all non-bank financial inter-mediaries (i.e., credit unions, savings and loans institutions, and so on). Some of these institutions were relatively powerful, yet they had far less collective influence than the commercial banking sector. Bills that applied to state-chartered commercial banks were coded 3. Generally, the state-chartered banks were smaller than nationally chartered commercial banks, and as a group they controlled far less capital. A code of 4 was given to bills dealing with nationally chartered commercial banks. A code of 5 was given to bills governing the behavior of both state and national banks, as well as central banks. Finally, bills that applied to all the different financial institutions within the data set were coded as 6. Clear-cut divisions existed between each of the different possible codes, producing an ordinal scale where ascending numerical scores reflected greater economic impact.

Salience

Operationalizing the category of salience to the universe affected was more challenging because there were no clear lines of demarcation between codes. A code of 1, for bills with zero/low salience to the universe affected, was defined as a minor change to existing laws. A code of 2 was given to bills of medium salience to the universe affected, such as those that shifted the parameters of what was an acceptable enterprise but did not create important new institutions or new areas of banking activities. For example, a bill that changed the reserve requirements of national banks would be coded 2. A code of 3 was reserved for bills that were highly salient to the universe affected, defined as bills that shifted the locus of regulatory decisionmaking or opened new areas of banking. A code of 4 was given to bills that created new financial intermediaries and new regulatory institutions, such as the Federal Reserve System.

Balance of Power

In the contemporary period, the main source of intersectoral competition is between commercial bankers and thrift institutions (credit unions, mutual savings banks, and savings and loan associations). However, for much of the period studied, disagreements between large money center commercial banks holding national charters and the smaller state-chartered commercial banks provided the most heated conflicts. In some ways operationalizing the third category was similar to doing so for the second category. A code of 1 meant that the bill in question only minimally affected the balance of power within the financial community. This was again narrowly interpreted. A code of 2 was given to bills with a moderate effect on the balance of power, defined to mean that the bill shifted the parameters of conflict or changed the extent of an existing burden on one group, but did not open new areas of competition or impose totally new burdens on one sector. For example, a bill that changed the level of federal taxes levied on state banks would be coded as a 2. A code of 3, for bills with a high impact on the balance of power, involved impositions of totally new burdens on one sector or expansions into new areas for competition. Bills coded as a 3 fundamentally redefined the balance of power within the financial community. The highest code of 4 was reserved for bills that created new competing financial institutions.

Outside Impact

The final category was impact on actors outside the financial community. Once again, a code of 1 was used for bills having zero/low impact. A code of 2 was given to bills with a medium impact on actors outside the financial community, applied when the effect on outside actors was significant but generally secondary to developments within the financial community. A code of 3, which meant that the bill had a high impact on actors outside the financial community, was applied to bills designed to achieve some important social objective that need not have been related to the well-being of the financial community.

Coding Reliability

Because I coded the House and Senate bills separately, I needed a way to ensure consistency over time in my coding. I did this by recoding every bill a second time. Initially, I coded all the House bills first and then only later coded the Senate bills, so the second time I checked all the bills introduced in a given year against each other. I did not separate the House and Senate bills, but checked whether they were similarly coded. If a discrepancy emerged, I rethought my coding of that particular type of bill and then looked up all bills dealing with the issue and recoded them. The loss of time was offset by greater consistency over time and across chambers.

An Overall Measure of Importance

These four dimensions were then incorporated into one overall measure of a bill's importance. To prevent a disproportionate effect of any categorization on the overall measure of importance, all four categories were put on a standard four-point ordinal scale. Otherwise, the six-point scope category would carry too much weight while the three-point outside impact category would carry too little. After converting all the categories to the four-point ordinal scale, I added up the numerical scores for each bill in each of the four dimensions. Because higher scores for each of the four categories were associated with greater importance, the total numerical scores provided an interval measure of overall importance. For some statistical tests these scores were later divided into minor, routine, and important categories. The minor category was composed of the lowest 25% and the highest category was composed of the upper 25% of the scores. The remaining 50% comprised the routine category.

While no overall measure of importance can completely avoid the problem of coder subjectivity, this measure clearly captures the multidimensional aspects of importance far better than any single measure. The care exercised in devising the ordinal scale and the re-checking also ensure reliability.

Bill Duplication

A final bill characteristic with which I had to grapple was the problem of bill duplication. In the last twenty-five years, duplicate bills have often been introduced during a Congress. If each is counted separately, the effectiveness of support from key actors can be underestimated. For example, if ten bills are introduced to enact a policy that a president favors and one passes, the way that the bills are counted can profoundly affect the rating of presidential effectiveness. If each bill is counted separately, the president is successful on only 10% of the initiatives he favors, but if the other duplicate bills are excluded the president is considered 100% effective. A duplication variable was created to avoid this problem. A code of 1 was given to original bills, and 2 was ascribed to all subsequent duplicate bills that did not pass. When a duplicate bill passed, it was given a code of 3, and the original bill was changed from 1 to 2. I was thus able to ensure that no bills that passed were eliminated from consideration and that no overcounting occurred.

Characteristics of Bill Sponsors

Once I had gleaned this information from a particular bill, I turned my attention to characteristics of the bill's chief sponsor, specifically party affiliation, committee membership, and chairmanship. I wanted to see if these three characteristics were related to the type of bills introduced and the extent of action taken on the bills.

Political Party Membership

To determine the partisan affiliation of a bill's sponsor, I looked in the *Biographical Directory of American Congresses* (1971) and copies of various years' *Congressional Directory*. In some cases where representatives and senators belonged to more than one party at the time they sponsored banking bills, I noted all the parties. The parties and their codes are listed below:

1 = Democratic Republican
2 = Jacksonian Democrat
3 = Whig
4 = National Republican
5 = Democrat
6 = Republican
7 = Conservative
8 = Anti-monopolist
9 = Readjuster
10 = Populist
11 = Independent
12 = Farmer Labor
13 = Radical
14 = Greenback
15 = Union Labor
16 = People's
17 = Farmers' Alliance
18 = Fusionist
19 = Progressive

20 = Unionist
21 = Popular Democrat (Puerto Rico)

American political parties have never been particularly cohesive ideologically, so the partisan affiliation of a bill's sponsor is sometimes an inaccurate indication of policy preferences. For example, Dixiecrats often took positions closer to the Republican Party than the national Democratic Party. Party affiliation of a sponsor can also be misleading when a measure is supported by both major parties. For these reasons, I also identified the parties of all co-sponsors and calculated the percentage of Democrats. Since co-sponsorship was not allowed in the Senate until the Seventy-fourth Congress and in the House until the Ninetieth Congress, when virtually all members were Democrats or Republicans, accounting for other parties was not a problem.

Committee Membership

Early committee membership lists were available in Goldman and Young's *Congressional Directories 1789–1840* (1973), and more contemporary information came from the CIS Serial Set and subsequent *Congressional Directories*. For the purpose of data entry, committee membership was coded as a 1 and non-membership as a 0. The specific committees with jurisdiction over banking bills changed over time in each Chamber. In the House of Representatives, banking bills were handled by the Ways and Means Committee before 1865, and by the Committee on Banking and Currency from 1865 to 1975. In 1975 this was renamed the Committee on Banking, Currency, and Housing. Two years later the committee received its current name—the Committee on Banking, Finance, and Urban Affairs. Until 1913, the Senate's equivalent was the Finance Committee. Jurisdiction over banking was then transferred to a new committee, the Committee on Banking and Currency, whose name was changed in 1970 to the Committee on Banking, Housing, and Urban Affairs, the name it still uses. I used the same references to determine whether a bill's sponsor also chaired one of the relevant committees. Again, for the purpose of data entry, I coded chairs as a 1 and non-chairs as a 0.

I also created an additional sponsorship variable, for which a code of 0 signified that the sponsor was not a member of the committee, 1 that the sponsor was a member of the committee but not the chair, and

2 that the sponsor was the chair. This sponsorship variable allowed me to distinguish the effects of committee membership from chairmanship. For the time-series analysis, these categorical variables were replaced by interval variables designed to measure the number of bills sponsored by different groups of legislators, such as the number of bills introduced by chairs in a given Congress.

Committee Staff

One way to measure the institutional development of the committee system within Congress is through the growth of professional staff permanently attached to the standing committees. Even though clerks and, occasionally, professional experts were employed by the various committees as early as 1856, permanent professional staff did not become part of the congressional infrastructure until the passage of the Legislative Reorganization Act of 1946 (Schneider 1980: 531–32). It and subsequent acts provided for a cadre of policy professionals to be attached permanently to each of the standing committees within Congress.

Congress had conflicting goals when it increased the number of staff (Malbin 1981: 134). Although the impact of increases in staff on legislation has not been systematically analyzed, these permanent policy professionals could affect legislation in a variety of ways. Entrepreneurial staff could clog the system with too many initiatives, or congressional effectiveness could be enhanced by the addition of professionals who are better able to craft comprehensive legislation.

I created a staff variable to answer these types of questions. The variable is interval in character and measures the number of permanent staff attached to the House Banking Committee for each year. I used the House figures only because more complete records exist for number of staff on the House Banking Committee than on the Senate Banking Committee.[1] The years before 1947 are coded zero, since there was no permanent professional staff. I was unable to obtain the figures for four of the years since 1947, and to account for those years I used the midpoints of the years before and after the missing year.[2]

Action Taken on Bills

Finally, I tried to determine how far each bill traveled toward passage. This was especially difficult for the period before publication of the

Congressional Record. Copies of the bills obtained from the Library of Congress showed whether a bill passed the chamber in which it had been introduced, and sometimes, but not always, it also indicated whether the measure was passed into law. After I ascertained that a measure had passed at least one chamber I followed the bill's progress in the *Congressional Globe* and *House Journal,* and I also checked the *Statutes at Large* for each applicable year. These were double checks on the information obtained through other sources. The publication of the *Congressional Record* in 1873, with its index titled "History of Bills," made the task much easier. The index, which describes all action taken in each session of a particular Congress, must be reviewed to determine whether a bill introduced in the first session was acted on in subsequent sessions of the same Congress. I coded the outcomes in the following manner:

1 = no action taken
2 = passed the House of Representatives
3 = passed the Senate
4 = passed the House and Senate
5 = approved by the president

A code of 1 was given to bills that were passed by neither the House nor the Senate. A code of 2 meant that the bill was passed by the House of Representatives but not by the Senate, and those that passed in the Senate but not the House were given a code of 3. Bills that passed in both chambers but did not become law were given a code of 4, and those that were enacted were assigned a code of 5. The five categories were collapsed into fewer categories for much of the statistical analysis.

Additional variables designed to measure the number of bills passed and vetoed in each Congress were created. The variables measuring the number of bills passed in each Congress were used as dependent variables in the time-series models. The veto variable was used as a measure of interbranch conflict.

Presidential Position

The foregoing research deals with only half the problem. Because this project seeks to explain the dynamics of executive-congressional interaction, the presidential side of the equation must also be examined.

Determining Presidential Position

I investigated a variety of ways to ascertain which legislation presidents supported. In the contemporary period, publications such as the *Congressional Quarterly* identify initiatives with presidential support, but they have only been published in the postwar period. I wanted to identify legislation supported by presidents throughout the entire period covered by this research. Party platforms can be found going back to 1840, but platforms are truer measures of "party positions" than of presidential positions.

The measure used for presidential positions on banking legislation was their actual written and spoken comments on banking. I have gone through all published records of presidents' papers, messages, and speeches. Fortunately, there are some excellent government compilations of this material. The federal government between 1911 and 1913 published a twenty-volume collection entitled *Messages and Papers of Presidents,* which includes the messages, speeches, and letters of all presidents through Taft. The Government Printing Office began a similar series entitled *Public Papers of the Presidents* (1930–86) with the Hoover presidency, covering all subsequent presidents except Franklin Roosevelt.

The presidencies of Warren G. Harding, Calvin Coolidge, Woodrow Wilson, and Franklin Roosevelt remained to be investigated. Material on the last two was not difficult to find. President Wilson published his papers privately as *The Messages and Papers of Woodrow Wilson* (1924), and Roosevelt's papers were also privately published under the title *The Public Papers and Addresses of Franklin D. Roosevelt* (1938–50). There are no general collections of Harding's or Coolidge's papers, although partial collections can be found in *Speeches and Addresses of Warren G. Harding* (1923), and a volume of Coolidge's speeches entitled *The Price of Freedom* (1924).

To find out more about Coolidge, I read through the Library of Congress's microfilm of the *Calvin Coolidge Papers* (1965), and the introduction explained that President Coolidge was a private man who burned most of his papers. To supplement the partial collections of Harding and Coolidge papers, I read through their "State of the Union" messages and inaugural addresses and all their messages and speeches reprinted in the *Congressional Record.* Since both men were adherents of the Whig notion that presidents should function strictly as administrators and there is no indication that either man had any interest in banking legislation, I believe that I have identified their positions and that their inclusion in the data set is justifiable.

Short of spending a lengthy period doing research at presidential libraries, I am satisfied that I have identified the presidents' public positions on all the banking issues they confronted. Although archival research would help identify private as opposed to public presidential positions, strong support or opposition to legislation is likely to appear in publicly written or spoken comments. After all, part of leadership is rallying support for a particular position, so one would expect this leadership to be publicly manifested.

Coding Presidential Position

I noted every reference that a president made to banking and cross-referenced them with the bills that I had already catalogued. I coded each bill according to a five-point ordinal scale of presidential positions:

1 = strong opposition
2 = generalized opposition
3 = no public position
4 = generalized support
5 = strong support

A code of 1 was given to bills that a president strongly opposed, meaning bills that a president strongly lobbied against or actually vetoed. A code of 2 was given to bills that were contrary to a president's expressed position but were neither specifically identified by name nor lobbied against extensively. If the president expressed no public position on a bill, it was coded 3. Bills that were generally consistent with a president's public position, but that he had not specifically endorsed by name, were given a 4. A code of 5 was reserved for bills that had strong presidential support, either through specific endorsements or extensive lobbying.

In some instances generalized support/opposition and strong support/opposition were hard to distinguish. After an initial decision to keep the five different codes because they conveyed more information, I ultimately collapsed them into three—opposition, no position, and support—for much of the data analysis. There were both substantive and statistical reasons for collapsing presidential support down into three categories. First, the level of support or opposition is not necessarily exogenous. The degree to which a president pursues his preference on a bill is likely to be a function of that bill's chance of passage. If the measure is not likely to pass in one chamber, the president will probably not waste his political capital on that measure and will not strongly support it. If, however, there is a chance that the bill will pass, the president will be tempted to exert more effort and exhibit "strong" support. Second, there were too few cases in each of the five cells to ensure sufficient confidence in the results. As with the earlier fourfold coding used to measure importance, I cross-checked the coding a second time to provide consistency across the two houses and over time.

For the times-series analysis, the categorical presidential position variables were replaced by interval variables designed to measure the number of bills with presidential support or opposition in a given Congress.

The Institutional Presidency

I was also very interested in distinguishing between the effectiveness of individual presidents and the institutionalized presidency. The material discussed above considers only the support and opposition of individual men occupying the office of the president. It does not measure the impact of the executive branch as a whole. In the contemporary period, thousands of legislative proposals are forwarded from different parts of the executive branch to the Office of Management and Budget for clearance (Light 1982: 4). I wanted to discover the impact of this expanded executive branch on the fate of policy initiatives.

Unfortunately, the legislative priorities of the broader executive branch are impossible to determine for the entire time period covered. From 1823 through 1832, vague Treasury Department recommendations were scattered throughout the Treasury Department Annual Reports. For the period from 1833 through 1864, I was unable to find any such recommendations in the Treasury Department's reports. Reports from the Comptroller of the Currency contain recommendations for the period between 1865 and 1932, but not thereafter. The Treasury Department made some recommendations from 1919 through 1932, but most were drawn from the Comptroller of the Currency's reports.

After 1932 Treasury's recommendations contained less and less about banking, probably because independent banking regulatory agencies were created outside the executive branch of government. Recommendations from these agencies could not be used to measure the effectiveness of the institutionalized presidency in passing legislation.

William Sherman, the archivist responsible for banking records at the National Archives in Washington, D.C., verified that no reliable public records were kept of executive branch banking proposals. Furthermore, he indicated that it would be extremely difficult, if not impossible, to obtain the private records for the time period covered (Sherman interview, July 27, 1990).

Party Control Variables

Some method to measure party control was necessary to discover whether one party's control of both houses of Congress and the presidency increased the chances of presidential success on legislative initiatives. The first step was to enter into the data set which parties controlled the House of Representatives, Senate, and presidency during each session of Congress.

For some statistical tests I used this information to create a three-point ordinal measure of party control. A code of 1 was given to all cases when one chamber of Congress was controlled by one party and the other chamber was controlled by another party. When the same party controlled both congressional chambers and a different party controlled the presidency, a code of 2 was assigned. When the same party controlled the House, the Senate, and the presidency, a code of 3 was given.

1 = divided Congress
2 = united Congress
3 = united government

Economic Variables

To test whether the pattern of executive-congressional interaction is different during a crisis, I had to devise a measure of crises. Since most crises have economic consequences or causes, I decided to use measures of changes in the underlying economy as a proxy for crises. However, economic time-series data stretching back to 1823 are not easy to find. The *Historical Statistics of the United States: Colonial*

Times to 1970 (U.S. Bureau of the Census 1975) is apparently the best source, but its records are incomplete. Virtually all scholars in the field use this as the basis of their economic time series.

The longest relevant time series were those documenting changes in the prices of wheat, corn, and wool from 1800. The agricultural prices, deflated using 1983 figures, were used to measure the well-being of the farming sector. The number of business failures and bank failures per year were used as more general measures of the nation's economic condition.

Other variables, such as the consumer price index, the gross national product, bank deposits, unemployment, population, and the money supply, were poor predictors. I also tried using lags and rates of change for most of these variables. All the series were extended with data from subsequent *Statistical Abstracts of the United States* (U.S. Bureau of the Census 1972–87).

Notes

1. The figures used to construct this variable were obtained from Ornstein, Mann, and Malbin's *Vital Statistics on Congress, 1991–1992* (1992), Schneider's "Congressional Staffing, 1947–78" (1980), and Fox and Hammond's *Congressional Staffs* (1977).

2. Using the midpoints gave me more plausible figures than I was able to obtain by the more commonly accepted method of regressing the bank committee staff figures against another variable that was likely to move in conjunction with it. I tried regressing the bank staff variable against the total staff figures for all House committees. This procedure gave me figures for the missing years that were higher than the numbers for the surrounding years. The probable reason for this distortion is the addition of three new committees since 1947, which caused the total number of House staff and the number of banking staff to diverge in the later years.

Bibliography

Ackerman, Bruce. 1991. *We the People: Foundations*. Cambridge: Harvard University Press.

Ameniya, Takeshi. 1981. "Qualitative Response Models: A Survey." *Journal of Economic Literature* 19, no. 4 (December): 1483–1536.

American Banker. 26 January 1898. "Postal Savings Banks." By J.H. Thiry, 132–34.

American Bankers Association. 1905. *Proceedings of the Thirty-first Annual Convention*. Pp. 138–48.

———. 1908a. *Proceedings of the Thirty-fourth Annual Convention*. Pp. 274–86.

———. 1908b. *Postal Savings Committee Letter* (24 November).

———. 1911. *Proceedings of the Thirty-seventh Annual Convention*. P. 382.

———. 1912. *Proceedings of the Thirty-eighth Annual Convention*. Pp. 320–24.

———. 1913. *Report on the Federal Reserve Bill* (September).

American Political Science Association Committee on Political Parties. 1950. *Toward a More Responsible Two-Party System*. New York: Rinehart.

Amlund, Curtis Arthur. 1969. *New Perspectives on the Presidency*. New York: Philosophic Library.

Anderson, Donald F. 1968. *William Howard Taft*. Ithaca, N.Y.: Cornell University Press.

Andrews, William G. 1960. "Democracy and Representation in the Senate." *South Atlantic Quarterly* 59: 461–68.

Barber, James David. 1977. *The Presidential Character*. Englewood Cliffs, N.J.: Prentice-Hall.

Barker, Benjamin, and Stanley H. Friedelbaum. 1966. *Government in the United States*. Boston: Houghton Mifflin.

Berch, Neil. 1992. "The Item Veto in the States: An Analysis of the Effects over Time." *Social Science Journal* 29, no. 3: 335–46.

Bicha, Karel D. 1976. *Western Populism: Studies in an Ambivalent Conservatism*. Lawrence, Kans.: Coronado Press.

Birnbaum, Jeffrey H., and Alan S. Murray. 1987. *Showdown at Gucci Gulch*. New York: Vintage Books.

Blocker, John G. 1929. *The Guaranty of State Bank Deposits*. Lawrence: School of Business at University of Kansas.

Bond, Jon R., and Richard Fleisher. 1980. "The Limits of Presidential Popularity as a Source of Influence in the U.S. House." *Legislative Studies Quarterly* 5, no. 1 (February): 69–78.

————. 1990. *The President in the Legislative Arena*. Chicago: University of Chicago Press.

Brady, David W. 1985. "A Reevaluation of Realignments in American Politics: Evidence from the House of Representatives." *American Political Science Review* 79, no. 1 (March): 28–49.

————. 1988. *Critical Elections and Congressional Policy Making*. Stanford, Calif.: Stanford University Press.

Brady, David W., and Philip Althoff. 1974. "Party Voting in the U.S. House of Representatives, 1890–1910: Elements of a Responsible Party System." *Journal of Politics* 36, no. 3 (August): 753–75.

Brady, David W., Richard Brody, and David Epstein. 1989. "Heterogeneous Parties and Political Organization: The U.S. Senate, 1880–1920." *Legislative Studies Quarterly* 14, no. 2 (May): 205–23.

Brinkley, Alan. 1982. *Voices of Protest: Huey Long, Father Coughlin, and the Great Depression*. New York: Knopf.

Brownlow, Louis. 1937. *Report of the President's Committee on Administrative Management*, 74th Cong., 2nd sess. Washington, D.C.: Government Printing Office.

Bryan, Mary Baird. 1925. *The Memoirs of William Jennings Bryan*. Chicago: John C. Winston.

Burnham, Walter Dean. 1986. *Democracy in the Making*. 2d ed. Englewood Cliffs, N.J.: Prentice-Hall.

Cameron, David R. 1978. "The Expansion of the Public Economy: A Comparative Analysis." *American Political Science Review* 72, no. 4 (December): 1243–61.

Chamberlain, Lawrence. 1946. *The President, Congress and Legislation*. New York: Columbia University Press.

Chandler, Alfred D. 1965. *The Railroads: The Nation's First Big Business*. New York: Harcourt, Brace & World.

Charnwood, Lord. 1917. *Abraham Lincoln*. 3d ed. New York: Henry Holt.

Chicago Banker. 5 February 1910.

Cobb, Roger W., and Charles D. Elder. 1983. *Participation in American Politics*. 2d ed. Baltimore, Md.: Johns Hopkins University Press.

Cohen, Michael, James March, and Johan Olsen. 1972. "A Garbage Can Model of Organizational Choice." *Administrative Science Quarterly* 17 (March): 1–25.

Collie, Melissa P. 1985. "Voting Behavior in Legislatures." In Loewenberg, Patterson, and Jewell 1985, 471–518.

Congressional Quarterly Weekly Report. 12 April 1980. "New Banking Law Will Lift Interest Rate Ceilings, Tighten Monetary Control." By Gail Gregg, 964–65.

————. 2 February 1985. "Banking Deregulation Issues Await Action; Hurdles Remain." By Jacqueline Calmes, 187–88.

————. 7 January 1989. "Reagon Added Luster but Little Clout to Office." By David Rapp, 3–12.

Coolidge, Calvin. 1924. *The Price of Freedom*. New York: Charles Scribner's Sons.

————. 1965. *Calvin Coolidge Papers*. Microfilm Collection. Washington, D.C.: Library of Congress.

Cooper, Joseph. 1960. "Congress and Its Committees." Ph.D. dissertation, Harvard University.

Copeland, Gary W. 1983. "When Congress and the President Collide: Why Presidents Veto Legislation." *Journal of Politics* 45, no. 3 (August): 696–710.

Coren, Robert W., et al. 1989. *Guide to the Records of the United States Senate at the National Archives*. Washington, D.C.: National Archives and Records Administration.

Corwin, Edward S. 1957. *The President: Office and Powers*. New York: New York University Press.

Coughlin, Charles. 15 January 1933. Radio Broadcast.

Cutler, Lloyd N. 1988. "Some Reflections about Divided Government." *Presidential Studies Quarterly* 18, no. 3 (Summer): 485–92.

Danhof, Clarence H. 1969. *Change in Agriculture: The Northern United States, 1820–1870*. Cambridge: Harvard University Press.

David, Paul. 1967. "The Growth of Real Product in the United States Before 1840: New Evidence, Controlled Conjectures." *Journal of Economic History* 27, no. 2 (June): 151–97.

Davidson, Roger H., Walter J. Oleszek, and Thomas Kephart. 1988. "One Bill, Many Committees: Multiple Referrals in the U.S. House of Representatives." *Legislative Studies Quarterly* 13, no. 1 (February): 3–28.

Degler, Carl. 1963. "The Ordeal of Herbert Hoover." *Yale Review* 52 (Summer): 563–83.

Derthick, Martha. 1979. *Policymaking for Social Security*. Washington, D.C.: Brookings Institution.

Duluth Times. 4 December 1890.

Eccles, George S. 1982. *The Politics of Banking*. Provo: University of Utah Press.

Economic Policy Commission. 1933. *The Guaranty of Bank Deposits*. New York: American Bankers Association.

Edwards, George C. III. 1976. "Presidential Influence in the House: Presidential Prestige as a Source of Presidential Power." *American Political Science Review* 70, no. 1 (March): 101–13.

————. 1980. *Presidential Influence in Congress*. San Francisco: W.H. Freeman.

————. 1989. *At the Margins: Presidential Leadership of Congress*. New Haven, Conn.: Yale University Press.

————. 1990. "Studying the Presidency." In *The Presidency and the Political System*, 3d ed., ed. Michael Nelson, 29–45. Washington, D.C.: Congressional Quarterly Press.

Edwards, George C. III, and Stephen J. Wayne. 1990. *Presidential Leadership: Politics and Policy Making*. 2d ed. New York: St. Martin's Press.

Eulau, Heinz. 1985. "Introduction: Legislative Research in Historical Perspective." In Loewenberg, Patterson, and Jewell 1985, 1–14.

Fenno, Richard F., Jr. 1973. *Congressmen in Committees*. Boston: Little, Brown.
———. 1991. *The Emergence of a Senate Leader: Pete Domenici and the Reagan Budget*. Washington, D.C.: Congressional Quarterly Press.
Fiorina, Morris. 1992. *Divided Government*. New York: MacMillan.
Fisher, Louis. 1975. *Presidential Spending Power*. Princeton, N.J.: Princeton University Press.
———. 1985. *Constitutional Conflicts between Congress and the President*. Princeton, N.J.: Princeton University Press.
———. 1987. *The Politics of Shared Power*. 2d ed. Washington, D.C.: Congressional Quarterly Press.
Ford, Henry Jones. 1898. *The Rise and Growth of American Politics*. New York: Macmillan.
Fortune. 28 August 1978. "Foreign Banks Are Cracking the Facade of U.S. Banking." By David C. Cates, 94–99.
Fox, Harrison W., and Susan W. Hammond. 1977. *Congressional Staffs: The Invisible Force in American Lawmaking*. New York: Free Press.
Galambos, Louis. 1975. *The Public Image of Big Business in America, 1880–1940: A Quantitative Study in Social Change*. Baltimore, Md.: Johns Hopkins University Press.
Gamm, Gerald, and Kenneth Shepsle. 1989. "Emergence of Legislative Institutions: Standing Committees in the House and Senate, 1810–1825." *Legislative Studies Quarterly* 14, no. 1 (February): 39–66.
Glass, Carter. 1927. *An Adventure in Constructive Finance*. New York: Page.
Goldin, Claudia, and Frank Lewis. 1975. "The Economic Cost of the American Civil War: Estimates and Implications." *Journal of Economic History* 35, no. 2 (June): 299–326.
Goldman, Perry M., and James Sterling Young, eds. 1973. *Congressional Directories 1789–1840*. New York: Columbia University Press.
Goodwyn, Lawrence. 1978. *The Populist Moment*. Oxford: Oxford University Press.
Gormley, William T., Jr. 1989. *Taming the Bureaucracy: Muscles, Prayers, and Other Strategies*. Princeton, N.J.: Princeton University Press.
Greene, William H. 1983. *Econometric Analysis*. 2d ed. New York: Macmillan.
Hammond, Bray. 1957. *Banks and Politics in America*. Princeton, N.J.: Princeton University Press.
———. 1970. *Sovereignty and an Empty Purse: Banks and Politics in the Civil War*. Princeton, N.J.: Princeton University Press.
Harding, Warren G. 1923. *Speeches and Addresses of Warren G. Harding, President of the United States, Delivered During the Course of His Tour from Washington, D.C., to Alaska and Return to San Francisco, June 20 to August 2, 1923*. Washington, D.C.: James W. Murphy.
Harmon, Kathryn Newcomer, and Marsha L. Brauen. 1979. "Joint Electoral Outcomes as Clues for Congressional Support of U.S. Presidents." *Legislative Studies Quarterly* 4, no. 2 (May): 281–99.
Hechler, Kenneth W. 1964. *Insurgency: Personalities and Politics of the Taft Era*. New York: Russell and Russell.
Heclo, Hugh. 1977. *A Government of Strangers: Executive Politics in Washington*. Washington, D.C.: Brookings Institution.

Hepburn, A. Barton. 1924. *A History of Currency in the United States*. Revised ed. New York: Macmillan.

Hess, Stephen. 1988. *Organizing the Presidency*. Revised ed. Washington, D.C.: Brookings Institution.

Heyn, Edward T. 1891. "Postal Savings Banks." In *Annals of the American Academy of Political and Social Sciences,* vol. 8, 461–90.

Hibbs, Douglas A. 1982. "The Dynamics of Political Support for American Presidents among Occupational and Partisan Groups." *American Journal of Political Science* 26, no. 2 (May): 312–33.

Hicks, John D. 1931. *The Populist Revolt: A History of the Farmers' Alliance and the People's Party*. Minneapolis: University of Minnesota Press.

Hinckley, Barbara. 1971. *Stability and Change in Congress.* New York: Harper and Row.

Hoff, Samuel B. 1991. "Saying No: Presidential Support and Veto Use, 1889–1989." *American Politics Quarterly* 19, no. 3 (July): 310–23.

Hofstadter, Richard. 1985. *The Age of Reform: From Bryan to FDR*. New York: Alfred A. Knopf.

Homer, Sidney. 1977. *A History of Interest Rates*. New Brunswick, N.J.: Rutgers University Press.

Hoover, Herbert. 1934. *The State Papers and Other Public Writings of Herbert Hoover*. Garden City, N.J.: Doubleday, Doran.

Huitt, Ralph K. 1954. "The Congressional Committee: A Case Study." *American Political Science Review* 48, no. 2 (June): 340–65.

Huntington, Samuel P. 1973. "Congressional Responses to the Twentieth Century." In *The Congress and America's Future,* ed. David B. Truman, 306–26. Englewood Cliffs, N.J.: Prentice-Hall.

Iden, V. Gilmore. 1914. *The Federal Reserve Act of 1913*. Philadelphia: National Bank News.

Johannes, John R. 1974. "The President Proposes and Congress Disposes—But Not Always: Legislative Initiative on Capital Hill." *The Review of Politics* 36, no. 3 (July): 356–70.

Johnson, Donald Bruce, and Kirk H. Porter. 1973. *Party Platforms 1840–1972*. Urbana: University of Illinois Press.

Jones, Charles O. 1968. "Joseph G. Cannon and Howard W. Smith: An Essay on the Limits of Leadership in the House of Representatives." *Journal of Politics* 30, no. 3 (August): 617–46.

Kearns, Doris. 1976. *Lyndon Johnson and the American Dream*. New York: Harper and Row.

Keller, Morton. 1988. "Powers and Rights: Two Centuries of American Constitutionalism." In *The Constitution and American Life,* ed. David Thelen, 15–34. Ithaca, N.Y.: Cornell University Press.

Kemmerer, E.W. 1911. *The United States Postal Savings Bank*. Boston: Ginn.

Kennedy, Peter. 1979. *A Guide to Econometrics*. Cambridge: MIT Press.

Kennedy, Susan Eastbrook. 1973. *The Banking Crisis of 1933*. Lexington: University Press of Kentucky.

Kernell, Samuel. 1986. *Going Public: New Strategies of Presidential Leadership*. Washington, D.C.: Congressional Quarterly Press.

Kettl, Donald F. 1986. *Leadership at the Fed*. New Haven, Conn.: Yale University Press.

Kiewiet, D. Roderick, and Mathew D. McCubbins. 1988. "Presidential Influence on Congressional Appropriations Decisions." *American Journal of Political Science* 32, no. 3 (August): 713–36.

King, Anthony. 1975. "Executives." In *Handbook of Political Science,* eds. Fred Greenstein and Nelson Polsby. Vol. 5, 173–255. Reading, Mass.: Addison-Wesley.

King, Gary, and Lyn Ragsdale. 1988. *The Elusive Executive.* Washington, D.C.: Congressional Quarterly Press.

Kingdon, John W. 1984. *Agendas, Alternatives, and Public Policies.* Boston: Little, Brown.

———. 1989. *Congressmen's Voting Decisions.* 3d ed. Ann Arbor: University of Michigan Press.

Klebner, Benjamin J. 1974. *Commercial Banking in the United States.* Hinsdale, Ill.: Dryden Press.

Koenig, Louis W. 1971. *Bryan: A Political Biography of William Jennings Bryan.* New York: G.P. Putnam's Sons.

Kolko, Gabriel. 1963. *The Triumph of Conservatism.* New York: Free Press.

Krehbiel, Keith. 1988. "Spatial Models of Legislative Choice." *Legislative Studies Quarterly* 13, no. 3 (August): 259–319.

Krooss, Herman E. 1983. *Documentary History of Banking and Currency in the United States.* 4 vols. New York: Chelsea House.

Kuhn, Thomas S. 1970. *The Structure of Scientific Revolutions.* 2d ed. Chicago: University Of Chicago Press.

Laughlin, J. Laurence. 1912. *Banking Reform.* Chicago: National Citizens League.

———. 1933. *The Federal Reserve Act: Its Origins and Problems.* New York: Macmillan.

Lee, Jong R. 1975. "Presidential Vetos from Washington to Nixon." *Journal of Politics* 37, no. 2 (May): 522–46.

Lee, Susan Previant, and Peter Passell. 1979. *A New Economic View of American History.* New York: W.W. Norton.

LeLoup, Lance T., and Steven A. Shull. 1979. "Congress Versus the Executive: The 'Two Presidencies' Reconsidered." *Social Science Quarterly* 59, no. 4 (March): 704–19.

———. 1993. *Congress and the President: The Policy Connection.* Belmont, Calif.: Wadsworth.

Leuchtenburg, William E. 1983. *In the Shadow of FDR.* Ithaca, N.Y.: Cornell University Press.

Lewis, Anne L. 1978. "Floor Success as a Measure of Committee Performance in the House." *Journal of Politics* 40, no. 2 (May): 460–67.

Light, Paul Charles. 1982. *The President's Agenda: Domestic Policy Choice from Kennedy to Carter (with Notes on Ronald Reagan).* Baltimore, Md.: Johns Hopkins University Press.

———. 1985. *Artful Work: The Politics of Social Security Reform.* New York: Random House.

Link, Arthur S. 1954. *Woodrow Wilson and the Progressive Era, 1910–1917.* New York: Harper and Brothers.

Lippmann, Walter. 1955. *Essays in the Public Philosophy*. New York: Mentor.

Livingston, James. 1986. *Origins of the Federal Reserve System*. Ithaca, N.Y.: Cornell University Press.

Loewenberg, Gerhard, and Samuel C. Patterson. 1979. *Comparing Legislatures*. Boston: Little, Brown.

Loewenberg, Gerhard, Samuel C. Patterson, and Malcolm E. Jewell, eds. 1985. *Handbook of Legislative Research*. Cambridge: Harvard University Press.

Lowi, Theodore J. 1964. "American Business, Public Policy, Case Studies, and Political Theory." *World Politics* 16, no. 4 (July): 677–715.

———. 1985. *The Personal President*. Ithaca, N.Y.: Cornell University Press.

Maass, Arthur. 1983. *Congress and the Common Good*. New York: Basic Books.

McCloskey, Robert G. 1960. *The American Supreme Court*. Chicago: University of Chicago Press.

McFaul, John M. 1972. *The Politics of Jacksonian Finance*. Ithaca, N.Y.: Cornell University Press.

Madison, James, Alexander Hamilton, and John Jay. 1987 (orig. 1788). *The Federalist Papers*. New York: Penguin Books.

Malbin, Michael J. 1981. "Delegation, Deliberation, and the New Role of Congressional Staff." In *The New Congress*, eds. Thomas E. Mann and Norman J. Ornstein, 134–77. Washington D.C.: American Enterprise Institute for Public Policy Research.

Manley, John F. 1970. *The Politics of Finance: The House Committee on Ways and Means*. Boston: Little, Brown.

Manufacturer's Record. 14 February 1891.

Marcus, Sheldon. 1973. *Father Coughlin: The Tumultuous Life of the Priest of the Little Flower*. Boston: Little, Brown.

Marmor, Theodore R. 1970. *The Politics of Medicare*. New York: Aldine.

Matsunaga, Spark M., and Ping Chen. 1976. *Rulemakers of the House*. Urbana: University of Illinois Press.

Matthews, Donald R. 1960. *U.S. Senators and Their World*. New York: Vintage Books.

Mayhew, David R. 1974. *Congress: The Electoral Connection*. New Haven, Conn.: Yale University Press.

———. 1991. *Divided We Govern*. New Haven, Conn.: Yale University Press.

Mezey, Michael L. 1979. *Comparative Legislatures*. Durham, N.C.: Duke University Press.

———. 1989. *Congress, the President, and Public Policy*. Boulder, Colo.: Westview Press.

———. 1991. "The Legislature, the Executive, and Public Policy: The Futile Quest for Congressional Power." In *Divided Democracy: Cooperation and Conflict Between the President and Congress*, ed. James A. Thurber, 99–122. Washington D.C.: Congressional Quarterly Press.

Moe, Ronald C., and Steven C. Teel. 1971. "Congress as Policy-Maker: A Necessary Reappraisal." In *Congress and the President*, ed. Ronald C. Moe, 32–52. Pacific Palisades, Calif.: Goodyear.

Murphy, James W., ed. 1923. *Speeches and Addresses of Warren G. Harding*. Washington, D.C.: Government Printing Office.

Neustadt, Ricahrd E. 1960. *Presidential Power: The Politics of Leadership*. New York: John Wiley and Sons.

Nordhaus, William. 1975. "The Political Business Cycle." *Review of Economic Studies* 42 (April): 169–90.

North, Douglass C. 1961. *The Economic Growth of the United States, 1790–1860*. Englewood Cliffs, N.J.: Prentice-Hall.

Oleszek, Walter J. 1989. *Congressional Procedures and the Policy Process*. 3d ed. Washington, D.C.: Congressional Quarterly Press.

Ornstein, Norman J., Thomas E. Mann, and Michael J. Malbin. 1992. *Vital Statistics on Congress, 1991–1992*. Washington, D.C.: American Enterprise Institute.

Patterson, Eugene, ed. 1979. *Congressional Quarterly Almanac 1978*. Washington, D.C.: Congressional Quarterly Press.

Peppers, Donald A. 1975. "The 'Two Presidencies' Eight Years Later." In *Perspectives on the Presidency*, ed. Aaron Wildavsky, 462–71. Boston: Little, Brown.

Peretz, Paul. 1983. *The Political Economy of Inflation in the United States*. Chicago: University of Chicago Press.

Peters, Ronald M., Jr. 1990. *The American Speakership: The Office in Historical Perspective*. Baltimore, Md.: Johns Hopkins University Press.

Peterson, Mark. 1990. *Legislating Together*. Cambridge: Harvard University Press.

Philadelphia Record. 27 May 1933.

Pindyck, Robert S., and Daniel L. Rubinfeld. 1981. *Econometric Models and Economic Forecasts*. 2d ed. New York: McGraw-Hill.

Pious, Richard M. 1979. *The American Presidency*. New York: Basic Books.

Polsby, Nelson W. 1969. "Policy Analysis and Congress." *Public Policy* 17, no. 3 (Fall): 61–74.

———. 1971. *Congress and the Presidency*. 2d ed. Englewood Cliffs, N.J.: Prentice-Hall.

Polsby, Nelson W., Miriam Gallaher, and Barry Spencer Rundquist. 1969. "The Growth of the Seniority System in the U.S. House of Representatives." *American Political Science Review* 63, no. 3 (September): 787–807.

Porter, Glenn. 1973. *The Rise of Big Business, 1860–1910*. Arlington Heights, Ill.: AHM.

Postal Savings Act. 1910. *Statutes at Large*, vol. 36, part 1, chap. 386.

Price, David E. 1972. *Who Makes the Laws? Creativity and Power in Senate Committees*. Cambridge, Mass.: Schenkman.

Primack, Martin L. 1962. "Land Clearing under Nineteenth Century Techniques." *Journal of Economic History* 22, no. 4 (December): 484–97.

Ranney, Austin. 1954. *The Doctrine of Responsible Party Government*. Urbana: University of Illinois Press.

Ripley, Randall B. 1969. *Power in the Senate*. New York: St. Martin's Press.

———. 1984. *Congress, the Bureaucracy, and Public Policy*. Homewood, Ill.: Dorsey Press.

Rockoff, Hugh. 1974. "The Free Banking Era: A Reexamination." *Journal of Money, Credit, and Banking* 6 (May): 141–67.

———. 1975. "Varieties of Banking and Regional Economic Development in the United States: 1840–1860." *Journal of Economic History* 35, no. 1 (March): 160–81.

Rohde, David W., and Dennis M. Simon. 1985. "Presidential Vetoes and the Congressional Response: A Study of Institutional Conflict." *American Journal of Political Science* 29, no. 3 (August): 397–427.

Romasco, Albert U. 1975. "Hoover-Roosevelt and the Great Depression: A Historiographic Inquiry into a Perennial Comparison." In *The New Deal: The National Level,* eds. John Braeman, Robert Bremmer, and David Brody, 3–26. Columbus: Ohio State University Press.

Roosevelt, Franklin. 1938–50. *The Public Papers and Addresses of Franklin Delano Roosevelt.* New York: Random House.

Rose, Peter S., and Donald R. Fraser. 1985. *Financial Institutions.* 2d ed. Plano, Tex.: Business.

Rossiter, Clinton. 1960. *The American Presidency.* Revised ed. New York: Mentor.

Rostow, Walter W. 1960. *The Stages of Economic Growth: A Non-communist Manifesto.* Cambridge: Cambridge University Press.

Rundquist, Barry S., and Gerald S. Strom. 1987. "Bill Construction in Legislative Committees: A Study of the U.S. House." *Legislative Studies Quarterly* 12, no. 1 (February): 97–113.

Salamon, Lester M., et al. 1975. *The Money Committees.* New York: Grossman.

Schamel, Charles E., et al. 1989. *Guide to the Records of the United States House of Representatives at the National Archives.* Washington, D.C.: National Archives and Records Administration.

Schattschneider, E.E. 1942. *Party Government.* New York: Holt, Rinehart, and Winston.

———. 1961. *The Semi-Sovereign People.* New York: Holt, Rinehart, and Winston.

Schlesinger, Arthur M., Jr. 1945. *The Age of Jackson.* Boston: Little, Brown.

———. 1957. *The Crisis of the Old Order, 1919–1933.* Boston: Houghton Mifflin.

———. 1958. *The Coming of the New Deal.* Boston: Houghton Mifflin.

Schneider, Judy. 1 April 1980. "Congressional Staffing, 1947–78." In *Final Report,* ed. House Select Committee on Committees, 96th Cong., 2nd sess., H. Rep. 96–866, Appendix 1, pp. 482–92.

Schroedel, Jean Reith, and Bruce Snyder. 1992. "People's Banking: The Promise Betrayed?" Paper presented at the annual convention of the American Political Science Association, Chicago.

Sharp, James Roger. 1970. *The Jacksonians Versus the Banks.* New York: Columbia University Press.

Shaw, Albert, ed. 1924. *The Messages and Papers of Woodrow Wilson.* New York: Review of Reviews.

Sherman, William. 27 July 1990. Interview.

Shull, Steven A. 1978. "Presidential Congressional Support for Agencies and for Each Other: A Comparative Look." *Journal of Politics* 40, no. 3 (August): 753–60.

Sinclair, Barbara. 1989. *The Transformation of the U.S. Senate.* Baltimore, Md.: Johns Hopkins University Press.

Skladony, Thomas W. 1985. "The House Goes to Work: Select and Standing Committees in the U.S. House of Representatives, 1789–1828." *Congress and the Presidency* 12, no. 2 (Autumn): 165–87.

Skowronek, Stephen. 1982. *Building a New American State.* Cambridge: Cambridge University Press.

————. 1984. "Presidential Leadership in Political Time." In *The Presidency and the Political System,* 3d ed., ed. Michael Nelson, 117–61. Washington, D.C.: Congressional Quarterly Press.

————. 1986. "Notes on the Presidency in the Political Order." In *Studies in American Political Development,* vol. 1, eds. Stephen Skowronek and Karen Orren, 286–302. New Haven, Conn.: Yale University Press.

Smith, Rixey, and Norman Beasley. 1939. *Carter Glass: A Biography.* New York: Longmans, Green.

Smith, Rogers. 1990. "The New Non-Science of Politics: On Turns to History in Political Science." Paper prepared for the Comparative Studies of Social Transformations Conference, Ann Arbor, Michigan 5 October.

Smith, Steven S. 1989. *Call to Order: Floor Politics in the House and Senate.* Washington, D.C.: Brookings Institution.

Smith, Steven S., and Christopher J. Deering. 1990. *Committees in Congress.* 2d ed. Washington, D.C.: Congressional Quarterly Press.

Sperlich, Peter W. 1975. "Bargaining and Overload: An Essay on Presidential Power." In *Perspectives on the Presidency,* ed. Aaron Wildavsky, 406–30. Boston: Little, Brown.

Spitzer, Robert J. 1983a. "Presidential Policy Determinism: How Policies Frame Congressional Responses to the President's Legislative Program." *Presidential Studies Quarterly* 13, no. 4 (Fall): 441–57.

————. 1983b. *The Presidency and Public Policy.* University: University of Alabama Press.

Stanwood, Edward. 1898. *History of the Presidency from 1788–1897.* Boston: Houghton Mifflin.

Stephenson, Nathaniel Wright. 1930. *Nelson W. Aldrich: A Leader in American Politics.* New York: Charles Scribner's Sons.

Straussman, Jeffrey D. 1985. *Public Administration.* New York: Holt, Rinehart, and Winston.

Strom, Gerald S. 1990. *The Logic of Lawmaking: A Spatial Theory Approach.* Baltimore, Md.: Johns Hopkins University Press.

Sullivan, Lawrence. 1936. *Prelude to Panic.* Washington, D.C.: Statesman Press.

Sullivan, Terry. 1988. "Head Counts, Expectations, and Presidential Coalitions in Congress." *American Journal of Political Science* 32, no. 3 (August): 567–89.

Sundquist, James L. 1968. *Politics and Policy: The Eisenhower, Kennedy and Johnson Years.* Washington, D.C.: Brookings Institution.

————. 1980. "The Crisis of Competence in Our National Government." *Political Science Quarterly* 95: 183–208.

————. 1981. *The Decline and Resurgence of Congress.* Washington, D.C.: Brookings Institution.

Swenson, Peter. 1982. "The Influence of Recruitment on the Structure of Power in the U.S. House, 1870–1940." *Legislative Studies Quarterly* 7, no. 1 (February): 7–36.

Swift, Elaine K., and David W. Brady. 1991. "Out of the Past: Theoretical and Methodological Contributions of Congressional History." *PS: Political Science and Politics* 24 (March): 61–64.

Taft, William H. 1916. *Our Chief Magistrate and His Powers.* New York: Charles Scribner's Sons.

Taylor, Frederick E. 1971. "An Analysis of Factors Purported to Influence the Use of and Congressional Responses to the Use of the Presidential Veto." Ph.D. dissertation, Georgetown University.

Temin, Peter. 1969. *The Jackson Economy*. New York: W.W. Norton.

Thaysen, Uwe, Roger H. Davidson, and Robert Gerald Livingston, eds. 1990. *The U.S. Congress and the German Bundestag: Comparisons of Democratic Processes*. Boulder, Colo.: Westview Press.

Trescott, Paul B. 1963. *Financing American Enterprise: The Story of Commercial Banking*. New York: Harper and Row.

Troy Standard. 26 November 1890.

Tufte, Edward. 1978. *Political Control of the Economy*. Princeton, N.J.: Princeton University Press.

Tull, Charles J. 1965. *Father Coughlin and the New Deal*. Syracuse, N.Y.: Syracuse University Press.

U.S. Bureau of the Census. 1975. *Historical Statistics of the United States: Colonial Times to 1970*. Washington, D.C.: Government Printing Office.

———. 1972–87. *Statistical Abstracts of the United States*. Washington, D.C.: Government Printing Office.

U.S. Congress. 1841–1986. *Congressional Directory*. Washington, D.C.: Government Printing Office.

———. 1841–1986. *Congressional Record*, 43rd–99th Congresses. Washington, D.C.: Government Printing Office.

U.S. Congress, House. 1873. *An Act to Establish National Savings Depositories*. 43rd Cong., 1st sess., H.R. 797.

———. 1876. *An Act for the Establishment of Post-Office Savings Banks for Small Sums with Government Security*. 44th Cong., 1st sess., H.R. 1840.

———. 1886a. *An Act to Provide for the Security of Deposits in National Banks*. 49th Cong., 1st sess., H.R. 3740.

———. 1886b. *An Act to Provide for the Security of Deposits in National Banks*. 49th Cong., 1st sess., H.R. 5683.

———. 1886c. *An Act to Provide for the Security of Deposits in National Banks*. 49th Cong., 1st sess., H.R. 6240.

———. 1886d. *An Act to Create a Board of Management of the Revenue and Currency, Institute a Monetary System in Harmony with the Republican Principle of Hovernment, Establish an Equitable Standard of Distribution to Capital and Labor, and for Other Purposes*. 49th Cong., 1st sess., H.R. 7666.

———. 1908. *An Act to Establish a Simple and Scientific Monetary System Founded upon Gold, Guaranteed Bank Notes and Silver, with Uniform Banking and Bank Reserves in Gold Coin or Its Equivalent; to Guarantee All Deposits and Note Issues; and to Fix Certain Rules and Regulations Whereby the Financial Operations of the Government Shall Cease to Be a Disturbing Factor in Our Trade and Commerce*. 60th Cong., 1st sess., H.R. 12677.

———. 1910. *An Act to Establish a Complete Financial and Banking System for the United States of America*. 61st Cong., 2nd sess., H.R. 23707.

———. 1913a. *An Act to Provide for the Establishment of Federal Reserve Banks, for Furnishing an Elastic Currency, Affording the Means of Rediscounting Commercial Paper, and to Establish a More Effective Supervision of Banking in the United States, and for Other Purposes*. 63rd Cong., 1st sess., H.R. 6454.

————. 1913b. *An Act to Provide for the Establishment of Federal Reserve Banks, for Furnishing an Elastic Currency, Affording the Means of Rediscounting Commercial Paper, and to Establish a More Effective Supervision of Banking in the United States, and for Other Purposes.* 63rd Cong., 1st sess., H.R. 7837.

————. 1933. *An Act to Provide for the Safer and More Effective Use of the Assets of the Banks, to Regulate Interbank Control, to Prevent the Undue Diversion of Funds into Speculative Operations, and for Other Purposes.* Pub. L. 66, 73rd Cong., 1st sess., H.R. 5661.

U.S. Congress. House. Committee on Banking and Currency. 1934. *Hearings on Legislation to Extend the Temporary Plan for Deposit Insurance.* 73rd Cong., 2nd sess., p. 102.

U.S. Congress. House. Committee on the Post Office and Post Roads. 1910. *Hearings on the Subject of Postal Savings Banks.* 61st Cong., 1st sess., pp. 4 and 171.

U.S. Congress. House. Subcommittee Number Two of the House Committee on the Post Office and Post Roads. 1909. *Hearings on the Subject of Postal Savings Banks.* 61st Cong., 1st sess., p. 113.

U.S. Congress. Senate. 1910. *An Act to Establish Postal Savings Depositories for Depositing Savings at Interest with the Security of the Government for Repayment Thereof, and for Other Purposes.* 61st Cong., 2nd sess., S. 5876.

————. 1913. *An Act to Provide for the Establishment of Federal Reserve Banks, for Furnishing an Elastic Currency, to Afford Means of Rediscounting Commercial Paper, and to Establish a More Effective Supervision of Banking in the United States, and for Other Purposes.* 63rd Cong., 1st sess., S. 3099.

————. 1918. *An Act to Amend and Reenact Sections 5235 and 5236 of the Revised Statutes of the United States by Providing for a Guaranty Fund for Payment of Certain Deposits, and for Other Purposes.* 65th Cong., 2nd sess., S. 4426.

U.S. Congress. Senate. Committee on Banking and Currency. 1913. *Hearings on HR7837 and S2639.* 63rd Cong., 1st sess., vol. 2, p. 1039.

————. 1932–1934. *Hearings on 72nd Cong.* (1st & 2nd Session, parts 1–6) *Pursuant to Senate Resolutions 84 and 239; 73rd Congress* (1st and 2nd sessions, parts 1–18) *Pursuant to Senate Resolutions 56 and 97;* on *Stock Exchange Practices,* p 1–8, 267.

U.S. President. 1897. *A Compilation of the Messages and Papers of the Presidents, 1789–1897.* New York: Bureau of National Literature.

————. 1965. *Inaugural Addresses of the Presidents of the United States.* Washington, D.C.: Government Printing Office.

————. 1930–86. *Public Papers of the Presidents.* Washington, D.C.: Office of the Federal Register, National Archives and Records Service.

Van Deusen, Glyndon G. 1959. *The Jacksonian Era.* New York: Harper and Row.

Walker, Jack L. 1977. "Setting the Agenda in the U.S. Senate: A Theory on Problem Selection." *British Journal of Political Science* 7, no. 4 (October): 423–45.

Wanamaker, John. 1891. *Postal Savings Banks.* Washington, D.C.: Government Printing Office.

Warburg, Paul M. 1930. *The Federal Reserve System: Its Origin and Growth.* 2 vols. New York: Macmillan.

Watson, Richard A. 1988. "The President's Veto Power." In *Annals of the American Academy of Political and Social Sciences*, vol. 449, 36–46.

West, Robert Craig. 1974. *Banking Reform and the Federal Reserve 1863–1923*. Ithaca, N.Y.: Cornell University Press.

Wiebe, Robert H. 1967. *The Search for Order: 1877–1920*. New York: Hill and Wang.

Wildavsky, Aaron. 1966. "The Political Economy of Efficiency: Cost-Benefit Analysis, Systems Analysis, and Program Budgeting." *Public Administration Review* 26 (December): 292–310.

Wilensky, Norman. 1965. *Conservatives in the Progressive Era*. Gainesville, Fla.: University of Florida Monographs.

Williamson, John B., D.A. Karp, and J.R. Dalphin. 1977. *The Research Craft*. Boston: Little, Brown.

Willis, H.P. 14 April 1911. *Journal of Commerce*.

Wilson, Joan Huff. 1975. *Herbert Hoover, Forgotten Progressive*. Boston: Little, Brown.

Wilson, Woodrow. 1911. *Constitutional Government in the United States*. New York: Columbia University Press.

———. 1924. *The Messages and Papers of Woodrow Wilson*. New York: Review of Reviews.

———. 1956 (orig. 1885). *Congressional Government*. New York: Meridian Books.

Wonnacott, Ronald J., and Thomas H. Wonnacott. 1979. *Econometrics*. 2d ed. New York: John Wiley and Sons.

Woodward, Augustus B. 1825. *The Presidency of the United States*. New York: D. Van Veghten.

Zeidenstein, Harvey G. 1980. "Presidential Popularity and Presidential Support in Congress." *Presidential Studies Quarterly* 10, no. 2 (Spring): 224–33.

———. 1983. "Varying Relationships Between Presidents' Popularity and their Legislative Success: A Futile Search for Patterns." *Presidential Studies Quarterly* 13, no. 4 (Fall): 530–50.

Index

About the Author

Jean Reith Schroedel (Ph.D. 1990, Massachusetts Institute of Technology) is an assistant professor at the Center for Politics and Policy at the Claremont Graduate School. She received the Western Political Science Association's Pi Sigma Award for her paper "Legislative Leadership over Time." Her primary research interest is in congressional decisionmaking. She is also author of many articles and a book, *Alone in a Crowd: Women in the Trades Tell Their Stories,* dealing with race and sex discrimination in employment.